The Meininger Theater
1776-1926

Theater and Dramatic Studies, No. 4

Bernard Beckerman, Series Editor

Brander Matthews Professor of Dramatic Literature
Columbia University in the City of New York

Other Titles in This Series

The Meininger Theater
1776-1926

by
Steven DeHart

UMI RESEARCH PRESS
Ann Arbor, Michigan

Plate 30 is printed with permission of the
Cologne (W. Germany) Theater Museum; all
other illustrations are from the author's
collection.   misleading

Produced and distributed by
UMI Research Press
an imprint of
University Microfilms International
Ann Arbor, Michigan 48106

Library of Congress Cataloging in Publication Data

DeHart, Steven, 1947-
   The Meininger Theater: 1776-1926.

   (Theater and dramatic studies ; no. 4)
   Revision of thesis (Ph.D) —John Hopkins University,
1979.
   Bibliography: p.
   Includes index.
   1. Meininger Hoftheater. 2. Georg II, Duke of Saxe-
Meiningen, 1826-1914. 3. Theater—Germany—
Meininger—History. 4. German drama—19th century—
History and criticism. I. Title. II. Series.

PN2656.M52H63 1981   792'.0943'22   81-11453
ISBN 0-8357-1227-3   AACR2

Contents

List of Plates

Preface

Who were the Meininger, and why do they so often merit mention in histories of the theater? Many who have encountered the term "Meininger" associate it with certain key words such as realism, ensemble, or mob scene. Others may recall some connection with the work of Antoine or Stanislavsky. Such vagueness is not lessened by the multiplicity of terms referring to the group. A sampling from theater histories stretches from "the Meininger," the "Meiningen players," and the "Duke of Meiningen Company" to "the court players of the Duke of Saxe–Meiningen," "the company of the Duke of Meiningen under its producer Kronegk," and "the Meiningen players under the direction of Chronegk and under the patronage of the Duke of Saxo–Meiningen." All these titles have one common element—the place name Meiningen. This small Thuringian town, now seven kilometers inside the German Democratic Republic northwest of Coburg, lent its name to a local theater troupe that was to exercise an influence on the stage extending far beyond the provincial borders.

The name Meiningen came to stand for both good and ill in the theater world. To be sure, Meiningen was noted for reasons other than its resident drama company, but it is largely thanks to Duke Georg II and his work in the theater that Meiningen remains more than an unimportant name on the map. Because of Duke Georg and his company of actors, Meiningen still captures the attention of all who are interested in the drama of the nineteenth century. In spite of earlier scholarly investigations, however, the complete story of the Meininger, their preparations and performances at home and abroad, and their influence on others has remained unfamiliar.

This study of the Meininger was undertaken primarily to fill in factual information not reported by previous scholars both about Duke Georg and about his theater, and to pull together the results of prior works about the group. The Meininger had an important impact on the European theater, and an understanding of the group helps illuminate theater history. Three main areas have been investigated: the history of the Meininger theater, the theater's influence on others, and the group's critical reception.

The "reforms" associated with the Meininger were actually reflections of ideas and undertakings found in other European theatrical circles during the second half of the nineteenth century. Past writers have called the Meininger either innovators or clumsy copiers, but they can more accurately be described as refiners. Oftentimes, a concept adopted by the Meininger was changed as a result of their work so that it appeared to be a new idea or technique. The Meininger were influenced by the spirit of their time, and, acting as a catalyst for many ideas concerning stage reform, made their influence felt on the theater. However, one cannot consider the Meininger apart from the man who was their *spiritus* — Duke Georg. His theater can, indeed, be regarded as a reflection of his own understanding and ambitions. The Duke was every bit as much a product of his time as his theater was, and through his work he helped determine the direction the stage would take as the nineteenth century came to a close.

My thanks go to Drs. William H. McClain and E. Wayne Bundy for introducing the work of the Meininger to me, and for their helpful discussions and ideas concerning the theater. Mention should be made of the libraries and archives that made their resources available to me and without whose assistance my research would not have been possible: The Bavarian State Library, Munich; the Munich Theater Museum, and especially its director, Georg Laub; the library of the University of Munich; the theater collection of the Austrian National Library, Vienna; the Theater Science Institute of the University of Cologne; the Walter Unruh Theater History Collection, West Berlin; the manuscript division and literature archive of the German State Library, East Berlin; the Eisenhower Library of the Johns Hopkins University, Baltimore; and the Library of Congress, Washington, D.C. I was unable to obtain a visa to visit Meiningen, presumably due to its proximity to the border between East and West Germany. Whatever material is there (although Georg Laub has suggested that all materials pertaining to the Meininger have been moved to Leipzig) will have to serve future research. Finally, especial thanks to my wife Ganie, who offered guidance, support, editorial skills, and encouragement.

Introduction

It is not the tailor or the scenery painter, not the much–acclaimed costume book of our learned Professor Weiss—that they give us a dramatist's creation in well–rounded and complete fashion: that is the secret of the Meininger.

Karl Frenzel, Berlin critic, 1874[1]

This exaggeration in the treatment of the external aspects would destroy the stage if it became generally accepted. The form that is shown to us is so visually captivating that one no longer asks about a play's content. I have no appreciation for this type of beauty.

Paul Lindau, Berlin critic, 1874[2]

The weather may have been calm on the night of the Meininger Theater's guest appearance in Berlin during 1874, but a storm was brewing among the city's critics. Karl Frenzel and Paul Lindau held the most extreme opinions of the group, and their statements reflect the way in which the Meininger and their productions divided the theater and critical worlds into camps. The Meininger, according to contemporary opinion, either possessed the solution to all problems of the mid–nineteenth century theater or constituted the most artistically destructive force ever to appear on the stage. Duke Georg II, their leader and patron, was likewise considered either a theatrical genius or a royal dilettante. As is generally the case, however, investigation some years removed from the general furor shows that neither extreme opinion is completely justified, although previous studies of the Meininger have tended to be either a panegyric or a denunciation of the group.

The standard work on the history of the group is Max Grube's *Geschichte der Meininger* (1926), which has appeared in English translation by Ann Marie Koller as *The Story of the Meininger* (1963). Grube was a member of the Meininger theater and provides interesting anecdotes, but he lacks critical distance and is often overenthusiastic in his praise of the group's accomplishments. Other books dealing with the history of the Meininger are: Karl Grube, *Die Meininger* (1904); Hans Herrig, *Die Meininger, ihre Gastspiele und deren Bedeutung für das deutsche Theater* (1880); and Robert Prölss, *Das Herzoglich Meiningen'sche Hoftheater und die Bühnenreform* (1878). The treatises by Herrig and Prölss give first–hand accounts of the Meininger, but they were written before much of the group's history had taken place. Karl Grube had been a member of the troupe, but his book describes little more than his own experiences in the town of Meiningen and his opinions of fellow actors.

American dissertations on the Meininger have included: Anne Louise Hirt, *The Place of Georg II, Duke of Meiningen in the Unfoldment of Theatre Art* (University of Southern California, 1940); Helmuth Winfrid Hormann, *From Weimar to Meiningen: A Century of Theatrical Direction in Germany* (Cornell, 1943); and Ann Marie Best Koller, *Georg II, Duke of Saxe–Meiningen, and the German Stage* (Stanford, 1965). There have also been several German dissertations on the group, including: Gerhard Jeschke, *Die Bühnenbearbeitung der Meininger während der Gastspielzeit* (Munich, 1922); Alfred Kruchen, *Das Regieprinzip bei den Meiningern zur Zeit ihrer Gastspielepoche* (Danzig, 1933); Heinz Isterheil, *Die Bühnendekorationen bei den Meiningern* (Cologne, 1938); Marianne Jansen, *Meiningertum und Meiningerei* (Berlin, 1948); and Thomas Hahm, *Die Gastspiele des Meininger Hoftheaters im Urteil der Zeitgenossen* (Cologne, 1970). The works of Jeschke, Kruchen and Isterheil deal in detail with the playbooks used by Duke Georg, his directing techniques, and the Meininger set decorations; Hahm's treatise discusses the reception of the Meininger in Berlin and Vienna. The other studies mentioned have dealt in a more generalized fashion with the troupe's history, although they limit their discussions to the tours of 1874–1890, with some also mentioning specific developments in staging techniques.

The reception of the Meininger in the Netherlands is discussed in H. H. J. de Leeuwe, *Meiningen en Nederland: Proeve van vergelijkende Toneelgeschiedenis* (1959). Well researched and admirably documented, this work also limits its focus to the period between 1874 and 1890.

Rather than being concerned solely with what pieces the Meininger performed, where the performances took place, and what technical differences existed between Meininger performances and those of other companies, this study of the group includes historical and literary aspects as well. The discussion has been developed to help clarify mistaken ideas concerning the Meininger and to recall many lost or forgotten facts about the group and its principals.

There is some primary source material freely available in the Federal Republic of Germany in the form of correspondence, costume sketches, and set designs, and this material includes many items of interest to theater specialists. In addition, another type of primary material, invaluable for constructing a historical narrative but generally ignored by those concerned only with technical aspects, is available. Theater people are, fortuitously, seemingly vain. Dozens of those connected with the Meininger Court Theater in various capacities felt that the world would be interested in their experiences, and published volumes of reminiscences. In addition to books, many wrote autobiographical articles that were published, for the most part, in theater journals. Footnotes in this work will reflect the use of many published reports, yet these reports are hardly useful when standing alone. Many of them are first–hand accounts of situations and events at the Meiningen theater, and constitute an important source of information. These reports are not generally available, especially outside Germany, and when put together and sifted, reveal much about Georg and his theater. Such accounts were as necessary for the completion of this work as were the archival sources consulted. Through a compilation of the reports that many have left behind, the history of the Meininger can now be told in more detail than has heretofore been done.

Plate 1. Georg II, Duke of Saxe-Meiningen (1826–1914)

His intimate friends called him "Candle-ends,"
And his enemies, "Toasted-cheese."
Lewis Carroll
The Hunting of the Snark

1

Georg and the Beginnings
of the Meiningen Theater

Es gibt viele Meinungen—aber nur ein Meiningen. Wie viele über mich
herzogen, ich kenne nur einen Herzog.

Richard Wagner[1]

Richard Wagner is remembered today chiefly for his new art form, the music
drama, which he was able to create in large measure through his understanding
of the theater and the needs of the theater–going public. Georg II, Duke of
Saxe–Meiningen, is remembered not for creating a new art form, but for
reforming an existing institution, also through an understanding of the theater
and its audience.

In their own ways, Georg and Wagner were pursuing the same end: a
unification of the elements of the drama and the lifting of dramatic
presentations above commercialism. Wagner's search for an ideal aesthetic
system and Georg's strivings toward more perfect translation of dramatic
works into stage productions both broadened the realm of the possible in the
theater.

W. J. Henderson has provided a useful categorization of Wagner's aims.[2]
These were, in brief: to reduce music from the center of attention to one
element within the drama; to make a synthesis of all dramatic elements
working together for the expression of the poet's ideas; to give the libretto
dramatic flow; and to remove the lyric drama from the realm of commercial
speculation, making it more reflective of and influential on the intellect of the
audience. Wagner held lofty ideals for the theater, and his creations served as
the embodiment of those ideals. He professed the Schillerian view that the
theater should serve as a moral institution. Viewing the theater in the light of
his own work, the master of Bayreuth said in 1863: "Let us therefore determine
that the opera should be an artistic institution that contributes to the
ennoblement of public taste through continuously good and correct

presentations of musical–dramatical works."[3]

While Wagner was pursuing his goals at Munich and Bayreuth, Georg was directing his own preparations for theater reform in Meiningen. They knew each other and were familiar with each other's work. When the motto that begins this chapter was written, each had already spent years developing his plans. Wagner was then starting a new theater tradition in Bayreuth; Georg had been carrying out his own reforms in Meiningen for eleven years.

Georg's Ancestors and the Early Meininger Theater

The theater tradition that was later to develop into the troupe known as the Meininger began in 1776. That year Duke Karl August of Saxe–Coburg–Meiningen had a stage constructed in the third floor ballroom of his Meiningen castle. There the court circles presented amateur comedies that had been printed locally.[4] A theater company was not established in Meiningen until September 6, 1781, when a group of commoners performed *Die Jagd* (by Weisse; music by Hiller) on Duke Karl's stage. On that day, a civic association *(Bürgerverein),* composed of young court officials, musicians, and their families, was founded. The society used the castle stage for its dramatic performances until the early nineteenth century.

Duke Karl, who was an acquaintance of Goethe,[5] died in 1782. He was succeeded by his younger brother Georg Friedrich Karl (1761–1803), known as Georg I. The new duke also inherited the theater and continued to participate in amateur dramatics.[6] Georg I was of some importance to the literary world as well through his friendships with Schiller and Jean Paul.[7]

The first professional theater company to visit Meiningen was J. F. Schönemann's in 1785. Sondershausen came in 1787; Weber, in 1790; and Hasslock, in 1795.

When Duke Georg I died, his son, Bernhard, was only three. The government was placed in his wife's hands[8] until the young Prince Bernhard Erich Freund (1800–1882) attained the age of majority.[9]

In 1821, Bernhard took the reigns of government in Meiningen. He too had the family interest in the theater, and ten years later opened the Meiningen Private Theater as part of the festivities of his decennial. The money for the theater's construction was raised through the sale of stock. Shares cost fifty guilders, and purchasers had the option of buying shares paying either four percent, three percent, or no interest. Eighty-Five of Meiningen's citizens bought four percent notes, 87 took three percent shares, and 252 desired no interest.[10]

December 17, 1831, saw the premiere performance in the new theater, a production of Auber's comic opera *Fra Diavolo*. Productions at the private theater were done by traveling companies, who paid Bernhard up to one thousand guilders per month in rental from box office receipts. The first such company was directed by Bethmann. Other troupes were led by Hahn, Roeder, and Böhmly.[11] Duke Bernhard's financial support of the theater amounted to 250 guilders per month for the payment of orchestra members.

In 1859, at his son's urging, Bernhard changed his theater from a private theater to a court theater.[12] With this step, the Duke authorized greater expenditures for costumes and scenery, for resident actors, and for the newly created post of director *(Intendant)*. To this position he named his military adjunct, Carl, Baron von Stein. Additionally, Jean Bott, a violinist of some repute, was engaged as music director. Bott attempted to increase the stature of Meiningen as a center of the arts by writing an opera, "Aktaea, das Mädchen von Korinth," which premiered in Berlin in 1862, without success.[13]

Duke Bernhard's stage presented the usual variety of pieces—tragedies, comedies, operettas, and operas. When the current company was too weak in number to perform an opera, the choir was augmented by the addition of some of the Duke's soldiers. If necessary, the actors had to join in the singing and the singers became extras for the dramas.[14] Needless to say, performance quality often left something to be desired.

Besides making his theater available for the productions of traveling companies, Bernhard himself wrote light comedies that reportedly entertained his obedient subjects.[15] He also had an interest in music, and played the violin. The orchestra, the Meininger Hofkapelle, was under Bernhard's patronage, and repeatedly attracted Franz Liszt as guest conductor.[16]

Duke Bernhard's preoccupation with his theater may have contributed to his downfall. The upheavals of the 1840s had passed his land by with little turmoil, and he may have closed an eye to the political developments of the day. When the Seven Weeks' War of 1866 broke out between Prussia and Austria, Bernhard turned against his neighbors and sided with the Austrians, which led to a sudden occupation of the duchy by Prussian troops. Under pressure, Bernhard abdicated in favor of his son, Georg, whose own story had begun forty years before.

Georg's Early Life and Education

April 2, 1826, was a day of celebration in Meiningen; an heir to the throne had been born. The new crown prince was given his grandfather's name—Georg. By the time he was nine, Georg was considered ready for formal education. In September 1835 Moritz Seebeck, director of the Meiningen *Gymnasium,* was entrusted with the instruction of the prince, especially in the field of science.[17] It is unfortunate that more was not recorded concerning Seebeck and his pedagogical efforts with Georg. Koch, Georg's biographer in the *Deutsches Fürstenbuch,* expressed a high opinion of Seebeck's work with the young prince.[18] In fact, Koch goes so far as to state that Seebeck is primarily responsible for Georg's position in the realm of the arts, for it was Seebeck who first recognized his young charge's talents and began their development.

Georg became interested in acting while still a child. In an interview with a London reporter, Georg later recalled how theatrical presentations in which he participated fostered his love of the theater.[19] These small plays were produced with the assistance of family members in the great hall of the castle in the presence of the entire household and sometimes citizens of the town.

At the age of sixteen Georg began to study art. His first instructor in this field was the court painter, Paul Schellhorn, whom Max Grube called "not exactly a towering, but a conscientious artist."[20] The prince's favorite illustrated book was reportedly a collection of costume drawings from "Lalla Rooth," a pageant presented during 1821 in Berlin.[21] Georg's earliest artistic efforts are no longer available for evaluation; but Grube, whose objectivity is clouded somewhat by his enthusiasm for Georg and the Meininger, had apparently seen these first drawings. He testifies that even at that early stage they demonstrated "astonishing diligence and an extraordinarily sure eye."[22] The drawings reproduced here (plates 2 and 3), while not Georg's earliest, tend to substantiate Grube's claim.

Duke Bernhard, meanwhile, was having Landsberg Castle built in the Werra valley near Meiningen. He had engaged the artist Lindenschmitt for the interior ornamentation. Since Georg was no longer working with Schellhorn, he began receiving drawing instruction from Lindenschmitt.[23] As Georg later related, "I . . . am indebted to the father of the painter Lindenschmitt, who now lives in Munich, for my training in drawing."[24]

In 1844 Georg began his university studies. During his first year as a student, spent in Bonn, he studied law, archaeology, church architecture (with Kinkel), and history (with Dahlmann and Arndt).[25] As befitted a prince, Georg used his semester vacations for travel. In March 1845 he visited Paris, where he attended performances of Molière at the Théâtre Français,[26] and London, where he saw Shakespeare produced by Charles Kean at the Princess Theatre.[27]

Georg's third semester was spent at Leipzig. There he studied law and economics, but more important for his development, lived in the same house as Felix Mendelssohn-Bartholdy.[28] According to one account, the young student often discussed music with the composer.[29] These discussions certainly must have deepened Georg's appreciation and knowledge of music, and his friendship with Mendelssohn no doubt gave him added incentive to attend the concerts at the Leipziger Gewandhaus under his friend's direction. There he became acquainted with the idea that orchestral performances should, where possible, conform to the original intentions of the composer. The same attitude of fidelity later became one of Georg's leading principles in the presentations of his theater. Following the semester in Leipzig, Georg had no further contact with Mendelssohn, who died in 1847.

After his Leipzig semester, Georg entered the army. Berlin became his residence for several years, where he was a member of the Cuirassers of the Guard. As a member of royalty and a great-grandson of Friedrich Wilhelm II, Georg was naturally drawn to the Prussian court. There he had the opportunity of meeting leading figures of the day, including the artists Peter von Cornelius and Wilhelm von Kaulbach, who began his huge set of murals for the Berlin Neues Museum in 1847.[30] Grube reports that Georg studied under these artists;[31] Prasch explains, however, that they only advised him, in particular concerning an historical canvas on the subject of the Battle on the Lechfeld in A.D. 955.[32]

While in Berlin, Georg also became acquainted with Giacomo Meyerbeer, the Prussian *General-Musikdirektor,* [33] whose association helped Georg further cultivate his musical interests. He particularly enjoyed the concerts of the cathedral choir. Georg's residency in Berlin was briefly interrupted in 1849, when he fought in the Schleswig-Holstein campaign as a major in the Meiningen contingent.[34]

Early in 1850 Georg asked for the hand in marriage of Charlotte, Princess of Prussia, who was a niece of Queen Victoria of England. Following a visit to Meiningen, they were married in Charlottenburg on May 18th of that year;[35] he was then twenty-four and she, nineteen. As a wedding gift she presented him with Villa Carlotta on Lake Como, which he used throughout his life as a retreat. The young couple often visited relatives in London. During these visits Georg frequently attended the theater, where he became increasingly familiar with the Shakespearean revivals and stage reformation being carried out by Charles Kean.[36]

Even though Duke Bernhard ran his theater as he saw fit, Georg occasionally was able to apply some of his acquired knowledge in the field of dramatic art. During the fifties he undertook the presentation of Gluck's *Iphigenia in Aulis.* [37]

Although it was his first venture into theatrical production, Georg did not hesitate to make one reform. He designed all the costumes and had them specially made, a break with the tradition of every actor and actress providing his or her own costumes. Georg's goal was to create a unity of costuming, instead of a parade in which each actor tried to outdo the others in splendor.

The costumes for this opera became known as the "Crown Prince's wardrobe," and later formed the foundation of the Meininger troupe's costume department.

Georg's love of Gluck and his high aspirations for the theater soon led him into conflict with his father's wishes. Georg was usually not one to protest, but when he heard that Offenbach's *Orpheus in the Underworld* would be presented on his father's stage, he rose up in righteous indignation.[38] He maintained that the operetta was a travesty of Gluck's *Orpheus,* and wrote to the director that the presentation would ruin the public's appreciation of that work, should it ever be done in Meiningen. The prince had quite likely already had an unsuccessful confrontation with his father because of *Orpheus,* since he closes his letter on a note of resignation: "I see with sorrow that nothing can be done to avoid the calamity."

The usual state of affairs during this time, though, found Georg paying more attention to his family than to his father's theater. Charlotte and Georg had three children, but the second, Georg's namesake, died before reaching the age of three. Hardly two months later, Georg was dealt another blow when his wife died.

By this time Georg was 29 years old, and certainly sufficiently mature to have been of some service to his father in state affairs. Such experience would have been invaluable training for one who would some day become the ruler of his people. Yet Duke Bernhard did not permit his son to participate in the functionings of government.

There are at least two possible explanations for Bernhard's refusal. First, Bernhard was 55 years old, in excellent health, and foresaw no immediate possibility of Georg's becoming Duke. Second, some rivalry may have existed between father and son. Bernhard became ruler at the age of 21. He had had no opportunity to attend the university and he apparently had little understanding of things artistic. It was, after all, thanks to his son that the theater in Meiningen had changed in any way during his reign, but from the *Orpheus* incident it seems evident that father and son did not see eye to eye on the theater.

Perhaps Bernhard resented the opportunities for education and travel that his son had enjoyed. When he saw Georg becoming knowledgable in many fields, he tried to maintain his superior position in one field, in this case government, by denying his son an opportunity to gain experience in that area. Besides, Georg had studied with known liberals in Bonn, and Bernhard may have feared that his son's judgment had become tainted thereby.

Bernhard's mistrust did not extend to cutting his son off financially, though. In spite of their differences, Georg continued to receive an income as crown prince and military officer that enabled him to continue his travels and humanistic interests.

Because he had no opportunity to serve a political role as crown prince, Georg resumed his studies of music and art following his wife's death. Kaulbach, his Berlin acquaintance, sent two painters to work with him: Karl Lossow and Andreas Müller.[39] Not being needed in Meiningen, Georg decided to travel through Italy with Müller to study the art treasures in museums and churches.[40] Their trip lasted until the next year, since Georg frequently decided to retire to his Villa Carlotta in order that he might better assimilate the art history he was studying.

On October 23, 1851, he married the nineteen–year–old Princess Feodore von Hohenlohe–Langenburg. Their two children were born in 1859 and 1861.[41]

During this period Georg turned his attention to the field of music, especially church chorale music. In the summer of 1860 the prince attended a church service in Bad Salzungen, a town in the northern end of the duchy. He was impressed with the chorale music he heard there and requested a meeting with Leonhard Mühlfeld, the conductor, and Bernhard Müller, the choir-master. At that meeting, Georg expressed his approval of their efforts, and offered to help them. At Georg's expense, Müller traveled to Berlin, Dresden, and Leipzig to study the choirs there and to Rome to hear the choir of the Sistine Chapel.[42] In 1862 the results of Müller's studies were heard in a concert at Salzungen, which at Georg's request was repeated in Meiningen.

Georg was so pleased with the choir that he sent it on tour throughout the duchy, as well as to Thuringia and Franconia, where it served as a model for local choirs. In most of the towns in the duchy of Saxe–Meiningen, choirs were started that had the same composition as the Salzungen choir.[43] Typically, Georg's interest in the Salzungen choir was not limited to financial support but included criticism and guidance for improving the choir's performances. He also designed and purchased uniforms for the choir boys.[44]

The sudden flurry of musical activity in Salzungen attracted attention from far beyond the town's usual circle of influence. One musician who was involved with the preparations for the chorale performances asserted that the first step toward formation of protestant chorale societies *(Kirchengesangvereine)* was taken in Salzungen.[45]

In Georg's work with the Salzungen choir can be seen the pattern he followed throughout his life. A performance caught his attention, and he began to plan ways of improving upon what he saw and heard. He did not rely merely on his own abilities or those of the local people involved, but offered financial support so that the world's leading talents in that field might be consulted. Finally, what had been learned was applied in performances, staged so that others might learn from them.

That Georg took his role as an educator and shaper of the tastes of his people seriously is seen in a letter to Bernhard Müller dated December 19, 1860, concerning the crown prince's ideas and goals for the performance of chorale works.[46] In this letter, he expresses the opinion that only those works should be performed that would be uplifting to the congregation. He condemns the practice of letting public taste determine the level of performance, reasoning that the level of taste declines continuously as performance standards are lowered to meet the common demand. Conversely, if a high level of performance, based on artistic considerations, is maintained, then the public's taste will ultimately rise to meet that standard.

Georg's Elevation to Duke

The next significant event in Georg's life occurred in 1866. That year was marked by war, new alignments among the German states, and a new ruler in Saxe–Meiningen. The question of Schleswig–Holstein had led to the Seven Weeks' War between Prussia and Austria. Under Duke Bernhard's rule, Meiningen sided with Austria. When hostilities ended in August, Bernhard steadfastly refused to acknowledge Prussia's victory. As a result, Prussian troops were sent to occupy Meiningen and convert the tiny recalcitrant state to the Prussian way of thinking. Bernhard felt pressure not only from the outside troops but also from his own people, who wanted the Prussians to leave. Within a month, Bernhard abdicated.

On September 20, Prince Georg became Georg II, Duke of Saxe–Meiningen and Hildburghausen, to Jülich, Kleve and Berg, also Engern and Westphalia, sovereign Prince of Saalfeld, Count in Thuringia, Margrave of Meissen, Count of Henneberg, Kamburg, the Marches and Ravensburg, Lord of Kranichfeld and Ravenstein.[47] Georg immediately recognized Prussia's power, and in his first public address to the provincial legislature urged that Meiningen join the Prussian–dominated North German Confederation. Peace resulted. Meiningen joined the Confederation, and the occupying troops were removed.[48] Bernhard, who lived fifteen more years, remained in Meiningen with no political authority.

The first political matter of more than purely local importance to gain the attention of the new duke concerned the future German Kaiser. By December 1866, Georg had written to the neighboring dukes that he felt the time was ripe for the sovereigns of the German states to call for the elevation of the Prussian king to the position of Kaiser. To his cousin, Duke Ernst of Saxe–Coburg–Gotha, he wrote that the king would be more likely to accept the Kaiser's crown from the hands of the nobility of Germany than he had been to accept it from the Frankfurt Parliament. Georg also believed that the minor states would fare better under a German Kaiser than they would if they remained dominated by the power of Prussia:

> What are your views . . . on the question of whether we princes should unitedly offer the title of Kaiser to the King of Prussia? It would be accepted from the hand of the princes, but not from the hand of the Parliament. With a German Kaiser, southern Germany would be drawn in, and we would cease being, so to speak, Prussia's vassals, since the German Kaiser is quite different from the King of Prussia. We would keep our sovereignty the same as in the time of the German Reich; our position as princes against the draft constitution would not undergo any change: but we would be in a better position with a Kaiser of Germany than with the King of Prussia as President of the Confederation.[49]

To Duke Karl Alexander of Weimar, another cousin, Georg expressed the pragmatic view that a Kaiser would watch out for the interests of all who lived in his empire, whereas the King of Prussia would justifiably place Prussian interests first:

> The Kaiser will also take an interest in the welfare of those of his empire who do not live within the borders of his native state, while it would be impossible for the King of Prussia to do so.
>
> In the meantime, we have received the draft constitution of the North German Confederation, and the time appears to me to be ripe for considering whether we princes should decide to unitedly offer the Kaiser's crown to the King of Prussia, to be passed on to his descendants.[50]

To Georg, then, goes the distinction of being among the first, if not the first, of the German sovereigns to suggest that the nobility offer the Kaiser's crown to the Prussian king.[51] Thus, it appears that Georg possessed more political acumen than his father recognized. Not only did he succeed in bringing peace to the duchy where his father had brought Prussian troops, but he also demonstrated his awareness of the political trading necessary to protect his subjects from undue outside influence. He joined the Confederation, knowing that such action would bring about the departure of the occupying forces. He also immediately recognized that Prussia would ultimately dominate all other German states and that it was in his own interest to cultivate Prussian favor and try to persuade the Prussian king to accept the role of protector of the smaller German states.

During the first year of Georg's reign as Duke, his interest in music resulted in the inauguration of a series of ten "historical concerts." These concerts presented music in chronological order of composition, and were designed by Georg to educate his citizens in the history of music.[52] As a result of the attention drawn to Meiningen by the historical concert series, the Allgemeiner deutscher Musikverein (German Music Association), with Franz Liszt as its director, decided to hold its sixth *Tonkünstlerversammlung* in

Meiningen in 1867.[53] The Meininger Hofkapelle, under the direction of Emil Büchner, was the principal company for the festival's performances. That same year saw the first of the Meininger music festivals, events that later drew considerable attention.[54]

Although orchestral performances were to remain one of Duke Georg's primary interests, the opera met a different fate. It had been Bernhard's favorite theatrical form, but Georg saw that the financial demands of maintaining both an opera and a theater at a high artistic level would be too great. As a result, he dissolved the Meiningen opera and turned his attention to the art form that was to become his greatest love—the theater.[55]

Ellen Franz

The years 1866–1874 saw many changes at the Meininger Hoftheater. There were new directors, new managers, the acquisition of more scenery and costumes, and an influx of new talent. The new talent included two who, with Georg, became the molders of the Meiningen court theater during its most famous period.

The first, Ellen Franz, was born May 30, 1839. She was the only daughter of Dr. Hermann Franz, a teacher at the cathedral school of Naumburg, and his English wife. When Ellen was eight, the family moved to Berlin, where her father founded the Royal Trade School and served as its first director.[56] She received an excellent education, becoming fluent in five languages.[57] Her parents moved in the upper echelon of Berlin society and were good friends of Franz Liszt and Hans von Bülow. Liszt's daughter, Cosima, became Ellen's childhood friend and playmate, while Bülow was Ellen's piano teacher.[58]

Ellen's first encounter with the theater was at the age of sixteen, since her parents did not permit her to attend performances before then. She seems to have been quite taken with what she saw, for she insisted on visiting the theater regularly thereafter. Not satisfied with being only a spectator, Ellen began to learn women's parts from the plays of Schiller and Goethe.[59] She also persuaded Minona Frieb-Blumauer of the royal theater to give her instruction in diction.[60] Her parents became alarmed at the new interest their daughter was showing in the theater, since active participation on the stage was not considered proper for a young lady of her social position. They wanted her to abandon all interest in the theater, but her friends, Heinrich Marr of Hamburg's Thaliatheater, Franz and Cosima Liszt, and Hans von Bülow, encouraged her to become an actress. In the end, friends had a greater influence than parents, and Ellen joined the ranks of the thespians.[61]

She began her career in Coburg, where Liszt had arranged for her engagement. From there she moved to Stettin and Oldenburg, then to Mannheim. Friedrich von Bodenstedt, then Georg's director, was impressed by her acting when he visited Mannheim and offered her a contract at the Meininger theater.[62] She accepted, much to the sorrow of the Mannheim public, which regarded her as a favorite. The *Neue Badische Zeitung* exceeded its usual praise of her in its report of her final performance in Mannheim:

> The capacity house demonstrated respect for the departing artiste, such as we have seldom seen. There was a most sincere mood among the audience, which only sorrowfully sees this respected artiste depart.[63]

On October 20, 1867, Ellen Franz first appeared on the stage in Meiningen; within a short time she had become one of the leading ladies of the Meiningen company (plates 4 and 5). Her arrival in Meiningen was one of many changes that took place at Georg's theater as his zeal for the stage continued unabated during the next several years. By 1872 he had guided his company to a position from which it was beginning to attract the attention of theatergoers beyond the borders of Meiningen. Then, on February 10, his second wife, Feodore, died suddenly at the age of 32. After a period of mourning, Georg again took up his work at the theater, only to become embroiled in a father–son rivalry similar to the one that had earlier kept him from participating in the duchy's government. This time the disagreement was over a woman.

Perhaps Georg had his own blind spot in political matters, for at about the same time as Fräulein Franz came to Meiningen, the citizenry had begun to question the extent of their new duke's devotion to the theater. After Feodore's death, the popular attitude went beyond mere questioning. The general populace seemed to more or less openly disapprove of the attention Georg was paying to Ellen Franz, who by this time had been a member of the Meiningen company four and one–half years. Gossip became rampant that the Duke was seriously attracted to a commoner, and, even worse, to an actress. Georg decided to avoid the appearance of favoritism, and replaced Ellen with another actress, a certain Frau Swoboda.[64] She was met with warm enthusiasm by the Meiningen public, but the next day there appeared a bitter denunciation of Swoboda in the newspaper. The anonymous author was soon discovered to be none other than Georg.

The gauntlet thus being thrown down, a "battle" soon ensued, with father and son as principal opponents. After the publication of Georg's article critical of Swoboda, the lady's supporters had an "extra" printed calling for a show of solidarity in support of the public's new–found favorite. Their demonstration was to include the presentation of flowers after the next evening's performance.

In reaction, Georg issued a decree banning the sale of flowers in Meiningen. The "opposing forces," led by Georg's father Bernhard, who strongly disapproved of his son's friendship with Ellen, hastily telegraphed to florists in Gotha. Enough flowers arrived by train the next day to cover the stage when the final curtain fell.

The "Swoboda War" continued to escalate. It soon reached its high point with the publication in the official government newspaper of a vitriolic attack on Georg for his previous newspaper review of Swoboda's performance. The article went on to call for public demonstrations against the Duke. Incensed, Georg ordered an immediate investigation into the identity of the anonymous writer. The investigation soon bore fruit. The author was Georg's father, Bernhard Erich Freund.

Georg decided he had had enough of this petty fighting. While Meiningen was celebrating Frau Swoboda's acting, he traveled to nearby Bad Liebenstein and advised Ellen to do the same. When she arrived, Georg granted her the title of Helene, Baroness of Heldburg. The day was March 18, 1873; Georg was about to take decisive action designed to quash the rumors flying about Meiningen and prove to his father once and for all that he was the master of his own affairs. That night Georg and Helene were married in a room of his Liebenstein villa by the superintendant of the nearby village of Schweina. Ludwig Chronegk, a member of the Meiningen theater, had been invited to accompany Georg. He had become Georg's confidant, and was to serve as a witness for the marriage ceremony. The superintendant could not allow this, though, since Chronegk, being Jewish, was forbidden by law from serving in this capacity. As a result, the witnesses at the Duke's wedding were two of his household servants.

When news of the morganatic marriage was telegraphed to Meiningen, top government officials immediately tendered their resignations. Georg's two oldest children refused to have anything to do with his new wife, but the children of his second marriage immediately accepted her as their step-mother.[65] Georg's action soon won public approval as well. After a brief period of adjustment, most of Meiningen's residents accepted Helene as a fitting companion for their Duke, and Georg went on to show that he could be the ruler his people needed while still giving attention to his interests in artistic fields.

Ludwig Chronegk

Georg and his new wife formed two–thirds of a "team" that was to lead the Meiningen theater to new heights of fame and accomplishment. The remaining member of the triumvirate was Georg's close friend Ludwig Chronegk (plate

7). Details of his life are rather sketchy, but his history appears to have been one of continual involvement with the theater. Chronegk was born in 1837 in Brandenburg an der Havel, and his theatrical career began in the Kroll–Theater in Berlin.[66] His specialties throughout his acting career were simpletons *(Dümmlinge)* and female impersonations in vaudeville sketches. The somewhat corpulent comedian moved on to Görlitz, Pest, Zurich, Leipzig, and back to Berlin's Königstädter Theater before being signed as a member of the Meininger theater in 1866 at the age of 29. His first appearance in his new home was in the premiere performance under the new Duke Georg II, so it can truly be said of Chronegk that he was with the Meininger from the very beginning.

The next year of Chronegk's life brought him a friendship that was to have great impact on his future. That friendship was with the new actress Ellen Franz. When Georg began turning to her for answers to questions concerning dramatic performance, it seemed only natural that Chronegk participate in the discussions. It was thus that Georg discovered qualities hitherto unseen in this insignificant actor whose motto was *"immer lustigk" [sic]* (always happy). The three became close friends, as shown by Chronegk's invitation to the wedding of Georg and Ellen. The rest of his life was bound up with the Meininger theater, where he quickly rose to a high position. His death was to have a telling impact on the theater.

With Georg, Helene, and Chronegk working together, and with Georg controlling purse strings and repertoire, the stage was now set for the Meininger theater's finest hour. The "Meininger" have often been regarded as if they suddenly sprang full-blown into being, served 16 years as a model for the German theater, and then vanished, but they were actually a result of the interaction of a very specific mixture of people and events. If Georg's life had been different, the "Meininger" might not have had the influence they did.

Georg was neither the first nor the last member of the nobility to turn his attention to the theater, but he was surely more than the dilettante some have called him. He received a thorough introduction to the arts when young, and if that had been all there were to his education, perhaps he would indeed have become a dilettante. Instead, he went on to study with noted revolutionaries in Bonn and discuss music with a leading contemporary composer. He was hurt by the loss of a child and two wives, and perhaps turned to music and theater to a greater extent than he would have otherwise in an attempt to compensate for this loss. His father, too, helped make him what he was, by showing no confidence in his abilities. Georg bided his time, knowing that he would someday probably be ruler of his own theater as well as of his people.

It is noteworthy that Georg chose his third wife from the theater, and that he trusted only one other person, Ludwig Chronegk, to know of his plans for marrying Ellen Franz. Without Georg, the Meininger never would have been; but without Ellen Franz und Ludwig Chronegk, the Meininger never would have become a significant part of theater history. March 18, 1873, was more than just the wedding day of Georg and Ellen. It was also the birthday of their "child." Paul Lindau called it "the birthday of the true Meininger art."[67]

2

The Meininger: 1866–1926

There's no greater life
Than a "walk-on's" life;
Chronegk and Georg have made it a joy.
To always cry "Hail, Caesar!"
And stand as a statue on a stair
Is a high and a wonderful form of employ.

Karl Grube[1]

The Meininger are best known for their European tours from 1874 to 1890. The history of their theater both before and after those seventeen years is important, though, because it shows the development of Georg's plans and his troupe's skills.

Georg's theater was a natural product of nineteenth century concern for the actual and observable. Developments in the theater world showed Georg the direction his stage would take. When he became Duke in 1866, he used his resources and the facilities of his Meiningen theater to create a stage that he felt could serve as an example to the rest of the world.

Their tours took the Meininger to 36 cities in 14 countries. These tours not only presented the Meininger to a vast audience, they also established a model for other traveling stages to follow.

When the Meininger ended their tours, much of the world lost track of their work. Although its influence was greatly diminished, the Meininger theater continued to maintain high standards. Georg's attitude toward the theater did not change, and his stage continued to be a center for productions that were especially notable for the richness and detail of their sets. The development and post–tour history of the Meininger are generally unfamiliar, but there is a wealth of facts and stories that illustrate how the Meininger came to be an important force in the development of the nineteenth century theater.

Nineteenth-Century Currents of Thought

When Georg II became director of the Meininger court theater in 1866, conditions at his theater were typical of those found in most German towns.[2] The usual theater of the time had a resident company that performed a number of plays each season. Each company, naturally, had actors and actresses of local fame, but the nineteenth century had witnessed the rise of the star system, in which performers of greater fame made guest appearances at theaters throughout the country.

Originally seen as a means of improving local productions, the star system eventually had the opposite effect. Players of lesser talent joined the truly first–rate performers on the touring circuit in order to meet the demand as the public's hunger for "stars" became insatiable. As the frequency of guest appearances increased, the local troupes degenerated into mere supporting companies. An audience could often be attracted only by the advertised appearance of a famous personality on the stage.

Virtuosity for its own sake became common, and two stars would sometimes appear on stage at the same time, declaiming to the audience and ignoring each other. The public most often came to see a "name" perform, and dramatic content was of only secondary importance. A performance of *Othello* can serve as an example.[3] Edwin Booth played the title role, and the German Dawison was cast as Iago. Othello spoke English; Iago, German. Poor Desdemona spoke either English or German, depending on her conversation partner.

At the smaller stages there were stars of second and third rank, and these, too, had their followings. Max Grube relates that the star system even extended into the animal world. When Grube was a member of a small traveling company, the director was informed of a star guinea pig by the name of Leichsenring who was available for a performance with the company (Imagine the posters: "R.'s theater, this week featuring the world–famous guinea pig Leichsenring!"). The talented rodent's fee was too great, though —five thalers—and the company was obliged to continue without its services.[4]

Most directors thought more of filling their own pockets than of fulfilling their audiences' needs. Expense was kept to a minimum by eliminating all but the most essential rehearsals, and the thought of constructing special scenery for a play seemed to occur to no one. Carried to its extremes, the desire to get a play on the stage as quickly as possible led to a production of Schiller's *Fiesco* that had been prepared in two days, including all memorization, and a *Kabale und Liebe* performance presented by completely new personnel after only 90 minutes of rehearsal.[5] Props were designed mainly for the opera; if the theater needed some for a drama, there was a choice between a knight's hall and an ordinary room, medieval and modern streets, a forest and an open field.

Even at the Prussian court theater *(Hoftheater)*, the most respected German stage, the situation was no different. Paul Schlenther, later director there, tells in a volume about the Prussian theater under Botho von Hülsen's direction that the scenery was often a completely unrelated mixture most notable for its anachronisms: "The year 500 was burdened with a Swiss–style house," relates Schlenther as an example. "The tower of Sestos looked across, in its Normanic glory, to a cottage that had been built in rustic, romantic style on Abydos."[6]

The attitude toward classical drama was that a few performances could be given each year as a concession to art. Realistic drama fared even worse. There was little room on the Berlin stage for a play that offered anything beyond light entertainment. As a result, the Hoftheater's repertoire included 21 pieces by Roderich Benedix and 19 by Charlotte Birch–Pfeiffer, two very prolific nineteenth–century playwrights whose works were generally based on stock situations and conflicts that were ultimately resolved to a happy conclusion.[7]

Although some trends in the theater seemed to be negative, positive changes were occurring on other fronts. A new concern for the circumstances of time and place led to new developments in staging during the nineteenth century. Interest shifted from the universal and idealistic to the individualistic. There was a new enthusiasm for the study of national and historical differences in architecture, literature, dress, and customs. The first history of costume appeared in the late eighteenth century, and in 1856 the first installment of Hermann Weiss's influential costume history was published.

The Hoftheater in Berlin was perhaps the first theater to emphasize the new interest in historical accuracy in an 1801 production of Schiller's *Maid of Orleans*. Under von Bruhl's management, this theater was to become an important force in the popularization of antiquarianism in Germany, although later in the century the theater's direction paid far less attention to the harmonious presentation of historical elements. In France, Hugo and Dumas *père* insisted upon historically accurate settings and costumes, while Charles Kemble's 1824 London production of *King John* was the first in England to claim historical accuracy in every detail of costuming.[8]

The next development took place in the area of set construction. With the new–found realism of spectacle—i.e., the visual elements—the wing–and–drop setting seemed inadequate for interiors. It was gradually replaced by the box set, comprising three walls and a ceiling. Steps toward creation of box sets had been taken in the late eighteenth century, and by the early nineteenth century it was in limited use throughout Europe, by Schröder in Hamburg and Küstner in Munich, for example. The box set was not consistently used, however, until the period of the Meininger. Related to the box set was Diderot's theory of the fourth wall, which described the stage as a room with the wall closest to the audience being transparent. More and more the action took place inside the proscenium, and the actors behaved as if they were in real rooms.

Innovations in stage lighting enhanced stage realism. In the 1820s, gas started to replace candles and oil lamps and was used almost universally by 1840. The gas table was perfected by 1850. This central panel of gas valves (operated by a technician known as the "gas man") permitted complete and instantaneous control of all lights. Soon thereafter the limelight and the carbon arc came into use, making possible special effects such as sun rays or moonlight.

The new brighter light emphasized the artificiality of painted scenery and props. In the 1830s, three–dimensional details were beginning to appear. Door knobs were added to doors, floors were carpeted, and real molding was attached to walls.

While the theater moved toward increased realism, philosophy was also moving in new directions, and both disciplines reflected a nineteenth century preoccupation with the observable elements of life. The conclusion that man's problems could be solved through systematic inquiry was becoming more and more popular. Observation of phenomena and prediction of results became important tools, and the world was thought to be understandable only through sensuous experience.

One of the most influential thinkers of the mid-nineteenth century was Auguste Comte. His theory of logical positivism argued that scientific methods can be applied to the study of societies (hence the term "sociology"), and that the social behavior of man is subject to law and rationally comprehensible. The key to knowledge, according to Comte, lies in precise observation and experimentation, for all social events must be understood in terms of cause and effect. Man's primary means of gaining knowledge, he maintained, is through his five senses.

Charles Darwin's thoughts on evolution had the effect of reinforcing the attractiveness of Comte's positivism. The ideas in *On the Origin of Species by Means of Natural Selection or the Preservation of Favored Races in the Struggle for Life* were first formulated in 1838 and finally published in 1859. Darwin's theses—that evolution is explained by the process of natural selection, and that evolution justifies belief in the descent of all species from a common ancestor—had several important implications for the realist of the nineteenth century. First, heredity and environment are the determinants of existance and the explanations for all character traits and actions. Second, the traditional ideas of God as creator cannot be supported. As a corollary, the concept of immortality is challenged and man seems to have only his present life in which to reach fulfillment. Third, since natural selection has in the past led to improvement of the species, the process of improvement will similarly continue in the future. Fourth, man is no longer set apart from the rest of the natural world, but is seen as just another object for observation and experimentation.

The movement known as realism was an attempt to better the lot of mankind by coming to a fuller understanding of the truth. Truth, however, was defined by such influential figures as Comte and Darwin as being only that knowledge gained through the five senses. The new regard for observation gained importance in fields other than science and philosophy as well. The theater, Brockett noted, responded by becoming increasingly concerned with realism and accuracy. Playwrights felt they should write of the society around them, since that was the "truth" they were able to observe.[9] In the area of stage production, the first steps in the direction of realism were toward historical accuracy in setting and costume.

By mid-nineteenth century the greatest progress in the field of realistic presentation on the stage had been made in London. Falconer rescued the Drury Lane Theatre from a businessman who had regarded it solely as a speculation. Under Falconer's direction the theater gained fame as a center for Shakespearean productions. He spared no expense in restoring the theater and providing authentic costumes, but his outlays proved too extravagant. The theater was forced into bankruptcy.

A kinder fate met the Sadler's Wells Theatre, which since 1804 had been devoted to "nautical drama" because a stage–sized water tank had been installed so that sea battles and rescues from drowning could be portrayed.[10] By the 1850s, though, Samuel Phelps had turned Sadler's Wells into a well–respected, serious theater. He sought to achieve a harmony between the spoken and the visual elements, always keeping in mind that the spectacle should not detract from the words and ideas of the play. Phelps was a thespian as well as a director, and he understood his actors' personal needs. By emphasizing their achievements, he was able to develop a true ensemble from the members of the company.

Charles Kean, son of the famous actor Edmund Kean, became director of London's Princess Theatre in 1850. Kean and his wife, Ellen Tree, acted in their own productions, but their real abilities lay in managing and directing. A Fellow of the Society of Antiquaries, Kean prided himself on the historical accuracy of his costumes, scenery, and props. For example, the audience attending his production of Byron's *Sardanapalus* saw a reproduction of Nineveh that corresponded to Layard's excavations of the ancient city. However, between 1850 and 1859 the Princess Theatre was most famous for its Shakespeare "revivals." Kean changed the presentations of the Bard's plays from collections of speeches accompanied by gestures to productions alive with visual components. The scenery and stage decoration became important supporting elements instead of merely annoying problems to be dealt with. Historical elements were presented with painterly skill on Kean's stage, i.e., he attempted to reproduce a scene in a manner similar to that of an historical painter such as Kaulbach. The composition was well–executed, and all parts were blended harmoniously into a whole. Kean believed in stage symmetry, and in order to present a pleasant "picture" he emphasized the stage's mid–line. By balancing elements on both sides of the imaginary line, the resulting picture was immediately pleasing, although in the long run such unfailing symmetry would prove boring.

Rehearsals at Kean's theater showed the same attention to detail as did the decoration. He believed in long rehearsals so that everyone knew his part thoroughly. Background research was necessary, and he consulted cultural and art historians for advice on costuming and scenery. The cost of such planning was understandably high, and led to a "long–run system." After 1855, Kean's troupe rarely performed a play fewer than one hundred successive times. Kean was fortunate enough to gain the patronage of Queen Victoria, which drew aristrocratic audiences to the theater and elevated his work in the eyes of the English public.

Crown Prince Georg of Meiningen had seen Kean's work in London during the 1850s, but another German, the actor Friederich Haase, was also much impressed during a visit to the Princess Theatre.[11] He saw only one performance, *The Merchant of Venice,* with Kean as Shylock and his wife as Portia, but in his description of the performance, Haase speaks of magnificent staging, lively stage action, and scenery that formed the perfect setting for the drama. His evening at the Princess Theatre lived on in his memory for years afterward.

In 1866 Haase had been engaged as director of the Coburg court theater by Duke Ernst II of Saxe–Coburg–Gotha. Haase won Duke Ernst's financial backing for a production similar to the one he had seen earlier in London. He hired two local artists, the Brückner brothers, to paint the scenery, had copies of Kean's costumes made especially for the production, and held rehearsal after rehearsal until he felt that the play had become second nature to all participants. When all was ready, Haase felt he had been faithful to the standard set by Kean. He was pleased, ". . . to have brought to life a production of *The Merchant of Venice* that was a well–done watercolor of the majestic oil painting that had made such a strong impression on me in London."[12]

Georg's Operation of the Meiningen Theater from 1866 to 1869

Duke Ernst had invited his cousin, the new Duke Georg II of Saxe-Meiningen, to the premiere performance, the date of which Haase failed to record. According to Haase, the Coburg public enjoyed his production, and the Duke invited him to a festive supper afterwards. The other guests were Georg, Friedrich von Bodenstedt, Baron von Meyern-Hohenberg of the Coburg theater, and cabinet officer Dr. Tempeltey. Discussion flowed freely in the intimate circle, and, in Haase's opinion, it was on that night that Georg decided to restore the classics to their place on the German stage. Haase wrote of the evening:

> On that evening . . . (Georg) most likely made his decision to devote to classical drama the artistic attention to detail that a few years later made the Meininger theater famous.[13]

The Meiningen theater season had usually begun in October, but the Duchy's political turmoil during 1866 forced postponement of the opening until November. Along with the theater, Georg had inherited his father's producer,[14] Carl, Baron von Stein, and his artistic director, Karl Grabowsky, who bore the title also of supervising director.[15] Grabowsky had been a member of Vienna's Burgtheater in 1849, and after traveling from stage to stage obtained his position in Meiningen. These two—Stein and Grabowsky—helped Georg present the 1866–67 season, although Stein had felt for some time that his training was inadequate to manage a theater.

After six weeks of preparation, the first play under the new Duke opened; *Hamlet* was presented on November 4. Shakespeare's tragedy was not new to Meiningen, but a recently hired member of the company was. Ludwig Chronegk, who would later become director of the Hoftheater, made his first Meiningen appearance in the role of Guildenstern. Other notable productions that season included Shakespeare's *Julius Caesar* and Sophocles' *Oedipus Rex, Antigone,* and *Oedipus at Colonus.* The Meiningen productions of Sophocles used the just–completed translations by Adolf Wilbrandt, who had requested through a colleague, a teacher of Georg's eldest son, that his work be given a trial at the Meiningen theater. Wilbrandt described his translations as the first attempt to translate Sophocles into German, adapt his plays for the modern (nineteenth century) stage, and replace the Greek metrical system with one more suited to German. Another of his stated goals, which may have made his translations especially appealing to Georg, was to individualize the chorus.[16]

Oedipus at Colonus was not performed until season's end, since Wilbrandt had originally translated only the other two dramas. The initial success was so great, however, that he immediately set to work, completing his translation of *Oedipus at Colonus* in the early spring of 1867.[17] The Meiningen audience apparently appreciated these classical productions; one account relates that the theater was sold out for the performances of Sophocles.[18]

From narratives about the early period of the Hoftheater under Georg's reign, one might gather the impression that the citizenry of Meiningen had been starved for classical drama, judging from the nature of the plays supposedly presented. The anonymous author of the introductory article in the 1926 *Festschrift* stated, for example, "the nature [of the 1866–67 repertoire] was definitely classical."[19] A count of the plays performed in Meiningen during the first season, however, shows the repertoire to have been evenly divided between plays that were considered classical and those that were simply popular entertainment.[20] The company performed five pieces by Benedix and one by Birch–Pfeiffer. There were "farces" and "domestic scenes," a "rustic portrait" and a "comical sketch," but there were also plays by Lessing, Goethe and Schiller. Near the end of the season, Georg produced the one–act play *Between the Battles* by Björnson, the Norwegian author, who was then unknown on the German stage. A mixture of classical and light pieces was far more likely to succeed than a strictly classical repertoire, since such a mixture was the custom at nearly every theater of the period. Far from suddenly breaking with past tradition by turning his theater into one where only classical drama would be performed, Georg continued to produce lighter, less demanding pieces in order to please the limited Meiningen audience, while at the same time working toward perfecting his productions of classical pieces.

By the time the season closed on April 15, 1867, Stein had convinced Georg that it would be in the theater's best interest for him to retire. The next day Friedrich von Bodenstedt joined the Meiningen company as the new director. Georg had invited Bodenstedt to Meiningen several times in the course of the first season, having anticipated Stein's leaving the theater. Bodenstedt liked conditions in Meiningen, and agreed to join the theater upon Stein's retirement. In so agreeing, the noted Shakespeare translator and author of the "Mirza Schaffy" poems left his Munich professorship, which caused some amazement among his colleages who viewed the practical side of the theater with some disdain.

The 1867–68 theater season opened October 20 with a performance of *Romeo and Juliet.* Bodenstedt demonstrated his thorough knowledge of Shakespeare by basing the production on Schlegel's German version, using his own translation where he felt it to be an improvement. As the season progressed, though, it became even less classically oriented than the previous season had been; almost two–thirds of the productions were farces, minor comedies and other light pieces including a "Vaudeville farce" and a "comic

Intermezzo." In spite of the opera's discontinuance, musical drama appeared on the Meiningen stage during the season. A "musical quodlibet," *Fröhlich* (Happy), was presented in November; three scenes from Gounod's opera *Romeo and Juliet* and act three of Wagner's *Lohengrin* were combined into one program with a Kotzebue one–acter in February; and in March an Offenbach operetta was performed.

The classical repertoire was extensively changed from the previous year's. Bodenstedt used his own translation of *Macbeth,* his adaptation of Schlegel's translation of *King John,* Schlegel's versions of *Richard II* (shortened because it proved to be too lengthy), *Henry IV* (Part I), *Cymbeline,* and *A Midsummer Night's Dream* (adapted by Tieck and Schlegel), and West's version of *King Lear.* Goethe, Schiller, Calderon, and Beaumarchis were represented, Kleist's *Das Käthchen von Heilbronn* had its first Meiningen performance, and the season closed with Aeschylus' *Orestia* trilogy.

It is, of course, impossible to judge the artistic success of all the theater's productions, but some eyewitness accounts remain. During the 1867–68 season, a lengthy report was given in the *Jahrbuch der deutschen Shakespeare-Gesellschaft* of the Meiningen theater's *King John* production.[21] The reporter contrasted Bodenstedt's work in Meiningen with Dingelstedt's in Vienna. In his opinion, both had the same goal with regard to Shakespeare; namely, to win wider acceptance of his plays among German audiences. Their means to this end differed, however. Dingelstedt shortened and adapted Shakespeare, whereas Bodenstedt merely translated, eliminating nothing from the original (although in performance Bodenstedt often felt free to eliminate characters or passages from plays).

With this background discussion completed, the reporter gave his impressions of the actual performance. He had seen only two of the actors before, and he feared that the company of unknowns would prove to be less than satisfactory. Quite the opposite was true. He found the individual performances to be better than merely adequate, while the ensemble worked to perfection. Thanks to the harmonious performance of all, from the leading roles to the smallest walk-on parts, the reporter became more aware of the story of the play and less aware of the performances of individuals. He commented, too, on the scenery and costumes, feeling that the scenery was nearly perfectly suited to the action, and that the historical accuracy of props, far from distracting with detail, helped put the audience in the proper frame of mind and demonstrated artistic sensitivity on the part of Georg and Bodenstedt. Grabowsky received praise, also, and the reporter felt that the entire *mise-en-scène* was in every respect superior to anything he had seen at Berlin's Hoftheater.

Whereas Dingelstedt's productions tended to increase dramatic tension and please the audience with virtuoso performances, Bodenstedt's productions flowed smoothly, with any disturbing or boring elements eliminated, so that his audiences found equal pleasure in every scene. Oechelhäuser felt, however, that Bodenstedt could have cut additional material from the text of *King John.* The performance lasted four hours, which was, in his opinion, too long. The reporter wondered whether performances such as those in Meiningen might be possible elsewhere, and came to the conclusion that they probably would not. The prerequisites for a Meiningen–like performance would be a company willing to work as a true ensemble, so that all parts were well–performed, a stage devoted solely to drama, and theater leadership that was devoted only to art and not to financial reward. The famous theaters of the time strove to attain only mediocre goals. To see Shakespeare performed well, the reporter felt that one would need to go to Weimar, Karlsruhe, or Meiningen, whose stages could serve as an example to the entire nation.

Bodenstedt had invited Ernst Possart from Munich to play the title role in *King John.* While Possart had some fame as an actor, this was not necessarily an attempt to revive the "star system" in Meiningen. As early as 1865, Georg had been corresponding with Bodenstedt, who was a friend of Possart. At that time, Georg was directing a performance of *Othello* for his father's birthday celebration, and Bodenstedt had recommended his friend to Georg for the role of Iago. The crown prince agreed to hire Possart for the December 17, 1865, production. Georg had been pleased with Possart's performance then, and when Bodenstedt suggested that his friend play the role of Johann, Georg readily agreed.

The day after the performance of *King John,* Bodenstedt informed Possart that Georg wanted him to remain in Meiningen long enough to repeat his performance. He also told his friend that the Duke wished to speak to him, perhaps about his plans for the Hoftheater. "He is working on plans," said Bodenstedt, "that could become epoch–making in the future of the German stage."[22]

Georg did indeed speak to Possart of his plans. He explained that he was formulating a program for presenting dramatic masterworks to the German public with authentic costuming and scenery. These performances were not to take place in Meiningen, though, since the town could not support repeated performances of the same piece. Even then Georg had a missionary–like zeal concerning his theater. As he put it to Possart, "If the mountain won't come to the prophet, then the prophet has to go to the mountain."[23]

As Georg had desired, *King John* was repeated December 21. The following day, Georg again requested Possart's presence, so that the actor could present scenes from *Richard II* and dine with the Duke's party. In the course of the supper, Georg and Bodenstedt had an argument concerning attempts to present characters in Schiller's plays in a realistic mode. They specifically discussed *Wilhelm Tell*. Georg felt that the long monologue "Durch diese hohle Gasse muss er kommen" ("He must come down this empty path") (act 4, scene 3) was out of character for Tell. Not wanting to tamper with Schiller's poetry, however, Georg suggested that the speech should remain in the play but that Tell recite it as if he were in great haste. Such a delivery would indicate that Tell shoots Gessler while in an emotionally charged frame of mind, whereas if Tell stops and ponders his imminent action, then he is guilty of premeditated murder.

Bodenstedt became quite vehement in his reaction to Georg's thoughts, replying that Schiller never intended to free Tell from the accusation of murder. Instead, Bodenstedt claimed, Tell is behaving as a soldier in battle, killing to support and defend his land. The hasty delivery suggested by Georg would destroy the effect of the monologue and succeed only in killing Gessler a few minutes sooner, while at the same time mortally wounding Schiller and his concept of freedom.[24]

There seems to have been considerable misunderstanding between Georg and Bodenstedt, going far deeper than differences of opinion about Tell's monologue. Georg had hoped that Bodenstedt would be able to take charge of the theater, and Bodenstedt assumed that Georg was a typical ruler who wanted a good theater and was willing to spend whatever was necessary to reach that goal, but who himself understood little about the arts. Paul Lindau, who knew Bodenstedt, wrote in his memoirs that in actuality the professor was virtually helpless in the practical matters of operating a theater.[25] Bodenstedt's duty as director and as a poet was to get to the heart of a dramatic work and then present the play in such a way that the audience could also see the author's intentions, but he seemed incapable of transforming the poetic ideal into physical reality on the stage. In fact, Georg was himself responsible for many of the productions done during Bodenstedt's tenure. Grabowsky and Georg kept the theater operating, and Bodenstedt felt that he was being interfered with from above and treated with disrespect from below. By November 1869, Bodenstedt decided that conditions had become intolerable, and asked for a release from his position as director. Georg granted him his wish and, feeling responsible for Bodenstedt's situation since he had invited him to Meiningen, gave him a lifelong pension.

Bodenstedt remained in Meiningen for some time, harboring a spirit of malice toward Georg and his court for the supposed injustices committed against him, and quite willing to express his feelings to anyone who would listen. During his Meiningen residency, for example, he received a request from Lindau for contributions to his new publication *Neues Blatt*. Bodenstedt obliged him, but the poetry he sent was so bitter and full of hatred that Lindau found it unusable and destroyed it. He could later recall only one passage, in which Bodenstedt complained about:

> The court flunkeys, who are lower in the realm of creation than the apes; they are the nastiest vermin that God, in his wrath, has created.[26]

Preparations for the Meininger Tours: 1869–1874

With Bodenstedt's departure from the Meininger theater, Georg took the duties of stage manager upon himself. He became responsible for the personnel, and when he was at the theater he directed the rehearsals through Grabowsky's mediation. Grabowsky remained nominal director, taking charge of rehearsals when Georg was not present. During the 1869–70 season Georg also embarked on a program designed to make the Meininger theater more widely known. In December 1869 he invited two guests to view performances at his theater: Hermann Köchly, professor of classical philology in Heidelberg, and Karl Frenzel, theater critic for Berlin's *Nationalzeitung.* [27] Georg recognized that a favorable reaction by these two acknowledged experts would increase Meiningen's fame, but he also wanted to hear their critical opinions of his work. The local press had no drama critic, and although Georg felt he was proceeding on the right course, he desired knowledgeable confirmation.[28]

Köchly, familiar with Roman civilization through his translations of Caesar's memoirs of the Gallic and Civil Wars, was favorably impressed by the historical accuracy of the costumes, weapons, and scenery in the Meiningen production of *Julius Caesar* on January 2, 1870. The scenery had been prepared by the Brückner brothers of Coburg and Händel of Weimar, and was based on Visconti's sketches of his archaeological excavations. Hermann Weiss, the costume historian, had been consulted before the costumes were made. He taught Georg, for example, that the patterns in Roman clothing had been woven into the material, and that the modern practice of sewing decorated panels to the basic material destroyed the natural drape of the clothing. Instead, he recommended painting the decoration directly on the cloth. Weiss also instructed the company in the proper way to wear Roman coats, togas, tunics, dresses, and peploses. The weapons were copies of original Roman weapons assembled by Napoleon III in the museum of St. Germain.

Frenzel arrived in Meiningen on New Year's Eve 1869, and met with Georg that evening to discuss the theater. The critic immediately liked Georg and approved of his plans; from that time forth he became a supporter of the Duke and his company.[29] The next evening he viewed the Meiningen performance of *The Taming of the Shrew,* and recorded his thoughts for later publication in the *Nationalzeitung.* [30] His overall impression was one of a harmonious production. Individual performances were less than perfect, to be sure, because few of the actors had had long acting experience. The costumes, though, transported Frenzel to the Italy of the early Renaissance. He felt that costumes from other theaters, usually of a generalized fashion with a few specific details added, came off second best in comparison to Georg's, which were obviously designed by someone with an artistic eye and an understanding of historical clothing. In his review he also countered the oft–heard argument that excellent staging distracted an audience's attention from the content of a play. His experience at the Meiningen theater was that the audience had its powers of imagination channeled in one direction, so that the sense of illusion was generally undisturbed and the resulting attention given the dramatic content by the audience was much greater.

Frenzel admitted that there were some disharmonious points. Three actors, Franz, Chronegk, and Weilenbeck, tried to keep up a tempo that the others on stage found difficult. As a result, the audience's expectation that the action would be as unified as the decoration was not realized.

The critic found the production of *Julius Caesar,* presented on January 2, to be even more to his liking. His one point of criticism was that the stage was too small to allow the mass scenes to be as impressive as they might have been otherwise. His further discussion was completely in praise of the production. Through skillfully planned and executed scenery, the five scene changes in the fifth act were eliminated; all parties were on stage at the same time, but were located at different elevations of the three–dimensional scenery. The mass scenes, in spite of the space limitations, were the best executed Frenzel had ever seen. The individual members of the crowd carried on their own conversations and wore individually differentiated clothing, yet all were part of a single cohesive group. From individuals a unified body had been created, and the controlled individuality was a sign of considerable planning, rehearsal, and effort. Chronegk was singled out by Frenzel as one especially responsible for the group's success, because he acted as leader of the chorus. The individual roles, as Frenzel had expected, were not as well played as the crowd scenes were, but in general he considered the production to have been highly successful. [31]

There is one other record still extant of theater conditions in Meiningen during the period immediately following Bodenstedt's departure. [32] The account grew out of Georg's March 1870 visit to Berlin. March 22 was the birthday of Wilhelm, King of Prussia, and Georg had gone to Berlin to offer his personal best wishes. During his visit, he had occasion to attend the Prussian Hoftheater, where the performances of Siegward Friedmann and

Ludwig Dessoir caught his eye. At evening's conclusion, Georg extended an invitation to the actors for a meeting the following day. Not only had neither one of them ever met a member of royalty before, but they also had never heard of Meiningen until then. The two were somewhat uncomfortable when they met Georg, for he received them in military uniform (plate 8). They were soon put at ease, though, because the Duke wanted only to talk of the theater. Friedmann and Dessoir were playing the roles of Brutus and Cassius in Berlin, and Georg invited them to play the same roles on his stage in Meiningen. They accepted his offer, and he arranged their leaves from the Prussian theater.

They arrived in Meiningen on March 30, and were informed that they would be required to join in the four rehearsals remaining before *Julius Caesar* was presented on April 3. Such a directive came as a surprise to the Berlin actors, because they had come from the city, where they had already rehearsed their parts assuming that they would be exempt from any rehearsals in Meiningen. They soon concluded, however, that there was nothing else to do in Meiningen, and they attended the rehearsals.

Friedmann recorded that Georg was present at the rehearsals, leading the sessions himself. He sat in the darkened balcony and called out his directions, which were passed on to the actors by Grabowsky. The "managing director" was actually nothing more than an intermediary, because Georg seemed to want to keep a distance between himself and the actors.

The intensive nature of the rehearsals surprised the guests from Berlin. Georg sometimes ordered scenes repeated several times, each time noticing small details he wanted improved. Although he devoted greater attention to the main roles than he did to the small parts, the correct performance of both was of equal interest to him, and his suggestions for improvement often went into considerable detail. The behavior of the crowd was also important to him, and he tried to eliminate any actions that, in his opinion, were at all inappropriate. The rehearsals may have been lengthier than usual because, although the Meiningen theater had presented *Julius Caesar* three years earlier, it had not been a permanent part of the Meiningen repertoire since then. (Friedmann incorrectly states otherwise.) Besides, Georg wanted Frenzel and Köchly to see as perfect a production as possible. Friedmann and Dessoir were very impressed by the rehearsals, and Friedmann compared the proceedings to Lessing's *Dramaturgy*. Dessoir was more ebullient in his praise, saying, "I call that *direction!* It seems to me as if we came from Podunk to a leading court theater!"[33]

The comparison Friedmann made between the costumes of the Prussian and the Meiningen theaters is important, because it shows that Georg had already developed costuming in 1870 that far exceeded the usual theaters' costumes in terms of historical accuracy. Dessoir and Friedmann had brought their own clothing from Berlin, but were asked to use local costumes so as not to disturb the visual unity on the stage. Their usual togas were, as Friedmann described them, about the size of a tablecloth. The Meiningen togas were 30 ells long and made of wool. The wardrobe master had to teach them how to put the togas on, but Dessoir was less successful than his compatriot. He was apparently too short for the expanse of material, and looked like a "Roman nutcracker in swaddling clothes" when he was dressed. After he recovered from his initial surprise at his costume, however, Friedmann felt that the heavy weight was useful to him. It dampened his gestures, he wrote, and made him a more reserved and dignified Cassius.

Alois Wohlmuth, who was with the Meiningen company 1872–73, had a completely opposite view.[34] He disliked the town, and he disliked the way the theater was run. In his opinion, the actors were thought of as available bodies and were of no use to Georg if they possessed any spirit of independence. The actor condemned the new type of theater director, epitomized by Georg, who wanted to manage everything himself and who gave the dramatic personnel only secondary importance, comparing such a director to a doctor who cures pain by killing the nerve rather than removing the cause.

Wohlmuth felt that no one in Meiningen had any feeling for the poetic elements of drama. When he played Friar Lawrence in *Romeo and Juliet,* for example, he was told exactly where he should stand so as not to hide a piece of scenery. In a contrary mood, he delivered his lines without feeling, with improper intonation, and prosaically. No one corrected him; everyone was concerned only with the "painterliness" of the scene. As another example, Wohlmuth mentioned that while Romeo spoke with Benvolio about Rosaline (act 1, scene 1), peddlers tried to sell him apples and oranges. To Wohlmuth, Georg's work was no better than that of the English directors who had tried to impress their audiences with scenery. He had an explanation, too, for the way in which Frenzel was seemingly duped: Georg bribed him by promising him titles and decorations!

By the time of the 1872–73 season, the Meininger theater was performing considerably more pieces that could be considered classics. Shakespeare was often represented, and Goethe's *Faust* received its first Meiningen performance, as did Grillparzer's *Sappho.* During that season the stage was used only once for opera, when *The Marriage of Figero* was performed with the assistance of members of the Coburg opera.

One of the most famous of the group soon to be known as the Meininger, Ludwig Barnay (plate 9), made his first appearance with the company during the same season. Ludwig Chronegk, a friend of Barnay since 1860, passed on to him Georg's invitation to perform with the company, which he did in the role of Posa in Schiller's *Don Carlos* on November 3, 1872.[35] Just as other guest actors had, Barnay found the rehearsals to be completely different from anything else he had experienced. He found that such attention was paid to detail that at times it seemed as if the company were rehearsing a piece for its premiere performance with the author in attendance. Barnay was also impressed by Georg's desire to have every detail of a performance correspond to the playwright's intentions as he understood them. Barnay not only found the physical accoutrements historically accurate, but also regarded the performances of all the actors as completely appropriate. Everyone and everything seemed to be on stage for the sake of harmony.

Barnay was invited to return on December 1, as well as on March 11 and 13, 1873. He later recalled how, during one of these visits, he disputed with Georg a psychological point about Hamlet's role, the result being that the Duke agreed to make the change Barnay had suggested. He also remembered that he wanted to wear his usual costume from the Thirty Years' War period in *The Taming of the Shrew,* but was afterward glad that he had been forced to wear the Renaissance-style costume provided in Meiningen. Barnay said that he learned from the first incident that Georg was not a tyrant in his own theater and that he accepted advice from any source if such advice would enhance the performance. The second incident led to a basic change in Barnay's acting style, although he recognized it as such only afterward. He realized that the qualities portrayed in a role should come from within the actor and not depend on his costume or physical surroundings. Barnay came to understand this when he saw he could tame the Shrew as well in a genteel costume as he could in coarse clothing, swinging his whip wildly. If nothing else, the Meiningen emphasis on correct outward appearance helped Barnay, destined to become one of Germany's most celebrated actors, develop a more refined style of acting.

Karl Frenzel was again Georg's guest twice during the 1872–73 season. In September 1872 the two met in Bad Liebenstein. During a stroll through the forest, Georg asked Frenzel for the first time if he thought the theater might have some success as a touring company.[36] They decided that Berlin was a possible first city to visit. The privileged status of the royal theater (Prussian Hoftheater) had just been revoked, and other companies were now permitted to present classical drama and tragedy in Berlin. Frenzel told Georg that the Friedrich-Wilhelmstädtisches and the Viktoria theaters would be available the next summer, and Georg confessed that his interest in a visit[37] went beyond his desire for critical attention and his belief that he had something to offer the German stage. He told Frenzel that he could no longer support the theater based on the income available in Meiningen, and if a new source of income were not found, he feared that his theater would stagnate.

In March 1873 Frenzel came to Meiningen to witness the performances of *The Merchant of Venice, Twelfth Night,* and *Macbeth.* [38] He afterward offered Georg his opinion that the theater could successfully compete in Berlin, and encouraged the Duke to make the necessary arrangements. Georg was tempted to agree then, because he needed money in order to add Schiller's *Fiesco,* which had not been done in Meiningen since 1867, and Kleist's *Hermannsschlacht* to the repertoire. Instead, he told Frenzel he would consider the matter further.

The week after Frenzel's departure, Georg married Ellen Franz in Liebenstein while Meiningen watched Frau Swoboda star in Moser's farce *Das Stiftungsfest.* After one more performance, the theater abruptly closed its doors one month early. During the off–season, Georg made a fundamental change in the theater leadership. Grabowsky was promoted to director *emeritus,* and Georg's friend Ludwig Chronegk was made regisseur.[39] In this position, Chronegk was the theater's artistic and administrative director, and he took charge of the theater's preparations for a possible guest appearance in Berlin.

The curious repertoire of the 1873–74 season hinted that something extraordinary was afoot. October, November, and December saw a continuous series of comedies and farces interrupted only by one performance each of *Julius Caesar* and Schiller's *Robbers,* as well as the Meiningen premiere of Otto Ludwig's *Der Erbförster.* The comedies probably required little preparation, leaving time for lengthy and repeated rehearsals of more serious works. In mid-December, the long rehearsals culminated in a series of performances somewhat weightier than had been seen earlier in the season. The Hoftheater presented Goethe's *Götz von Berlichingen,* Schiller's *Robbers,* Molière's *The Imaginary Invalid,* Shakespeare's *Twelfth Night,* and the more recent *Pope Sixtus V* by Julius Minding. The latter two were to become part of the repertoire for the first Berlin visit, which by this time had definitely been agreed upon by Georg and Chronegk.

In a letter dated December 23, 1873, the Meiningen director wrote to his friend Ludwig Barnay in strictest confidence that the theater would be appearing at Berlin's Friedrich–Wilhelmstädtisches Theater during May and June of 1874.[40] The reason for his letter, Chronegk explained, was that he wanted Barnay to take the leading roles in some of the Meiningen productions, and he wanted Barnay's approval before he told the Duke of his plan to engage his old friend. From Chronegk's letter it is evident that the repertoire for the visit had not yet been determined, because he offered Barnay the parts of Mark Anthony in *Julius Caesar,* Macduff in *Macbeth,* the title role in *Wilhelm Tell,* Heinrich von Navarra in Lindner's *Bluthochzeit,* and a role in an unnamed one–act play (Björnson's *Between the Battles).* Additionally, he told his friend that there would be many other pieces in which he would have no role. If Barnay agreed to his offer, Chronegk would arrange "try–outs" for him in Meiningen during the coming spring, so that Georg could give his final approval.

At about the same time, Georg was again corresponding with Frenzel. The Duke told the critic of his decision, and asked for his assistance in making arrangements to rent a theater and to publicize the theater's performances. The reason Georg chose the Friedrich–Wilhelmstädtisches Theater was that its stage was approximately the same size as Meiningen's stage; thus, the preparations would be made somewhat easier by familiar conditions.[41]

The new year, 1874, saw an increasing number of classical pieces tried out on the Meiningen stage: *Egmont, Emilia Galotti, Romeo and Juliet, The Learned Ladies, The Merchant of Venice, Minna von Barnhelm, Macbeth, Twelfth Night, Wilhelm Tell, The Imaginary Invalid,* and *Maria Stuart,* as well as the newer pieces *Pope Sixtus V* and *Bluthochzeit.* By the end of March, Barnay had had his tryouts and had been named an honorary member of the company, and a definite program had been agreed upon. The season closed with five of the six plays that would be presented in Berlin. *Julius Caesar,* the play most familiar to the members of the theater, was not repeated at season's end.

The First Meininger Visit: 1874

The time had come for the Herzogliches Hoftheater to become, as one wag put it, a "hin– und herzogliches Theater."[42] In mid–April, costumes, scenery, and props were shipped by train from Meiningen to Berlin. The members of the theater soon joined the properties at the Friedrich–Wilhelmstädtisches Theater. The younger actors were glad to visit the capital; the older members of the troupe were less enthusiastic about leaving the peace and quiet of Meiningen. All, however, were somewhat apprehensive about their chances of favorably impressing the Berlin public. Their theater had become the center of critical disagreement even before its first Berlin performance. Basing their arguments on Frenzel's reports and the stories of a few others who had visited Meiningen, Berlin's theater critics discussed the "principles" of the Meiningen theater and whether or not the "reforms" represented by the group's performances were valid.

While argument raged outside the theater, chaos seemingly reigned within. The local director tried to adapt the Meiningen scenery to the Berlin stage while the musical director was rehearsing the locally hired musicians. Chronegk had engaged local soldiers to act as extras, and he was spending hour after hour with them for days, trying to educate them in the ways of the

Romans. As Chronegk would finish with one group of five or ten, it would be assigned to a regular member of the company, who then acted as its leader. The wardrobe department was busily sorting the costumes and delivering them to the appropriate dressing rooms, while Grabowsky, who had accompanied the troupe, stalked the stage, "representing" the Duke. Georg, meanwhile, was in Meiningen. He chose not to join his troupe, not to be there to witness their success or failure, not to take part in the hectic preparations leading up to the guest performances. As director, he would normally have met with the local critics before the opening night to ask for their favorable reviews, but Georg did not want to become involved with the trappings of publicity. Just as he directed his rehearsals through an intermediary, so he also let his representatives carry out the more mundane details of the Berlin public performance.

Georg also saw no practical reason for his presence. He had trained his company as best he could. He had had costumes and scenery prepared according to his directions, and he had rehearsed the company until he was confident they were capable of performing well. The die was cast, and his presence in Berlin could have had no effect on the troupe's performance.

May 1, 1874, was slated as the opening night. Everything was finally in place, and the actors were costumed and milling about the stage, anticipating the curtain's rising. Into the swarm strode Chronegk, holding a telegram. When the crowd finally quieted, he read the Duke's last message to the company before its Berlin opening: "Good luck to all! Pfutz shouldn't take too long to die. Georg." His only concern seemed to be that a minor actor named Pfutz, who had invented his own death scene for the battle in the last act of *Julius Caesar,* would be too melodramatic and draw attention to himself. The lack of last–minute advice indicates that Georg had confidence in the course he had taken with his theater and its preparations for its Berlin performances. The telegram also reflects his familiarity and concern with every detail.

Max Grube, who had joined the Meininger theater in 1873 and who was to become one of its most devoted members, recorded his impressions of the theater's first Berlin performances.[43] His report from backstage is interesting because it differs in its point of view from the accounts left by critics. When the curtain went up at 7 p.m., the audience was at first surprised by the appearance of the stage set, he wrote. Whatever they might have been expecting, they were most certainly not expecting an historically accurate reproduction of the Roman Forum. New to them also was the plotting scene in Brutus's orchard (act 2, scene 1). The usual method of delivery in the scene was to speak forcefully; the Meininger used a stage whisper, since secret intrigue is not usually shouted for all to hear. The audience's reaction, Grube continued, was enthusiastic.

The battle scenes were also presented in a manner unfamiliar to the Berliners, wrote Grube. Those who took part in the stage fight were regular members of the troupe, not extras hired for crowd scenes. The actors were drilled in techniques of combat, so that they appeared to be actually fighting. If blood were accidentally spilled, the audience accepted it as a natural part of the battle. Additionally, wounded and killed were planned in the stage directions, completing the illusion that the actors were actually striking hefty blows. The portion of the stage where the battles took place was narrowed, giving the impression of a larger group than was actually on stage, and the battles took place in twilight and moonlight, so that the semi–darkness helped further the audience's impression that the battle was real.

Grube reported that the audience was especially impressed by the appearance of Caesar's ghost. In that scene (act 4, scene 3), Brutus's tent was dark red, and suddenly Caesar appeared against this background as if out of nowhere. The technique was simple. The actor's costume was of the same material as the tent wall, and he blended into the backdrop until an electric spotlight suddenly illuminated his face. Electric lighting was making its first appearance, and Georg had hired Baer of Dresden, one of the first masters of the new technical field, to develop special light effects for the Berlin performances.[44]

The effect of the carefully prepared production on the Berlin public was suprisingly widespread and far more favorable than most had thought possible. At evening's conclusion, repeated curtain calls were necessary. By the next day, Berlin's theater world was divided into two camps: Pro–Schauspielhaus (the Prussian royal theater, under von Hülsen's direction) and pro–Meininger.[45] In spite of the controversy among the critics, or maybe because of it, the people of Berlin thronged to see the provincial theater that was causing such a stir. The May 1 performance was attended mainly by theater critics, Berlin nobility, and friends of the theater who had come from Meiningen. The May 2 performance was more sparsely attended, but public interest waxed when the reviews were published, and May 3 was the first of many sold–out evenings.

Demand for tickets was so great that the visit, originally scheduled to close May 31, was extended through June 16. The original theater calendar was of necessity revised. *Julius Caesar,* originally scheduled for six consecutive evenings, was performed 10 times. The next play scheduled was *Pope Sixtus V.* Similar care and attention had been lavished on preparations for both productions, but Minding's drama proved to be unpopular and was replaced after four evenings by *Julius Caesar,* which was then repeated an additional 12 times. The next piece, *Twelfth Night,* had nothing of the splendor of *Julius Caesar's* staging, and none of the crowd scenes. Nevertheless, the comedy was well received, Grube claimed, and it demonstrated that the Meininger had those among their actors and actresses who could carry a performance without the aid of extras.

Albert Lindner's *Bluthochzeit* was the Meininger's fourth production. Several critics changed their line of attack, questioning whether the piece was worth performing. Whereas the Meininger had heretofore been criticized for presenting poor acting that they tried to cover up by the use of well–made scenery, critics now said that even the talents of the Meininger could do nothing to save a play that was poorly written.

Four evenings were occupied by Molière's *The Imaginary Invalid,* which bore signs of revision. Georg had eliminated the curtain between acts by having servants tidy the room with the curtain up.[46] While this technique was new to much of the audience, most seemed to find it an interesting change. Georg also eliminated the closing scene, however, replacing it with a rather flat line spoken by the invalid: "I want no more doctors in this house! And if Dr. Purgon comes, drop this large bottle on his head." On the same program with Molière was Björnson's *Between the Battles.* The Norwegian one–acter was fortunately the first part of the program. Grube said that Berlin audiences found the play strange and not to their liking, but that Molière made the evening a success.

The 1874 visit closed with *The Merchant of Venice.* The Meininger were least prepared to present Shakespeare's Venetian comedy, and scheduled its performance for only two nights. The play was not at all well received, and even Grube admits that the performance was poor in comparison to the later Meininger version of 1886.[47]

Georg's aspirations for the visit to Berlin had been met. First, he had needed additional income to finance the production of new pieces. By May 20, 15,500 guilders worth of tickets had been sold. Chronegk had calculated that the daily costs of the trip would be 500 guilders; thus, the entire month's expenses had been recouped by the time the month was two–thirds past. The additional 7500 guilders worth of tickets that were sold during the remainder of May were counted as profit.[48] Applying the same profit/cost ratio to the half month of June that the run was extended shows that the theater concluded its first Berlin visit with a profit of over 11,000 guilders.

Because the main financial reason for the Berlin performances had been to raise money for new productions, Georg kept the actors' salaries low. Barnay, for example, received only 600 guilders for the month he spent in Berlin, although Georg also rewarded him with a medal. As he explained in a letter to the actor, Georg was so pleased with the theater's trip that he had decided to create a medal for art and science, and awarded the first two of the series to Chronegk and Barnay.[49]

The second reason for the Meininger's visit to Berlin was to receive critical appraisal. The Meininger had undeniably caused a storm in Berlin, and the critics had been a very vocal part of the uproar. For every person supporting the Meininger there was another who disapproved of their efforts. Georg certainly had sufficient material to ponder during the summer.

The people of Berlin had seen the Meininger, and thus Georg's third goal had been fulfilled. He felt that he was leading the German theater in a new direction, and he especially felt that he was showing his countrymen how Shakespeare should be performed. He needed a wide audience for his efforts, and in Berlin the theater, seating approximately 800, had been sold out nearly every night. Over 37,000 spectators had witnessed Georg's work.

The new season opened in Meiningen at the beginning of November. Georg and Chronegk had agreed that there should be a second Berlin trip, and additional arrangements had been made for performances in Vienna and Budapest. The citizens of Meiningen were again offered only occasional light comedies during the early part of the 1874–75 season, since their theater was trying out new pieces for its upcoming guest appearances.

1875–1880

The Meininger theater had opened later than usual in 1874, and it also closed the season early, on April 4, 1875. Following a pattern that was to become traditional, the final month of the season was given over to the plays that would be presented on the upcoming tour. Four new plays, Kleist's *Hermannsschlacht,* Grillparzer's *Esther,* [50] Molière's *The Learned Ladies,* and Schiller's *Die Verschwörung des Fiesco zu Genua,* were added to the traveling repertoire for 1875, while one from the previous year, *Pope Sixtus V,* was eliminated.

The Meininger had booked the same Berlin theater for two months this time, and they were to perform from April 16 through June 15. Coming to Berlin in the spring became a tradition of sorts with the Meininger, leading the magazine *Kladderadatsch* to speculate that they were called the Meininger because they always came to Berlin during the month of *Mai.* [51]

The four newly–rehearsed plays formed the core of the second season. All four were to remain in the Meininger repertoire until the cessation of the tours.

Increased advance publicity in 1875 caused greater public awareness of the Meininger in Berlin, but it also led to a direct conflict with the Prussian Royal Theater. When von Hülsen heard that the Meininger would be performing *Hermannsschlacht,* he rearranged the schedule of the Schauspielhaus so that Kleist's play would be on both stages at the same time.[52] Although he succeeded in filling the theater for several evenings, attendance fell off so sharply when the Meininger began their *Hermannsschlacht* that von Hülsen cancelled his remaining performances.

The Meininger's second Berlin visit proved to be as successful as their first. Schiller's *Fiesco* was the center of their program, and played 22 of the 60 evenings they were in Berlin. Björnson's *Between the Battles* was received even more coolly than it had been the previous year, and was replaced after two performances by Grillparzer's *Esther. Julius Caesar* was repeated eight times.

Observing the traditional summer closing, Georg dismissed his actors until September, when they reassembled for their first appearance in Vienna, lasting from September 25 to October 31. Whereas Chronegk had been able to hire local soldiers as extras in Germany, the Austrian authorities forbade that country's soldiers to appear on the stage. Chronegk therefore had to hire anyone who showed an interest in the job. The repertoire in Vienna was composed of plays that the Meininger had done in Berlin, but the Vienna public did not warm to the group as the Berliners had. They felt, perhaps justifiably, that their own *Hofburgtheater* was superior to all other stages. Nevertheless, Dingelstedt, director of the Burgtheater, found much to his liking in the Meininger's *Imaginary Invalid,* which was performed but once. He adopted their *mise–en–scène,* and from that time forth the Burgtheater's placards for Molière's play proclaimed that their production was based on the Meininger version.[53]

When the Meininger played in Budapest November 3-19, Chronegk solved his problem with extras in a different way. For some reason, the bakeries of Budapest were closed, and so the Roman army of the Meininger was composed entirely of temporarily out–of–work bakers.[54] Chronegk had considerable difficulty making it clear to the baker army why they should care about Caesar and his fate. Finally the director lost his temper and threatened to beat his extras if they did not cooperate. His outburst had the desired effect, although a member of the troupe recalled being torn at the time between amusement and fear for Chronegk's safety when the short director began threatening the group of 100 strong young Hungarians.

Perhaps the most significant result of the 1875 tour was that the Meininger found that they could transport all their necessary equipment with them from city to city. The approximately 60 actors and actresses were accompanied by 20 to 30 mechanics, movers, and other assistants. The Meininger even had their own gas man who traveled with them. Special trains were required to transport people and material, since all scenery, costumes, and props traveled with the company.[55] This was something new in the theater. Prior to the Meininger, touring companies traveled by post coach, and it was always a minor miracle when actors, costumes, and scenery arrived in the right place at the right time. Ignoring the question of cost, travel by special rail car demanded considerable planning, but the ease with which touring companies traveled since that time is due primarily to the example set by the Meininger.[56]

For 1876 Georg added five new pieces to the traveling repertoire; two enjoyed great success, one was only moderately popular, and two were never again performed by the Meininger. *Das Käthchen von Heilbronn* by Kleist was received warmly, while Schiller's *Wilhelm Tell* was to become one of the Meininger's greatest successes.

Tell must have struck a responsive chord with the public, for it succeeded in spite of some serious faults. The central figure was portrayed as an average man, not as the hero of a national legend. Barnay, the Meininger's first Tell, especially tried to give the impression that the character was one whom a person could meet at any time walking down a Swiss street. Georg could not conceive of Tell as being otherwise; his earlier argument with Bodenstedt concerning Tell's character had laid the foundation for the 1876 production.

One notably unsuccessful revision in the Meninger version was made because Georg abhorred animals on the stage. In the scene disputed with Bodenstedt (act 4, scene 3), Armgard is supposed to throw herself before Gessler's horse, daring him to trample her as he has trampled freedom. In the Duke's production, however, Gessler walked down the "empty path," and, meeting Armgard, said, "Make way, woman, or my foot [instead of "horse"] will pass over you." Audiences invariably found the line amusing, and the high point of the play took on a completely different character than Schiller had intended. In spite of the production's deficiencies, *Tell* was extremely popular with audiences, and was eventually performed 223 times during the tours.

The other new plays of the 1876 season enjoyed lesser popularity. *Macbeth* was done according to the Schlegel/Tieck translation instead of the customary Schiller translation. When it did not succeed as other plays by Shakespeare had, it was dropped from the repertoire the following year. Otto Ludwig's *Der Erbförster* (The Hereditary Forester) had a rather limited run, closing after only two performances. Grube claims that the play was warmly received,[57] but in fact Georg had a great love of the outdoor life that was not necessarily shared by his audiences. Additionally, *Erbförster* was rushed into production. Whereas *Tell* had been rehearsed for three years before appearing on the Berlin stage, Ludwig's play had had only three performances in Meiningen before it was added to the traveling repertoire.

Georg had visited Scandinavia in 1875, and one of his souvenirs was a new interest in Nordic drama. The Meininger theater had been performing Björnson since 1867, and his *Between the Battles* was a regular feature on Meininger playbills. Now Georg had become acquainted with the work of a second Norwegian dramatist—Henrik Ibsen. While visiting Norway, Georg saw *Kongsemnerne (The Pretenders),* and investigated the locales where the play is set and the costumes of the region. He decided to add *The Pretenders* to his company's stock of plays, but the performance suffered from the Duke's impetuosity. There were only three trial runs in Meiningen, which were the first performances of Ibsen in all of Germany. The Meininger took Ibsen's play to Berlin, but it lasted only seven performances. Ibsen was present in Berlin for the 1876 Meininger visit, since it was the first time one of his plays had been done for a large German audience. He maintained a philosophical attitude toward the show's demise, saying that it closed only because the Meininger were leaving town.[58]

The 1876 tour was interrupted for the summer, and then continued in Dresden and Breslau from mid–September to mid–November. The plays that had had little success in Berlin were eliminated in the latter two cities, and the program was rounded out with successes from prior years. At the conclusion of the year's trips, Chronegk was promoted to managing director, which did not change his duties, but gave him more prestige.

In 1877 Georg decided his troupe could dispense with a visit to Berlin, where the company was already well–known, and instead widen its circle of influence by visiting Cologne and Frankfurt. Without the Berlin audience to act as a sounding board, Georg felt comfortable adding only one new piece to the repertoire that year. That one new play became another unsuccessful attempt at convincing audiences that they should share the Duke's love of plays about the outdoor life. The drama in question was Iffland's *Die Jäger* (The Hunters), performed by the Meininger near the end of their visit to Cologne. First seen in Meiningen in 1868, this genre picture was a personal favorite of the Duke. The people of Cologne did not share his taste, however, and the play was permanently dropped after two performances.

Besides the usual mixture of minor comedies and plays scheduled for the upcoming tour, there were also several benefits staged in Meiningen during the 1877–78 season. They included a concert for the widows and orphans fund; a celebration of Carl Eduard von Holtei's eightieth birthday to provide support for the playwright and former actor, who was living in poverty in Breslau; and, most interestingly, a benefit premiere of a play by Adolph L'Arronge for the Genossenschaft deutscher Bühnen–Angehöriger (German Theatrical Guild). The guild had been started by Ludwig Barnay in 1871 as a representative body of actors to counterbalance the Deutscher Bühnen–Verein (German Theater Association), an organization of theater owners and directors headed by Berlin's Botho von Hülsen. As a theater owner, Georg might have been expected not to support Barnay's group, but he not only disliked Hülsen, he also felt that the actors should receive more democratic representation. That is not to say that Georg had no rules at his own theater. He had a strict code with a list of fines that could be assessed against those who broke rules, but he did not see himself in the role of adversary to his actors.

December 19, 1877, was a notable day in Meiningen. That evening Schiller's *Robbers* was presented in finished form, ready to become part of future tours. Joseph Lewinsky had come from the Burgtheater to play the role of Franz von Moor, and special trains brought over 500 guests to the performance.[59] The costumes seen by the audience were to prove especially popular with students wherever the Meininger performed. Instead of the unidentifiable shabby clothing worn on other stages, the Meininger robbers wore uniforms modeled after those of the students at the Württemberg Military Academy, where Schiller had studied, and clothing similar to that of the robber bands seen in southern Germany during the period of Schiller's youth.

Also on the stage that evening was a young actor who would use the Meininger stage as a springboard to much greater fame. Joseph Kainz (plate 10) had been fired from the Leipzig municipal theater, but immediately found a position in Meiningen. There he was schooled in acting by Helene and was introduced to a new acting technique by Georg. That technique, which Georg repeatedly instructed the Meininger to use, required an actor to place himself entirely in the role given him, so that he was in every sense the means whereby the author's words took on life.[60]

Kainz received favorable notice from Frenzel when *The Robbers* opened in Berlin in 1878. He played the role of Kozinsky, but Chronegk took Frenzel's praise as a sign that Kainz could be entrusted with more important roles.[61] Emmerich Robert, a noted actor from Vienna's Burgtheater, had been engaged to take the leading role in Kleist's *Prince Friedrich von Homburg,* which was the Meininger's second new piece for 1878. Chronegk decided at the last minute that Kainz would alternate with Robert as the prince.

An unfortunate incident helped Kainz and the Meininger make Kleist's Prussian drama the "hit" of the season. While Kaiser Wilhelm I was riding through the streets of Berlin on May 11, an attempt was made to assassinate him. A young man shot at but missed the elderly German leader, and the people of Berlin became quite wrought up over the incident. The Meininger had fortuitously scheduled *Prince Friedrich* for that evening, and the theater was completely sold out.[62] Emotions were at a fever pitch, and all stood applauding as the orchestra played the national anthem prior to the curtain's rising. All who were present anticipated the play's last line, and when the words rang out, "Down with all enemies of Brandenburg!" ("In Staub mit allen Feinden Brandenburgs") the audience began cheering wildly. Kainz's and the Meininger's victory was complete.

Shakespeare's *The Winter's Tale* had recently become popular on the German stage thanks to Dingelstedt's translation. Flotow, who had collaborated with Dingelstedt, had written an extensive musical accompaniment and had choreographed the play. The customary costuming for the play was entirely white, in pseudo–classical style. Georg eliminated most music, used Tieck's translation, and designed costumes based on Botticelli paintings and Bohemian peasant clothing. The Duke thereby hoped to match the costumes better to the play's locales (Sicilia and Bohemia) so that his audiences might pay closer attention to the play's content and be less estranged by its apparent timelessness. With *The Winter's Tale* the Meininger proved that Shakespearean drama was their forte; the play became second only to *Julius Caesar* in popularity and was performed 233 times during the tours. Grillparzer's *Die Ahnfrau* completed the 1878 Berlin schedule.

During the performances in Berlin, Georg became embroiled in a lawsuit brought by one of his actresses.[63] On June 6, 1878, Therese Grunert told Chronegk during the break between the third and fourth acts of *The Winter's Tale* that she wanted to play Bertha in *Die Ahnfrau,* which was scheduled for the following evening. The casting had already been set—she was scheduled to have the part three days later—and Chronegk refused her request. She thereupon declared that she was indisposed and would be unable to continue that evening's performance, in which she was playing the role of Time. After some name–calling on both sides, Chronegk fired her, effective June 15, on the grounds of insubordination. She immediately complained to the theater association, which had legal authority in such disputes. Von Hülsen, the organization's president, repaid Georg for his previous lack of support by acting as counsel for Grunert. The association decreed that the actress could not be fired without compensation, no matter what the reason. She was awarded 900 marks damages plus five percent interest, and Georg was forced to remove a clause from his theater regulations that permitted "dismissal without compensation."

The other members of the troupe felt that an injustice had been perpetrated, and with their consent Georg resigned as a member of the theater association.[64] Von Hülsen's reaction was to pass a law that no actor who had been a member of the Meininger theater in 1878 could be hired at another stage until he or she had signed a document repudiating all support of Georg and his theater. The theater world was generally appalled at von Hülsen's blatantly prejudicial treatment of his rival director, and several publications, such as Kürschner's almanac *(Theaterjahrbuch),* called for von Hülsen's resignation and a boycott of the theater association. Peace was not restored between the association and the Meininger theater until 1909 when the association's journal printed a special "Meininger issue."

After closing in Berlin, the Meininger traveled to Frankfurt am Main. On the twenty–first day of their visit, July 10, they were to perform *Die Ahnfrau.* The theater was already half full when Chronegk stepped in front of the curtain shortly after six p.m. and told the audience that the evening's performance had been cancelled because of "technical difficulties." The real reason soon became apparent. Within a few minutes a conflagration had enveloped the roof of the theater. The cause of the fire was a break in the gas pipe above the stage lights. The Meininger quickly carried whatever costumes and scenery they could outside, and the fire actually damaged nothing of theirs. The water, however, destroyed the scenery for *Die Ahnfrau* and *Wilhelm Tell,* part of the scenery for *Julius Caesar* and *The Winter's Tale,* and many costumes, according to Chronegk's report.[65] Damage to the Meininger properties was 18,000 marks, which was covered by insurance.

The fire may have been an inconvenience to the Meininger, but it also gave theatergoers an opportunity to show their support of the troupe. In his report, Chronegk mentioned receiving an envelope addressed to "the Directorship of the Royal Meininger Acting Society in Frankfurt am Main." The envelope bore no return address, but contained two five-mark notes and a forget–me–not.

1881–1890

Although the tours continued as usual for the next two years, there were no additions to the repertoire until 1881, when the Meininger performed in London. That year they added to their stock of plays *Wallensteins Lager;* Goethe's *Iphigenia; Preciosa,* which was a melodrama[66] by Wolff with music by Carl Maria von Weber; and *The Taming of the Shrew.* [67] While in London the Meininger performed the first three of the aforementioned plays, as well as nine others. Three of the plays done in London were Shakespearean, one was by Molière, and eight were by German authors, including four by Schiller. All performances were given in German.

Georg and Chronegk had chosen the cavernous Drury Lane Theatre, seating over 3200, for their guest appearances. Chronegk was entrusted with the management of all details, as had become usual during the tours, even though he spoke not a word of English. His efforts in training the local supernumeraries were especially difficult because of the language barrier. Additionally, the Meininger did not arrive in London until May 27 and their run started on May 30, which left only the weekend to train the extensive crowds needed for Drury Lane's large stage.

The guest appearances opened with *Julius Caesar,* which attracted considerable attention. The Meininger benefitted from the Londoners' familiarity with the play, because the performance in German seemed not to hinder the audiences' understanding or appreciation of the drama, judging from the large attendance during the play's first run. *Julius Caesar* was also the first play the Meininger ever gave as a matinee. British law required theaters to close on Sunday, so Chronegk scheduled Saturday afternoon performances to help make up the difference at the box office. The first of these matinees was designated a "professional matinee," and was presented for the benefit of the London actors who could not attend the regular evening performances. Over three hundred actors and actresses attended, including, according to Barnay, the greatest stars of the British and American stage.[68]

One of the Meininger's 57 London performances comprised the third acts of *Julius Caesar, Wilhelm Tell,* and *The Winter's Tale.* There is no record of why Chronegk chose such a combination, although he was doubtless attempting to stem the tide of decreasing attendance.

Julius Caesar, which had been enjoying great success, was removed from the program after five performances because the Prince of Wales, who was the Meininger's patron during their London visit, decided that he was tired of Shakespeare and wanted to see Wolff's *Preciosa.* Although the melodrama was adequately performed,[69] it was in no way Shakespeare's equal. Public interest in the Meininger performances waned, in spite of the later return of *Julius Caesar* to the program. Besides *Julius Caesar, Wilhelm Tell* was considered to have been a success, and people came to see *Iphigenia* because it was written by Goethe. Chronegk hardly gave the other two Shakespeare plays a chance to succeed, and the remaining pieces on the calendar were unfamiliar to most Londoners. There were over 30,000 Germans living in London at the time, but it would have been a mistake to rely on them alone to fill the theater every evening. However, some support was forthcoming from the German community. Fifty of the leading German merchants of the city volunteered as extras in the productions of *Preciosa.*

Although there was some public enthusiasm at first, the Meininger's visit to London would have to be regarded as a failure. The press made favorable comments only about the costumes; all else—the acting, the choice of plays, even the scenery—was regarded as being below London standards. To the Londoners, the Meininger performances seemed heavily Germanic and often far different from the Shakespeare familiar to them. Clement Scott wrote in London's *Daily Telegraph* on June 30, for example, that there was nothing of the "true Shakespearean flavour," in the Meininger's *Twelfth Night,* pointing out that the humor was German, not English, and that even "the clown might be a peasant in a German beer–garden." Although the Meininger's supporters have long presented the London visit as the prime example of how well the troupe was received even under unfavorable circumstances—i.e., in a foreign country—the fact remains that in London they were unable to draw a full house.[70]

During the next five years, Georg reduced the theater season in Meiningen to an average length of only three months each year, while at the same time increasing the time the company spent on the road. New plays were added to the Meininger repertoire annually. As could be expected, some of the new plays had successful runs, while others became failures. Schiller was most favorably represented. *The Piccolomini,* which had almost vanished from the German stage, and *Wallenstein's Death* became staples of the Meininger schedule. The Meininger rarely performed the Wallenstein trilogy as other than a complete unit filling two successive evenings, and Georg once even scheduled all three for one evening, a plan that was thereafter abandoned due to the program's length. *Maria Stuart* also became popular with the Meininger's audiences. *The Bride of Messina* was the only Schiller play the group did not find to be a success.

Over the years there has been some speculation as to why Goethe and Lessing were not better represented in the Meininger's touring repertoire.[71] The conclusion has generally been drawn that either Georg had an antipathy for the two German classicists or he was so discouraged by the indifferent reception received by Goethe's *Iphigenia* and Lessing's *Miss Sara Sampson* that he assumed their plays would not draw an audience. An investigation of the theater calendar in Meiningen hints otherwise. Of Goethe's dramas, *Clavigo, Torquato Tasso, Egmont, Faust, Götz von Berlichingen,* and *Iphigenia* were performed in Meiningen, while Lessing was represented by *Emilia Galotti, Miss Sara Sampson, Minna von Barnhelm,* and *Nathan der Weise.* If Georg truly had had a dislike of Goethe's and Lessing's dramas, he would most certainly not have produced so many of them.

Karl Grube suggested a possible explanation for the exclusion of *Emilia Galotti* and *Nathan der Weise* from the Meininger tours. The two plays were part of the permanent repertoire of Berlin's Royal Theater, and, Grube maintained, Georg realized that the Meininger would suffer from a comparison.[72]

The overall reason for the absence of Goethe and Lessing from the Meininger stage tours, however, can be found in Georg's artistic and dramaturgical attitudes. During the tours, the Duke's real reason for maintaining a theater in Meiningen was to provide a stage for his company's rehearsals. He chose the plays to be added to the Meiningen repertoire, at least in the case of classical drama, according to the capabilities of his actors and actresses. If it became apparent to him that the Meininger could not perform a piece while meeting the standards he had set for its performance, Georg would not allow the piece to be viewed by the wider public. It appears likely that, given the personnel at his disposal, Georg felt that most of the plays of Goethe and Lessing would not have been done justice by the Meininger if he had added their plays to his troupe's tours.[73] The fact that he chose to produce one play of each was quite likely an attempt on his part to see if perhaps his estimate of his theater's ability was correct. The results, however, demonstrated the wisdom of his decision. The Meininger versions of *Iphigenia* and *Miss Sara Sampson* were never warmly received by the public.

Georg could be persuaded to produce a piece against his better judgment, though. Lord Byron's *Marino Faliero* was reputedly Helene's favorite drama. At her urging he added the piece to the traveling repertoire, using Arthur Fitger's translation. The play, written in 1820, had its German premiere in 1886 by the Meininger. In spite of Georg's efforts to please his wife, the play was never popular.[74] The Meininger presented it five times during their 1886 tour, and it was repeated only 14 times in the course of the next four years.

The 1886 tour took the Meininger to Barmen, Mainz, and Düsseldorf. While the troupe was performing in those cities, Chronegk and Georg were making arrangements to take the Meininger on a tour of America. In later years there came to be some confusion about whether the Meininger actually made the trip.[75] A visit to America had become synonymous with financial success in the nineteenth century; Fanny Gessler, Lola Montez, and Jenny Lind had demonstrated the profitability of performing in the United States. With an eye to improving the financial position of his troupe, the Duke had initiated negotiations for an American tour with Wesley Sisson, director of the Criterion Theater in Brooklyn, for his services as an agent. Georg was anxious to demonstrate his theater's skills in America, but he was aware of the risks he would run if there were no guarantee of recovering the costs incurred in transporting costumes, scenery, and personnel to America and back. A contract was drawn up that would have become effective if Sisson had deposited $20,000 in Meiningen by May 1, 1886. In mid–April Chronegk received a telegram saying that the contract had been approved by the German consul in New York. Chronegk received the contract in Barmen, where the Meininger were performing, on April 20. He then wrote to Georg that everything had been settled, and asked to be sent a telegram as soon as the money arrived in Meiningen. He began negotiating with the actors Possart of Munich and Beck and Felix of Barmen to accompany the Meininger on their visit to the new world.

While Chronegk was busy with his preparations, though, events were taking place on the other side of the Atlantic that would prove fatal to the plans for a visit to the new world. Even though the required deposit had not been raised by the promoters, tickets had already been printed and were being sold. Sisson had begun advertising that the Duke himself would accompany his players, although Georg had made it clear from the beginning that he would not come with them to America. Sisson wrote to Chronegk that he would be visiting Mainz, the Meininger's home during May, to become familiar with the company. Chronegk assumed that Sisson was acting in good faith and went ahead with his plans, even though no money had been forwarded to Meiningen. He chose the repertoire, comprising seventeen plays,[76] and calculated a profit of 532,000 marks from the visit, which was to last 150 performances.

When Sisson arrived, however, it was not to observe the Meininger. Instead, he tried to persuade Chronegk to sign the contract without any provision of a guarantee. When Chronegk refused, Sisson attempted to raise the required money in Berlin, Frankfurt, and Mainz. Unsuccessful in his attempts, he returned to America.

Chronegk had not given up hope for a visit to America. He thought that if he could go to New York himself, he might be able to arrange for the Meininger's performances. He booked passage and made plans to leave Düsseldorf on June 29. However, he suffered a stroke the day before his scheduled departure, and was immediately taken to Marienbad, where he remained for six months before recovering sufficiently to resume his duties at the theater. On July 10 he wrote to Georg that it appeared there would be no trip to America that year, but since he foresaw such a visit the following year, the contract talks should continue. By July 28, though, he wrote that it would be necessary to modify the contract. Sisson was in no position to guarantee all that Georg and Chronegk had hoped for.

Georg hired a new agent in America, Constantin von Grimm, and asked him to investigate the chances for his theater's success if it should come. The Meininger had received some unfavorable publicity because Sisson had refused to refund the tickets he had already sold to the expected Meininger performances. Grimm replied that the Meininger were assured of great success if they would make proper preparations, i.e., advance publicity, including an illustrated magazine about the theater, a program in German and English that included synopses of each act, and sufficient posters. Grimm felt that if an honest American manager could be found, the Meininger would have no need of an agent such as Sisson, and that their success would be so great as to warrant repeated visits.

Georg decided against continuing his plans to send his theater to America, though. He felt that conditions there were so different from those he knew in Europe that it would be unwise to risk the effort. His experience with Sisson had made him leery of American "representatives," and he felt that Chronegk would not be physically capable of making the trip. Some years later, a few members of the Meininger theater would undertake a visit to the United States on their own initiative (discussed on pp. 51 – 52). They represented themselves as the Meininger, and it is no doubt from this source that the confusion arose concerning whether the Meininger ever performed in America.

When plans for the five month long visit to America fell through, a large space in the normally busy schedule of the Meininger was left vacant. With Chronegk recovering from a stroke, there was no one to attend to the details that would have been required to arrange for substitute tours during the autumn of 1886. Instead, the Meininger enjoyed an extended vacation.

When the local season began in Meiningen during December of that year, Georg had prepared a theater festival, scheduled for shortly before Christmas. The festival consisted of performances of Echegaray's *Galiotto,* translated by Paul Lindau, Voss's *Alexandra,* and Ibsen's *Ghosts.* Georg had invited the two dramatists and the translator to the performances, and Berlin critics were also scheduled to be in attendance. Lindau, who had been the Meininger's most vocal opponent when they began performing in Berlin, had by this time become a staunch supporter of their theater and a friend of the Duke, his conversion no doubt aided by the Meininger adoption of his play *Johannistrieb.*[77]

The first two pieces presented no problem, but a storm of protest arose among the upstanding Meiningen citizenry concerning Ibsen's play. The performance Georg had scheduled for Meiningen was to be the first public performance of *Ghosts* in Germany. A single performance had been given on April 14, 1886, before a private audience in Augsburg, but the play had then been banned by the police. Georg felt no pressure from the so–called protectors of public morality, though, and he prepared a performance of the controversial play for his theater. Although virtually none of his subjects had read the Norwegian drama, all were bitterly opposed to it, since they assumed the play was immoral.

Grube recalled how the public expressed their displeasure but how Georg was able to make a success of the evening, much to Ibsen's satisfaction.[78] Almost no tickets were sold to the performance, because most people had decided to express their displeasure by refusing to attend. Georg knew that he could expect no support from his subjects for a drama they considered avant–garde, so he began giving away tickets to all who applied for them at the court offices. When that measure was not entirely successful, he passed out tickets to all government workers, along with the subtle hint that he was hoping for appropriate applause during the performance. The entire Meiningen police force, six men strong, was on hand to prevent a riot. There was none, but neither was there much applause, except from Georg and his circle. Before the performance, Georg had presented Ibsen with a medal;[79] afterward he gave a reception in the playwright's honor. Ibsen was, Grube relates, completely satisfied with the evening's events.

When the tours resumed in February 1887, audiences were treated to only one more performance of *Ghosts,* but to repeated performances of the Meininger's last great success—Schiller's *Die Jungfrau von Orleans* (The Maid of Orleans). Helene had found among the ranks of the Meininger actresses one who seemed to her in all ways perfect for the role of Johanna. Amanda Lindner (plates 11, 12 and 13), described as being tall and thin with a face of classic beauty,[80] became Helene's favorite. The eighteen–year–old actress received private lessons in speech and dramatic reading from Helene, who also saw to it that the Duke put Schiller's play into production. Georg devoted long hours to the set design, including the addition of a horse to the play.

Georg had no objection to a horse appearing on his stage as long as it was dead, and thought that the scene of Talbot's death (act 3, scene 6) would be an appropriate place to introduce one. He felt, Max Grube recalled, that a battle scene should show dead animals as well as dead people, so he had a stuffed horse placed on the stage. The horse was draped with a white blanket, and no matter where the stage hands pushed the beast, it remained the center of attention on stage.[81]

Finally Grube hit on the idea of having the horse be Talbot's. The same shot that wounded Talbot would have killed his mount, and so the scene opened with Talbot being pulled by soldiers from under the horse, then propped up against the horse's back to deliver his dying speech (plate 14).

The Meininger opened their eighth Berlin visit with *Die Jungfrau,* which was so warmly received that it played for 55 consecutive evenings. No one knew it at the time, but 1887 marked the last time the Meininger would play in Berlin. They concluded their final visit, appropriately, with their first great success, *Julius Caesar.*

The concluding trip of 1887 was to Dresden during November and December. While the Meininger were in Dresden, it was decided that they should perform *Ghosts.* The performance was heavily attended by the police, who afterwards made it clear to Chronegk that they hoped he would change his mind about future performances of Ibsen's "immoral" play. The police were powerless to directly forbid the play's performance, since the theater was operated by a Duke who was, besides, related to the Prussian royal family, but their tone left no doubt that officials found the play offensive. Not one to take unfair advantage of a situation, Chronegk removed *Ghosts* from the schedule. The Meininger performed the play only once more—during a visit to Copenhagen in 1889.

The next three years witnessed no successful additions to the repertoire; however, the Meininger took their theater to several new stops each year. In 1888 the Meininger visited Antwerp, Rotterdam, and Amsterdam, where they met with critical disapproval,[82] and Brussels, where André Antoine of Paris's Théâtre Libre saw them perform.

The shortest Meininger guest appearance occurred in 1889, when the theater visited Gotha for only two evenings. The visit was made in February during the regular season in Meiningen; it was Georg's only attempt to reach an audience close to home during the Meininger's famous period (1874–1890). The Meininger also made their only visit to Scandinavia the same year, playing one month each in Copenhagen and Stockholm.

The 1890 tour took place entirely in Russia, where St. Petersburg and Moscow saw the Meininger for a second time, with Kiev and Odessa added as new stops. The four visits, lasting from March to July, were showcase performances featuring many of the Meininger's most famous productions, as well as some that had enjoyed less acclaim. Georg and Chronegk hoped to demonstrate their theater's talents to the Russians, with as many as 16 plays being performed in one city.

The End of the Meininger Tours: 1890

No one except Georg realized it at the time, but July 1, 1890, was the end of an era. When the curtain fell on *Twelfth Night* in Odessa, the yearly Meininger tours came to an end. On August 10, Chronegk distributed a circular among the members of the theater informing them that Duke Georg had decided to discontinue his theater's traveling performances. All were given the choice of renewing their contracts under new conditions or of seeking employment elsewhere.[83]

Several factors had influenced Georg's decision to end the tours. Among the reasons was Chronegk's physical condition. Ever since his stroke in 1886, Chronegk had been unable to maintain the pace he had kept earlier. Indeed, Grube cites this as Georg's primary reason.[84] Paul Richard, who had been Chronegk's assistant for several years, was no doubt capable of continuing the work, but, according to Grube, Georg thought that it would have hurt Chronegk to see someone else take his place.

Some theater historians have suggested an additional reason for the discontinuance of the tours.[85] According to their view, Georg realized that he had done everything he wanted to do. A continuance of his theater's travels would have neither spread the fame of the Meininger further nor taught other theaters anything new, since everyone already knew about the Meininger and what they stood for. Grube supports this point of view, telling how he had asked Georg why the Meininger could not have a farewell performance in Berlin. Georg's reply showed that he believed his efforts had been completely successful. He answered, "It is no longer necessary. The German theaters have learned what they should."[86]

A third possible reason for the Meininger's cessation of their travels might have been their financial burden on the Duke. The financial success of their first visit to Berlin has already been discussed (pp. 35 – 36), and another source has recorded an example of the theater's profits during 1877.[87] In Breslau, where it was considered difficult for a theater to turn a profit, the Meininger filled the house 39 times, bringing in 130,000 marks at the box office. Paul Richard, the assistant director, records that the total income for all tours amounted to 6,322,978.47 marks.[88] There appears to have been no records left of actual expenditures, but one source tells that in Prague, the Meininger were charged rent of 12,400 guilders (24,800 marks) for one month, while the theater management from whom Georg rented the building paid only 12,000 guilders rent annually for the building.[89]

Paul Lindau assured his readers that Georg's theater had no financial worries.[90] He claimed that in spite of great costs, the income from the tours exceeded expenditures. He also pointed out that when a piece was dropped from the repertoire, the profit from the sale of surplus costumes and scenery was added to the profit from the box office in order to provide a contingency fund for lean years. As an aside, he mentioned the real reason the theater had no need to worry about its finances: Georg continually helped out the theater from his own private funds.

Two of the reasons mentioned—Chronegk's health and the costs—also appear in a letter written by Helene. In her letter, written shortly after Georg's decision, she says that the main reason for discontinuing the tours was Chronegk's poor health. Finances were also mentioned as a reason; the theater had been losing considerable sums of money, and Georg no longer felt justified in providing a subsidy. A third, rather surprising reason was that Georg and his wife no longer found any pleasure in directing their theater. They had come to regard it only as work, while others reaped all the benefits.[91]

Many have considered the history of the Meininger closed with the end of the tours. The scenery, which had been stored in a school building, was sold to other theaters.[92] Many of the actors moved to other stages, and those who remained became members of the Meiningen Hoftheater, the same uninfluential provincial stage it had been prior to 1874. Heinrich Laube was of the opinion that all theater reforms must come from a large city,[93] and for that reason Julius Bab seems justified in saying that as soon as the Meininger stopped performing in the great cities of Europe, their influence on the theater also ceased.[94]

For a history of the Meininger, however, the operation of the Meiningen theater after the tours had ceased will be of importance. Just as Georg's work during the years 1874 to 1890 reflected his personal growth toward a theory of dramatic presentation and his sincere efforts to put his theory into practice, so the Meiningen theater after 1890 should have retained many of the characteristics associated with the Meininger. The audiences in Meiningen were smaller and less discriminating, but if Georg had suddenly abandoned his theater to the dictates of local taste, if the Meiningen stage sets had evidenced less than painstaking attention to detail, if the repertoire had stagnated, Georg could justifiably be regarded as a dilettante whose only aims had been personal glorification and income. If, conversely, his court theater had continued in the tradition that had come to be associated with the Meininger, even though productions were necessarily limited by the reduced income from not playing in the large cities, then Georg would seem to have been quite serious in his work as a theater reformer.

Before following the post–1890 history of the Meininger theater, though, the matter of the Meininger in America merits final consideration. Christian Eckelmann, an actor who never performed under Georg's direction, has left an account of how he became one of the "Meininger."[95] He was unexpectedly granted the honor of becoming a member of the famous troupe, he said, when in 1891 he was hired by the "R——Brothers," who were organizing the "Meininger" visit to America and seemed to be hiring any unemployed actor in Berlin. Over four months later the group finally set sail. Eckelmann's description of his colleagues shows just how "official" the group must have been and how much America was to see of actual Meininger performances. "There were about thirty of us," Eckelmann reports, "including *genuine* Meininger, who had already been on many tours" (emphasis added). Who were these "genuine" Meininger? Eckelmann listed Karl Weiser, Carl Grube, Mathieu Pfeil, Anna Haverland, Hilmar Knorr, and Karl Machold. These were not names that usually came to mind when audiences thought of the Meininger; indeed, Paul Richard included only three of them, Grube, Haverland, and Knorr, in his listing of the members of the Meininger.[96] One wonders, then, about the veracity of Eckelmann's report that hundreds of small ships and boats, manned by members of New York's German associations, met the ship aboard which these ersatz Meininger arrived when it entered New York harbor.

According to the actor, the "Meininger" were a great success. The group opened in New York with *Julius Caesar,* which, he claimed, played only to sold–out houses. *The Robbers* was apparently on the playbill also, since Eckelmann stated that he played Franz Moor 38 times in one month, including matinees.

A review of the group's opening night performance, November 17, 1891, at New York's Thalia Theatre supports Eckelmann's contention that the foreigners were warmly received by their New York audience.[97] It is apparent from this review that there was a misunderstanding of the origins of the group, because the reviewer calls them "the dramatic company from the Court Theater of the Duke of Saxe–Meiningen" when they were actually only a group of actors who decided to represent themselves as the Meininger. In spite of the audience reaction, to the reviewer the "Meininger" became proof that realism on the stage left only an empty shell of the poetic intent of a play. He felt that the mob scenes were excellently presented, while the individual performances were, in general, poor.[98]

According to Eckelmann's account, the "Meininger" ended their run at the Thalia Theater after eight weeks. Their American tour continued by special train, just as the Meininger had traveled throughout Europe, and in the dining car they were allegedly provided "Thuringian bratwurst and Meininger beer." They made eight more stops, Eckelmann claimed: Philadelphia, Baltimore, Washington, Pittsburgh, Cincinnati, Chicago, St. Louis, and Milwaukee. A survey of the newspapers of those cities failed to discover any mention of the performances, however, and it thus appears likely that Eckelmann was guilty of exaggerating the impact the "Meininger" had on America.

The Meininger Theater after Chronegk: 1891–1899

In the same year as the pseudo–Meininger were crossing the Atlantic, Georg decided to retire Ludwig Chronegk from his position as director of the Hoftheater (plate 16). Chronegk, still in failing health, was replaced by his assistant Paul Richard. While Richard was director, Georg continued to produce plays that were his own favorites. In many cases, the playwrights were personal friends of the Duke. Richard Voss, for example, saw his play *König* done in Meiningen during January 1895. Georg also remained semi–active in the theater. In February 1895 he personally directed *Der Freischütz,* his favorite opera, according to a letter from his wife to Helene Jachmann, December 1, 1894, outlining Georg's plans for the coming year.[99]

Paul Richard held the post of director for five years, until Chronegk's death in mid–1895. At that time Georg's former opponent, Paul Lindau, was named director. Lindau's regime was marked by an ambitious program of new productions, the first of which was Christian Dietrich Grabbe's *Don Juan and Faust.* To be sure, Alfred von Wolzogen had produced the drama 20 years earlier in Schwerin, but Wolzogen had so completely revised the play that it bore only faint resemblance to Grabbe's original.[100] The March 6, 1896,

Meiningen production came on the heels of a January 1896 production in Nürnberg. Both productions attempted to restore the play to the form its author had intended, although the two directors were working independently.

Lindau's attempt to add *Don Juan and Faust* to the standard German theater repertoire was unsuccessful. Except for one production in 1899, there was no further interest in the play until Grabbe's one hundredth birthday on December 11, 1901.

The play is important to a history of the Meininger, though, for another reason. Photographic portraits had been made of individual members of the Meininger before, but Grabbe's drama marked the first time that photographs were made of an actual production by members of the Hoftheater. In these photographs (plates 17, 18 and 19) one can see the Meininger tradition of attention to detail. Pillars support architectural arches, the doors are real, and the windows contain glass. The furnishings are of a unified style and complement the painted scenery. The scenery itself is carefully proportioned and painted, so that the decorative elements have a three–dimensional effect. The box set with its ceiling is readily apparent in the pictures. The photographs also record the melodramatic (in the modern sense) quality of the acting, which many critics of the Meininger belittled.

Other plays both old and new were brought to Meiningen for the first time under Lindau's direction. Besides Grabbe's play, Immermann's *Tragedy in Tirol* and Lesewitz' *Julius von Tarent* were restored to their original form. The works of living authors, both those destined to become famous and those soon to be forgotten, were seen on the Meiningen stage. From the first group, Hauptmann *(The Sunken Bell),* Sudermann *(Modest Happiness),* Ibsen *(The Wild Duck* and *John Gabriel Borkman),* and Björnson *(Mary of Scotland)* were represented. Dramatists of lesser stature included Otto Erich Hartleben *(Das Ehrenwort),* Ludwig Fulda *(Jugendfreude),* Leo Ebermann *(Athenerin),* Wilhelm Jensen *(Der Kampf ums Reich),* and the teams of Schönthan and Koppel–Ellfeld *(Renaissance* and *Die goldene Eva),* and Blumenthal and Kadelburg *(Hans Hückebein* and *Weisses Rössel).* Lindau also used the Meiningen stage for his own works, such as his hastily–written play *Die Erste.*

In 1898 Meiningen again briefly enjoyed widespread attention because of its theater. Georg and Helene celebrated their twenty–fifth wedding anniversary in March of that year, and Lindau organized a special theater performance to honor the couple (plates 20 and 21). From far and near former Meininger came to join the current members of the Hoftheater in a presentation of Shakespeare's *The Merchant of Venice* (plate 22). All living veterans of the Meininger tours, with the exception of Joseph Kainz, returned to Meiningen for the March 13 engagement, for which they received no remuneration. Shakespeare's play had been chosen for the large number of roles it offered, but even so there were not sufficient parts to furnish a speaking role for everyone. Many who were accustomed to lead billing at other theaters therefore played walk–on parts.

Theater critics and former admirers of the Meininger joined the citizenry of the town in honoring the ducal couple. Lindau would have one believe that the evening's events were a complete surprise to Georg, but it would have been impossible to keep such elaborate preparations secret in a town of Meiningen's size.[101] The evening's playbill listed 55 parts, surely a record for a performance of *Merchant of Venice,* all of which were played by former Meininger. Many more actually appeared on the stage, but had agreed to come too late to have been listed on the program. Through the special performance the nation was shown the esteem in which the Duke was held by his actors, and many who had forgotten about the Meininger and their tours again read accounts of the enthusiasm with which the group's performances had often been greeted.

Following his success with *The Merchant of Venice,* Lindau wanted to try his hand at producing *Faust II.* He initially found no support forthcoming from Georg, but after much planning and pleading was able to win him over. Preparations began for an 1898 performance.[102]

Entitled "Faust's End," the production included the entire fifth act and nothing else of Goethe's original. All music was eliminated, with some exceptions as noted, and all singing parts were presented as stylized recitations. In a few instances, such as the conclusion of the "chorus mysticus," tones were vocalized as the words were spoken on stage. Sixteen vocalists were used, divided into four groups, each comprising a bass, a baritone, a tenor, and an alto. One group was placed in the lower right of the orchestra pit, another in lower left, the third and fourth on catwalks above and to the right and left of the stage. Whenever the choir produced its tones, everyone on stage looked in all directions, as if trying to discover the source of the sound. At the conclusion, all lifted their hands heavenward, trying to reach the *mater gloriosa* as the curtain fell.

Lindau also made other plans to create a true spectacle. He wanted to show Faust ascending into heaven, to have a shower of roses cover Mephisto, and to send an army of devils streaming forth onto the stage. As the tableau's crowning glory, Lindau wanted to show Mary, floating in the highest reaches above the stage, with cherubs at her feet.

It was not reported that Lindau was able to produce all the spectacular effects he wanted, but Georg told him to proceed and he would provide the funding. The running time of the last act was about ninety minutes, so the rest of the evening was filled by a presentation of Beethoven's Fifth Symphony.

The performance took place December 26, 1898. Lindau claimed that spectators, including the entire faculty of the University of Jena, came by the trainload.

The Meininger Court Theater in the Twentieth Century: 1900–1926

"Faust's End" was Lindau's last major contribution to the Meiningen stage. In March 1899 he resigned his post, the result of a misunderstanding between Georg and himself. Paul Richard was again named director. During Richard's second tenure, which lasted until 1907, the work of G. B. Shaw was first seen in Meiningen when the Court theater presented *Caesar and Cleopatra.* [103]

Schiller's one–hundredth death day was commemorated May 9, 1905. On that day, the University of Jena presented Georg with an honorary doctorate in honor of the glory he had brought to Schiller through the productions of his plays.[104]

Georg's eightieth birthday was celebrated in 1906, but Richard apparently did not take charge of the attendant festivities. Max Grube directed *Egmont,* presented on April 1 (plate 23). As was done eight years previously, former Meininger took leave from their theaters to join in the celebration honoring Georg. The evening proved to be one of the outstanding theater events of the year in Germany, even though the Duke was not present, but was instead vacationing on France's Cap Martin at the time.[105]

That same year, the Meininger took another tour. It has heretofore been assumed that the Meininger tours ended in 1890. While it is true that Georg stopped the practice of yearly tours at that time, occasional tours were made after 1890. A review in an Amsterdam weekly discusses a two week long visit by the Meininger to that city during April and May 1906.[106] These were no pseudo–Meininger as had appeared in America. The article includes portraits of four of the principals, and they were indeed listed as members of the Meininger theater during that year. Although the review is devoted mainly to a discussion of attendance figures, the repertoire is also mentioned. It comprised Lessing's *Minna von Barnhelm,* Sudermann's *Johannisfeuer,* and *Komtesse Guckerl* by Schönthan and Koppel-Elfeld.

Two significant facts emerge from the review. First, the members of the Meininger theater were still being referred to as the "Meininger," both by themselves and by others. This may be considered a sign that they were still attempting to carry on the traditions to which they were heir. Second, the choice of drama in 1906 was similar to the repertoire in Meiningen (as opposed to the touring repertoire) during the 1874–1890 period, being composed of a classical work, a new, somewhat controversial play, and a light, entertaining piece.

Otto Osmarr, who joined the Meininger theater as an actor in 1895, had just replaced Richard as director, and Georg was again at Cap Martin when the theater building burned to the ground March 5, 1908.[107] The fire broke out in the furnace room, spread to a closet in which candles were stored, and from there soon engulfed the entire building. The fire department was unable to check the flames, but all who were engaged at the theater, actors and actresses, technicians, musicians, and librarians, did their best to save the theater's properties. Some scenery, about half the costumes, and a few of the props, which had included many antiques from Georg's private collection, could be saved. The trophies and souvenirs from the tours, housed in a special room dedicated to the memory of Ludwig Chronegk, the entire library, and nearly all musical instruments were removed from the building. There were substantial losses, however, including many of the properties used on the tours, which could have been of inestimable value to scholars later investigating the Meininger.

Speculation immediately arose as to the fate of the Hoftheater. Some said Georg would close it, others said a new theater would be erected, and still others claimed Georg would turn his theater into a touring company without a permanent home. Paul Lindau, who was living in Berlin as an author, was concerned about the fate of his former home. He telegraphed his sympathy to the Duke, and, in a return letter, Georg clearly explained the future of his theater. He informed Lindau that he had already asked an architect to make suggestions for a new building, and one week later he wrote that a Meiningen contractor had been entrusted with the rebuilding.[108]

Georg solved the problem of finding a home for his theater during 1908 and 1909 by sending it on an extended tour. The court theater was resident in Gotha and Coburg from October 1908 until April 1909. Under the circumstances of the theater's burning, Georg might have been excused for not caring as he usually had about the quality of his troupe's performances. In a letter to Max Grube, though, Georg shows that his attitude remained unchanged.[109] Georg asked Grube to attend the opening night performance in Gotha on October 18 and to report to him on the way in which the play *(The Robbers)* was done. The Duke felt that if the first performance was poorly done or ill–received, the entire tour would be a failure.

It is very interesting to note why Georg felt compelled to send an observer. In his letter, he tells Grube that during the past year he had seen his theater perform only one or two times. The reason for his absence must surely be attributed to ill health. The first signs of deafness had appeared in the 1880s, and Georg's loss of hearing had progressed by 1906 to the point that he could not hear dialogue on stage. Too, he seemed to be growing weaker, and he was crippled with arthritis so that he could not stand erect and was able to walk only with the aid of a cane.[110] He had been forced to turn his theater entirely over to its director, and his lack of personal contact concerned him. Otto Osmarr had never seen the Meininger perform during their most famous era, and Georg feared that the Meininger traditions that he had so carefully forged during the nineteenth century might be fading. He felt that Grube might be able to tell him whether the twentieth century Meininger measured up to his standards.

Grube's report was generally encouraging. To him it was apparent that the theater was trying to live up to the reputation of its predecessors. It bore the stamp of the Meininger whom Grube had known, and the stage seemed as painterly as he remembered. One great difference, though, was apparent in the ensemble's unity. The members of the troupe showed little sign of being coached to reinforce one another, and instead of forming a harmonious whole, many individuals seemed bent on upstaging the others.

When Grube made his report to Georg, the Duke offered him the position of director beginning in 1909. He accepted, and thus directed the events surrounding the opening of the new theater. Georg had continued his practice of not taking funds from the Duchy's treasury for the theater, and so he alone bore the cost of the new building.[111] Reflecting the Duke's love of classical drama, his new theater was designed in the architectural style of a Greek temple. For the opening night, Georg had chosen the *Wallenstein* trilogy, and Meiningen once more played host to the elite of the German theater world.[112]

The reconstruction of his theater was Georg's last great accomplishment. He and Helene were able to spend only two or three months in Meiningen each year because of their health. The theater was entrusted to Grube, although the Duke and the director corresponded frequently on theater matters. A photograph of a 1910 performance of Keller's fragment *Therese* shows that Georg's influence continued to be felt (plate 24). Essential details of the set are similar to those seen in the photographs of *Don Juan and Faust,* and reflect Georg's ideas on scenery as recorded during the era of the Meininger tours. Grube tried to keep Georg and his wife at least partially active in the theater by reporting all the day–to–day details of the rehearsals and performances.

The couple responded by occasionally requesting a favorite play or attending a rehearsal. In 1910, for example, Helene had adopted Paul Heyse as her favorite dramatist. For the playwright's eightieth birthday, Helene wrote to Grube, instructing him to have the Hoftheater present the premiere of Heyse's latest play, *Vanina Vanini.* The performance took place March 15, and, in appreciation for her attention, Heyse dedicated the play to Helene.[113]

Georg's loss of hearing became so acute that it was almost impossible for him to participate in the theater or in any other activity. In 1912 Helene wrote to Cosima Wagner that Georg could hear less every day, and that it was impossible for him to carry on a conversation with more than one person.[114] (plate 25) To accommodate the Duke, the theater performed such pieces as *Kardinal,* based on a work by Gilbert Parker and adapted by Grube and Rudolf Lothar. The play greatly pleased the Duke, because the plot was relatively uncomplicated and he could follow the action without hearing the words once he had read the text.[115]

In 1914 Georg developed asthma, and by early summer his state of health was precarious. His doctor ordered him to Bad Wildungen for a rest cure, but no more could be done for him. He died at 2:25 a.m. on June 25. Burial was June 28, not in the royal mausoleum, but in a tomb he had designed himself, which was located under large trees in the city cemetery. Paul Lindau wrote his obituary.[116]

Helene died March 24, 1923. Thus, the celebration of Georg's hundredth birthday on April 2, 1926, became a remembrance of all who had worked together to make the Meininger famous.[117] The president of the German Theatrical Guild, an organization Georg had supported from its inception, delivered a graveside eulogy. On April 3, the remaining former Meininger were reunited on stage for the last time in a memorial performance. The play chosen was, appropriately enough, *Julius Caesar.* The history of the Meininger had come to a close.

3

The Meininger Legacy

"What an abundance of artistic delight the German people owe to this noble, beloved Prince and his wife!"

Peter Rosegger [1]

When Georg set about reforming the German theater, he had many models to follow. Forerunners of one or more aspects of his work go back to the mid–eighteenth century. Goethe had earlier described the situation in which Georg found himself: "Everything intelligent has already been thought; one only has to try to think it again."[2]

On the Meininger stage, audiences saw the latest developments in the areas of accuracy in costume and set design, reflecting the spirit of each particular play instead of dealing with a play's setting in general terms. Attention to detail had become more and more important on German stages since the 1730s, and was made increasingly necessary when plays were written that were set in places and times that were not far removed from the audiences' own experience.[3]

Effective use of supernumeraries and the development of ensemble players are associated with the Meininger theater, but developments in those areas can be traced back to Dalberg, Goethe and Klingemann in the late eighteenth and early nineteenth centuries. The development of a first–rate ensemble required a strong director, and as directors became more powerful, advances were made in other areas as well. Rehearsals became necessary tools for training a troupe, and fidelity to the words and intentions of an author took on increasing importance. Immermann in Düsseldorf and Laube at the Vienna Burgtheater placed great emphasis on the text, sometimes to the detriment of the stage decoration. Dingelstedt succeeded Laube at the Burgtheater, and changed the emphasis there to one of lavish and historically accurate sets.

Before coming to Vienna, Dingelstedt had been in Weimar. While there, he had devoted considerable time to Shakespeare, whose plays were presented at a noted festival in 1864. Prince, later Duke, Georg was one of the spectators at the Shakespeare festival, where he took notes on the historical aspects of the productions. Although he did not carry it out, Dingelstedt had been given the idea of taking his Shakespeare festival on the road, to show others how Shakespeare should be done.

Devrient was also influential on the German theater and on Meiningen. During his 1852–1869 tenure as director at Karlsruhe, he propagated the idea that individual roles should be subordinated to the whole, i.e., that a true ensemble should exist, and that a director must be faithful to the author's text.

In other countries, too, a movement toward theatrical historicity and verisimilitude could be noted. Houssaye, at the Comédie Française in Paris, had increased paid attendance by using Gobelin tapestries and expensive furniture on his stage beginning in 1849. Charles Kean, at the Princess Theatre in London, prided himself on historical accuracy,[4] and had a direct influence on Georg when the Prince attended performances at the Princess in the 1850s.

From the many influences and elements of dramaturgical reform that were prevalent in the mid–nineteenth century, Georg synthesized a "Meininger style," which was disseminated throughout Europe during his theater's tours. Parts of this style gained adherents at many theaters, especially in Germany, but also in France and Russia. Some directors successfully refined Georg's practices for use on their stages; others merely copied the Meininger without any attempt at integrating isolated principles into an overall artistic plan.

Georg's scope of influence was surprisingly wide. Besides affecting the further development of the theater, he was also of some importance in the realm of literature. To some authors, such as Rosegger, Georg was merely a friend. To others, such as Hauptmann, he was an inspiration. To still others, he was a patron who provided the first opportunity for the performance of their plays. In certain cases, a deeper working relationship developed between an author and Georg. Ibsen, for example, worked closely with the Duke in preparing his play *Ghosts* for its first public production in Germany.

Theatrical Successors

In 1908, Josef Dischner claimed that every German theater then in operation could trace some element of its success back to Georg and the Meininger.[5] Dramaturgy had changed somewhat during the 1880s in response to the new demands of naturalist drama. In Germany, some directors used the Meininger developments in realism to further the new trends. Others used poorly understood Meininger principles in clumsy ways to try to halt the acceptance of newer methods.

The first step toward naturalist theater reform in Germany came in 1883, when Adolph L'Arronge founded the Deutsches Theater in Berlin, modeling it upon the theater in Meiningen. L'Arronge was a champion of the Meininger and their style.[6] He claimed that no one was ever distracted from the content of a play by the richness of the Meininger stage, but that people were easily convinced by drama critics that the Meininger had misled them. Georg did care about the appearance of his stage, L'Arronge admitted, but his greatest contribution to the theater was the Meininger's unified productions.[7]

The most noteworthy element of a Meininger production was, according to L'Arronge, the crowd. He had never seen such effective use of extras elsewhere. He was impressed with Georg's utilization of the verve and intelligence of his young, inexperienced actors. In the opinion of L'Arronge, the fact that Georg's ensemble was able to present the ideas of a playwright in such a convincing manner was proof that Germany's other stages were neglecting their own development if they did not follow the Meininger example. Other stages, he felt, might well have actors who could present individual scenes more powerfully than the Meininger, but nowhere else, he believed, could one experience a play's full impact except on the Meiningen stage. The classics, Shakespeare and Schiller, he maintained, were the Meininger's strongest point, and it was precisely in that area that all other stages were weakest.

Even though the Meininger were, in L'Arronge's opinion, the best example to follow in all of Germany, few stages seemed to have benefited from their existence. As a result, he decided to form his own theater based on what the Meininger had taught him:

> The impression that the Meininger performances made on me is a lasting one, and the desire to further develop what they had taught me, thereby testing my own abilities, gave me the impetus to risk founding the "Deutsches Theater," together with several leading actors.[8]

L'Arronge's partner was Ludwig Barnay, and the principal actor was Josef Kainz, both formerly of the Meininger. With such assistants, in addition to his own predilections, L'Arronge naturally followed a course that had much in common with Georg's troupe.

Otto Brahm's reviews of the first season at the Deutsches Theater were overwhelmingly favorable.[9] He praised the acting and especially the decorations, recognizing the Meininger's influence. "The stimuli of the Meininger have had an effect here," Brahm said in his October 1, 1883, review of Schiller's *Kabale und Liebe,* "and the experiences of that company have been used appropriately here."[10] In later reviews (October 7 and November 12, 1883), Brahm again cited the influence, noting that the Deutsches Theater did not slavishly copy Georg's troupe, but took its strong points and refined them.

Barnay left the Deutsches Theater in 1884, and Brahm immediately noticed a decline in standards. In a review of *Wilhelm Tell* (September 30, 1884), he mentioned that the quality of acting had declined, and that the play often suffered because of the staging. He spoke of "pushing and shoving and

Meininger–like shouting,"[11] which he called "Meiningerism"—an attempt to compensate for lack of ability through overacting.

There had been some improvement by the March 27, 1886, production of *Antigone.* Brahm praised the way the scene had been brought to life by following the example of the Meininger in the area of staging.

By using the principles of the Meininger, the Deutsches Theater had a greater influence in Berlin than Georg ever did. This was true because of the permanent competition it offered the royal theater, which improved its staging and increased its respect for the plays of Shakespeare, Schiller, Lessing, and Kleist as a result.[12]

The Deutsches Theater did little, however, to address the needs of the naturalist movement. Although it raised the level of production in Berlin, L'Arronge's theater largely ignored new playwrights other than those who wrote in the tradition of Schiller.

The plays of the naturalist writers presented problems and depicted situations that seemed startling to European society. Believing that literature must either become scientific or perish, Emile Zola, principal spokesman of the French Naturalists, argued that literature should illustrate the laws of heredity and environment or record case studies. Zola compared the writer to the doctor, who does not seek to hide the cause of an infection, but brings it into the open where it can be examined. Similarly, the dramatist should seek out and reveal social ills so that they might be corrected. Some of Zola's followers went a step farther, saying that a play should be a "slice of life" transferred to the stage.

It fell to another playwright, though, to create a play embodying the principles of naturalism Zola had outlined. Henri Becque, in *The Vultures* (1882), first succeeded in presenting social problems in a modern, realistic milieu. In his play, there are no sympathetic characters, no obvious climaxes, and a cynical outcome.

Henrik Ibsen wrote his first play in 1850 and was appointed resident dramatist and stage manager at the Norwegian National Theater in 1851. Until 1877, Ibsen's plays were, for the most part, romantic verse–dramas about the Scandinavian past. In the 1870s Ibsen abandoned verse because it was unsuited for creating an illusion of reality. In *A Doll's House* (1879), Ibsen first shocked conservative readers by presenting Nora as a person in command of her life who walks out on her husband. *Ghosts* (1881) became a further rallying point for those who supported a drama of ideas. The allusion to venereal disease made *Ghosts* so controversial that it was banned in most countries.

In Ibsen's prose dramas, he refined Scribe's "well–made–play" formula, making it better suited to the realistic style. He discarded asides, soliloquies, and all nonrealistic devices. All exposition was motivated, and dialogue flowed in a natural pattern. Internal psychological motivations became more important than external visual detail.

Commercial, subsidized theaters closed their doors to the new dramatic works that were being written. Their directors felt that they could not afford to alienate the paying public. The result was the rise of "free stages," private organizations supported by subscriptions that provided a forum for works banned elsewhere. The model for such theaters was the Théâtre Libre, organized in Paris by André Antoine in 1887.

Germany's first "free theater," the Freie Bühne, was organized during 1889 in Berlin by a group of writers. The group was a democratic organization with officers and a governing council, and Otto Brahm was elected president. The Freie Bühne had no permanent actors in its employ, and gave its performances on Sunday afternoons so that actors working elsewhere could assist. The group exerted little influence on production techniques, since there was a new company for every play. Its main contribution was to give a hearing to those plays forbidden by the censor.[13]

Externally, the Freie Bühne had little in common with the Meininger. For Brahm, nature or truth was a faithful representation of a segment of reality, with particular emphasis on the cruder aspects of contemporary life, to the exclusion of any poetic adornment.[14]

In spite of the differences, there are those who point out areas where Brahm learned from Georg.[15] Brahm considered the essence of a play in fashioning scenery appropriate thereto. A shabby room was just as essential in Hauptmann's *Weavers* as an accurate reproduction of the Roman Forum was in *Julius Caesar*. Brahm also had a fine eye for detail, and when an actor came out of a storm into a room, he first had to step in a bucket of water so that his feet would drip on the floor.

The organizational pattern for the art theater—a theater that utilized the talents of unknown actors to form an ensemble under the hand of a strong director—came into being with the Meininger. Brahm adopted the idea in his own theater. He rehearsed his actors thoroughly, and tried to bring alive in them the specific atmosphere of the play they were performing.

Brahm mentioned the debt he owed the Meininger in his publication, *Die freie Bühne* ("The Free Theater"). He pointed out that his stage wanted to take the good that had come of Georg's work in one area—he was referring to the reawakened interest for classical drama among Germany's theatergoers— and expand it to cover all aspects of art: "Truth, for which Duke Georg so earnestly contended in a limited area of the theater,—the Freie Bühne demands it for the whole of dramatic art."[16]

The Freie Bühne came to an end in 1894, when Brahm was named director of the Deutsches Theater. He was succeeded in that position by Max Reinhardt in 1905. Reinhardt had become an actor at the age of nineteen and was familiar with nearly every school of drama and play production. Because of his eclecticism, he was able to reconcile many different styles at the Deutsches Theater. For him, each new production became a problem to be solved, not through the use of conventional, accepted solutions, but through clues given by the play itself.

Reinhardt was a clear successor to Georg's methods, because he believed that the director must control every aspect of play production. He prepared a promptbook for each play he produced, in which all details could be noted. Just as Georg had, Reinhardt received criticism that his actors were like puppets, and that his hand could be seen in everything.

Georg sent an observer to Berlin to judge Reinhardt's work. The Duke received a telegram informing him that Reinhardt was doing everything as he would have done it himself. In his *Midsummer Night's Dream,* for example, Reinhardt covered his stage with real grass and a forest of actual birch trees.[17] In Dischner's opinion, Reinhardt was, of all directors, the most like Duke Georg, because his greatest successes were the same plays for which Georg was most famous.[18]

A completely different type of troupe embraced the Meininger style in the 1870s. Munich's Gärtnerplatztheater followed Georg's principles of fidelity to an author's text, careful and thorough rehearsal, decorations that supported the text, and tours that demonstrated the troupe's prowess to other cities, including Berlin. The difference, however, was that Gärtnerplatz produced only local color pieces in Bavarian dialect. The outward results of their art were the same as those of the Meininger, but the works they produced were never considered critically significant.[19]

August Förster, director of the Leipzig municipal theater, was no great admirer of the Meininger; Julius Bab called him Heinrich Laube's star pupil.[20] Nevertheless, there was a certain "Meininger quality" to his productions of *Julius Caesar* and *Wilhelm Tell.* Förster liked to base his work on performances that had been given elsewhere; for those two works, he turned to the prior productions that had been most successful—those of the Meininger.[21]

There were other, less fortunate examples of Meininger influence in Germany. As Bab pointed out, imitation is successful only if done with understanding and with the intention of making someone else's work a part of an overall system.[22] The antiquarianism represented by the Meininger suited them well, for they used it to elucidate basic aspects of the plays they presented. On those stages where historicity and realism became the main focus, however, there was little artistic quality to speak of.

In Munich, for example, Ernst von Possart became director of King Ludwig's Court Theater in 1880. Possart's own tendency was toward excess in the area of decoration, but Ludwig's taste made matters worse. Although Ludwig often demanded performances at which he was the only spectator, he decreed that the stage set be built in a truly realistic fashion. This led to scenes where the actors could not even be seen because they were in the middle of a forest or inside a building. Possart learned to cooperate fully with Ludwig, who once became angry when it was suggested to him that the noise from an actual waterfall on stage (!) be dampened so that the actors could be heard.[23]

Julius Hofmann tried to imitate the Meininger in Cologne. In 1882, he negotiated with Henry Irving of London's Lyceum Theatre for the purchase of sets from *Romeo and Juliet* (plate 26). Irving had spent £8000 on the sets, but was willing to sell them for £2000. Hofmann, who regarded the theater only from its financial side, calculated that if he bought a Meininger–like set, he would enjoy Meininger–like success. Since he bid only 20,000 marks (£1000), though, the deal fell through.[24] Hofmann must have had a keen eye for scenery that would have been appropriate on the Meininger stage. Although Georg did not have a set like the one in plate 26, he later added one to his theater's stock.[25]

Paul Bonsdorf publicized the fact that he was emulating the Meininger. He directed theaters in Münster, Osnabrück, and Lübeck, but never enjoyed the financial solidarity needed to make a success of his attempts to imitate the Meininger. Because of the shabbiness of his costume reproductions, he earned the nickname "kattuner Meininger" ("calico Meininger"). Idealistic and true to the Meininger to the end, he rented Berlin's Nationaltheater, where he went bankrupt.[26]

The Dresdner Hoftheater, under Marcks's direction, was responsible for sullying the reputation of the Meininger. The theater's personnel were, for the most part, older actors who did not understand the Meininger's artistic principles. Marcks directed them in performances that featured excessive decoration and much shouting on stage.[27]

In 1904, Dr. August Bassermann became director of the Karlsruhe Court Theater. There he won acclaim for his Shakespeare productions, both because of his attention to the text and his effective use of crowds. In *Julius Caesar,* for example, 136 students had been engaged as supernumeraries. Because he was a reserve officer, Bassermann's direction was especially effective in battle scenes.

Bassermann also followed Georg's example by giving his extras small parts to interpret. The effect must have been distracting, though. Instead of speaking in a manner that would produce only background noise, Bassermann's extras spoke their parts clearly and even interrupted the main characters. During Anthony's speech, for example, the audience heard comments such as "What's that?" "We know that!" "Brutus is a murderer!" "That's right!"[28]

A May Festival was given every year in Wiesbaden by the local Hoftheater. Georg Hülsen–Häseler, Jr., was the director at the turn of the century, and he tried his best to satisfy Kaiser Wilhelm II, who always attended. The Kaiser's taste ran to the spectacular, and the Wiesbaden productions were much to his liking. Besides lavish productions of Wieland's *Oberon* and Gluck's *Armida, The Merchant of Venice* was done, based on the latest photographs of Venice. Everything was copied exactly from the original, and the actors were left to their own devices. The result was more an exhibit populated by declamatory actors than a play. Much was made of the claim that Hülsen–Häseler was following Georg's example faithfully, and the reputation of the Meininger suffered as a result.

Since the Meininger's tours took the troupe to foreign countries as well as to German cities, its influence was also felt abroad. William Archer, London's leading critic, was impressed by the Meininger when they visited in 1881, even though they performed only in German. He took umbrage, however, at the statement he read in a newspaper that Shakespeare had been introduced to the English repertory by the Meininger. Archer pointed out that, even ignoring Kean's revivals, Irving's Shakespeare revivals beginning in 1874 were both successful and totally unaffected by the Meininger's visit. "They did not teach us to understand Shakespeare," he said. "They did not even teach us to understand *Julius Caesar.*"[29] *Caesar* had been a success for the Meininger, yet when Beerbohm Tree revived that play in 1898, people still claimed it would not be a commercial success. In only one point did the Meininger leave an influence in London. Tree selected his Anthony on the basis of his ability to move the mob in the same way Barnay had in 1881. Archer, on the other hand, felt completely justified in declaring the Meininger's " . . . influence upon the English stage to have been practically nil."

The situation was different in France, where André Antoine organized the Théâtre Libre in 1887, originally as a forum for Zola's plays. Antoine, who had participated in various capacities at theaters since his childhood, joined the amateur company, named the Cercle Gaulois, of the gas company where he worked. Because of his experience and enthusiasm, he soon became leader of the group. To attract attention to the small theater, he wanted to hold a premiere, and obtained permission from Zola to present Hennique's dramatization of the novelist's *Jacques Damour.* Unfortunately, the members of the Cercle Gaulois refused to support Antoine's proposal.

Antoine and his supporters organized their own theater, where the works that other stages would not produce could find a home. The name chosen was the Théâtre Libre. The Théâtre Libre's guiding tenets were realism in subject matter, simplicity, naturalness, and verisimilitude in the expression of passions, in staging, and in acting. Antoine disapproved of the oratorical declamatory style then popular in French theaters. He also criticized the star system because it caused both author and public to favor the actor to the detriment of the play.

In July 1888, Antoine had taken his theater to Brussels for a guest appearance. While there, he saw a performance of the Meininger, about whom he had heard favorable comments. Most discussions of the Meininger's influence on Antoine have mentioned that he totally embraced their principles and that his productions became true works of art only after seeing their performances.[30] The sole basis for such a claim has been Antoine's 1888 letter to Françisque Sarcey.[31]

To be sure, much of the letter discusses the crowd scenes, for which Antoine had much praise. He found the practice of using trained actors as supernumeraries enabled the Meininger crowds to behave as true ensembles, much superior to anything seen in France. Instead of looking into the audience, all the extras watched the protagonists. Another scene that impressed him with its naturalness came in *Wilhelm Tell* (act 4, scene 3). Gessler's way was blocked by a beggar and two children who played the scene with their backs to the audience. Antoine considered it a simple and logical way to make the scene effective.

Antoine did not find all to his liking, though. He found the Meininger sets discordant and poorly painted. There were too many props, often put on the stage for no reason. The costumes were lavish and historical, but to Antoine they were also in bad taste. He could think of no documentary evidence to justify them. The stage carpet was the same in all scenes, and there were squeaking floorboards among the mountains, he related.

The special effects and lighting he found successful, up to a point. He mentioned a torrential rain, done by projection, that ceased abruptly instead of gradually stopping. A ray from the setting sun moved quite suddenly across a window at the very moment of a man's death, seemingly for the sole purpose of accenting the tableau.

He found the actors adequate, although several did not appear to be comfortable in their costumes. The mountaineers in *Tell,* he noticed, all had white hands and spotless knees.

Antoine had used a realistic approach to drama from the beginning of the Théâtre Libre, and had no doubt already equalled or surpassed the Meininger in the area of verisimilitude. The two theaters had basically different repertoires. The Meininger presented mainly classics, while Antoine was interested mostly in radical new plays that could not be produced in the commercial theaters. However, the performances at the Théâtre Libre reflected in some respects what Antoine found to his liking in Brussels. He began coaching his actors in more thorough fashion, in order to build an ensemble. He discouraged conventionalized stage movements and speech, and urged natural behavior among his actors.

The Meininger visited Moscow in 1885, but a twenty-two-year-old actor who had taken the name of Stanislavsky was too busy with other activities to take notice of them.[32] When they returned five years later, Stanislavsky was in the audience. He attended every performance, coming not only to look but also to study.[33] He commented that, for the first time, Moscow had seen historically real productions, well–directed mob scenes, fine outer form, and amazing discipline. He noticed, though, that there was little attention given to the acting, which he considered to be of rather low quality.

He especially admired Chronegk for his tyrannical methods of directing. Being a member of an amateur group, he felt that the group could benefit from such a strong hand: "We also wanted to give luxurious performances, to uncover great thoughts and emotions, and because we did not have ready actors, we were to put the whole power into the hands of the stage director."[34]

Stanislavsky learned to imitate Chronegk. Each sat at a table with a watch, waiting for the appointed rehearsal time. When it arrived, a bell was struck and the rehearsal began.[35] In Stanislavsky's own words, he became "a despotic director."[36] Then a whole generation of directors, who did not have the talent of Chronegk or Georg, imitated Stanislavsky. These new directors, in his opinion, treated the actors without feeling, much as if they were merely another prop.

In his 1893 production of Gutzkow's *Uriel Acosta,* Stanislavsky used what he had learned from the Meininger. The play was unusual for Moscow in the authenticity of its costuming and the excellence of its mob scenes.[37] The costumes then available in Moscow, even though copied from the Meininger wardrobe, were totally unacceptable. The tailors had so altered them that they were little more than variants of the only three styles in use in Moscow, which Stanislavsky dubbed "Faust," "Les Huguenots," and "Molière." Stanislavsky's troupe therefore made its own costumes.[38]

The Moscow Art Theater was founded in 1897, and its first performance took place in 1898. The play was Tolstoy's *Czar Fyodor.* The audience was surprised at the realistic setting. To some, it was merely an imitation of the Meininger and a display of archaeological details.[39] According to another account, though, Stanislavsky announced two principles that showed his clean break with the Meininger. He believed that a faithful representation of all props was unnecessary, as long as there were some authentic pieces to catch the eye. Likewise, the scenery did not have to be real, as long as the audience thought it was.

For a production of *Julius Caesar,* Stanislavsky followed many of Georg's suggestions. He sent two of his assistants to Rome to draw up blocking diagrams while consulting the layout of the actual Forum. The promptbooks noted speeches for everyone, even the twenty–eighth legionnaire in the last battle scene.[40] Actors were given custom–tailored costumes and taught how to wear togas. Much incidental stage business, such as trading at market, was introduced. The thunderstorm was so violent that the actors could not be heard above it.

By 1906, Stanislavsky's basic philosophy had changed. He came to regard the actor as the basic unit of the theater, and considered it necessary to devote the major part of his preparations to the area of acting.

That same year saw the Moscow Art Theater playing in Berlin. Stanislavsky appears not to have completely broken with his Meininger training, since the German critics all noted similarities. One even went so far as to praise Stanislavsky for proving that adaptations of the Meininger's work did not always have to demonstrate a degeneration of the original.[41]

The Art Theater was well received, especially after a visit by Kaiser Wilhelm. In honor of the occasion, the troupe was invited to dinner at the homes of Friedrich Haase and Gerhart Hauptmann. Haase had a small apartment, but he wanted to honor his Russian guests. He invited a man and a woman from every Berlin theater, a selective process that prompted Stanislavsky to refer to it as a Noah's Ark arrangement.[42]

Also present at the dinner were actors of the Meiningen troupe, who had assembled to rehearse *Egmont* for Georg's eightieth birthday. In recalling the events of the evening, Stanislavsky wrote, "Haase wanted to please me by introducing me to the actors who had given me so much pleasure in their time."[43]

After dinner the Meininger gathered around Stanislavsky's chair and insisted that he tell them of his creative work. Max Grube met the Russian director for the first time and found it fascinating that he was able to obtain results at a democratic theater—everything at the Art Theater was put to a vote—that were similar to those Georg obtained at his autocratic institution.[44]

Stanislavsky abandoned his despotic methods modeled after Chronegk, but he always retained the Meininger's drive for getting to the heart of a play:

Only with time, as I began to understand the wrongness of the principle of the director's despotism, I valued that good which the Meiningen Players brought us, that is, their director's methods for showing the spiritual contents of the drama. For this they deserve great thanks. My gratitude to them is unbounded and will always live in my soul.[45]

Literary Beneficiaries

When Peter Rosegger wrote his message of gratitude for Georg's artistic contributions, he was expressing feelings of affection for the Duke shared by many literary figures of the day. On the occasion of Georg's eightieth birthday in 1906, messages of congratulation poured into Meiningen from throughout Germany; among them were letters from Rosegger, Paul Heyse, and Paul Lindau.[46] Partly because of his position as Duke and partly because of his importance as a cultural figure, Georg became acquainted with many authors, both successful and aspiring. Although it was not a major goal of his stage to produce new dramas, Georg did provide certain playwrights the first opportunity to see their plays performed. Even dramatists who did not know him personally and who never saw their creations performed on his stage, however, felt his influence through the accomplishments of his troupe.

Gerhart Hauptmann never met Georg, yet, in his own opinion, he owed much to the Duke. In 1874 Hauptmann moved to Breslau to attend the same school as his older brother Carl. Gerhart was not the most capable of students, and he was under especial pressure during the 1876–77 academic year. His thoughts often turned to the theater, inspired, no doubt, by the presence of the Stadttheater directly opposite the school.

The Meininger scheduled their second Breslau appearance for October and November 1877. Carl obtained tickets for Gerhart and himself. Gerhart was fascinated by the experience of watching the Meininger, and recalled their impact on his youthful imagination in his book *Das Abenteuer meiner Jugend* ("The Adventure of my Youth"):

> One can judge what the experiences of *Macbeth, Julius Caesar,* the *Wallenstein* trilogy, and Kleist's *Hermannsschlacht,* performed by (the Meininger) theater, must have meant to my totally enslaved boy's soul, deprived of all illusion and, in its dark cravings, hungering for grand impressions.[47]

Hauptmann seems to have confused the facts slightly when he recalled the event sixty years later. In 1877, the Meininger performed *Macbeth, Julius Caesar,* and *Die Hermannsschlacht,* but not *Wallenstein.*[48] They did not perform *Wallensteins Lager* in Breslau until 1881; the entire *Wallenstein,* until 1882. By that time, Hauptmann was in Jena, so he must have seen the Meininger perform elsewhere also. Nevertheless, his attendance at Meininger productions had a lasting effect on him. In 1932, in another retrospective work, he wrote how seeing the Meininger had filled a void in his inner self with an intellectual power that stayed with him his whole life:

No word of veneration approaches the value of this experience for my emptied, starving soul. No word measures the extent of the intellectual wealth that those few hours gave me for my entire life.[49]

Later, in Berlin, Hauptmann had occasion to think of the Meininger again. He had just read Ibsen's *A Doll's House,* and decided that he should try to create such a powerful drama. He compared his own progress from simple to more complex ideas to the progress the theater had made from the Meininger, who marked the beginning of a new form of theatrical art, to the Deutsches Theater, where the Meininger traditions were perpetuated in more refined form.[50]

Although Georg's primary dramatic interest was in the classics, he was also responsible for the original performance of a number of serious contemporary plays, both on the Meiningen stage and during the Meininger tours. According to Witkowski, the 1870s were a particularly difficult time for German dramatists seeking production of their works, owing to the concern of theater managers for profit and the predominant popular taste for outward effect.[51] Many of Georg's productions satisfied the public's desire for spectacle, but that result was incidental, not intentional. His interest in the artistic state of the theater led him not only to seek improved performance of classic drama but also to mount productions of plays by contemporary authors who caught his attention. In some cases, such as that of Paul Lindau, Georg sponsored performances of plays by authors who were already his friends. More often, however, Georg or Helene became interested in a playwright they did not know personally and added one or more of his works to the Meininger repertoire. As a result of visits by such authors to Meiningen or through consultation on a play's production, close working relationships and friendships developed between the Duke and certain playwrights.

Georg's major contribution in the area of modern drama was his work with Ibsen. The Meininger are credited with being the first to produce Ibsen in Germany. This they did on January 30, 1876, when *Pretenders* opened in Meiningen.[52] The play was repeated in Meiningen in March and April, then taken to Berlin for the troupe's 1876 visit (plates 28 and 29).

Ibsen was present in Berlin for the opening of his play there on June 3. In a letter dated June 14, he tells a friend that the play was presented "with glowing splendor" by Georg and the Meininger.[53] According to Ibsen, the piece was warmly received by the audience, although the critics seemed somewhat envious of his success.

German productions of *The Vikings, The Pillars of Society, Lady Inger,* and *A Doll's House* followed the Meininger introduction of Ibsen into Germany. When Ibsen wrote *Ghosts* in 1881, however, it seemed for some time as if no European theater would consider the play.[54] A German translation was published in 1884, but it was not until April 14, 1886, that it was first presented in Germany. On that date, Felix Philippi sponsored a closed performance of the play in Augsburg, to which he invited a large group of Munich actors.[55] The play had been banned by all German censors, and only a private performance could be given without police interference.

Georg had found Ibsen's writing to be much to his liking in *Pretenders,* since it enabled him to use the historical resources of his theater. *Ghosts* was stirring up such a controversy that the Duke decided he would give the play a chance to become widely known and judged on its own merits.

Georg decided to make *Ghosts* part of a festival week that would also feature a play by Voss and one by Echegaray, translated by Paul Lindau. The Duke invited Ibsen, who was living in Munich, to attend the performances, which were to be held just before Christmas. At the same time, he wrote to him for advice on proper scenery.

The correspondence between Georg and Ibsen is an interesting example of Georg's methods. The Duke preferred to correspond on a sheet of paper that had been folded in the middle, thereby forming four pages. To preserve Ibsen's comments in a form useful to himself, Georg enclosed with his invitation a sheet on which Ibsen was to make his reply, using the first two pages. Georg could then write comments on the last two pages and file the sheet for future reference.

In his reply, Ibsen politely thanked Georg and Helene for their invitation and informed them that he would indeed be in attendance at the German public premiere of *Ghosts.* He then answered Georg's questions, describing the interior of the typical Norwegian country house he had intended for the setting of his play, going into detail about the style of furniture, type of stove, and color of wallpaper. In conclusion, he offered to be of assistance if Georg needed further information.[56]

When Georg received Ibsen's reply, he sketched the set for *Ghosts* on page three of the sheet (plate 30), and on page four wrote a letter to the Brückner brothers of Coburg, his scenery artists, ordering a closed set based on Ibsen's comments and the sketch on page three. The back of the set was to be a solarium, containing real flowers, and behind that was to be a Norwegian landscape. The backdrop with the landscape was already in Meiningen, since Georg had decided to use a mountain scene from *Wilhelm Tell.*

Georg's note to the Brückners was dated November 15, and the rehearsals were scheduled to begin December 3. On the same day, Chronegk sent a letter to the painters confirming Georg's order and requesting various pieces of scenery for other plays. He pointed out that *Ghosts* would be given in mid–December, thus giving himself some leeway if the scenery was not ready, and requested that the set be done a few days before then for the rehearsals.[57]

The most interesting aspect of the correspondence is that Georg seemed to be concerned only with the visual elements of the play. His letter to Ibsen asked only about how the scenery should be constructed, not about how the psychological content of the play should be developed. Georg seems to have been oblivious to the fact that Ibsen's play was a radical departure from the conventional drama usually done by the Meininger. He apparently presented *Ghosts* not because he wished to hasten the breakthrough of naturalist drama, but because he felt that the play would provide a pleasing "picture."

Chronegk sent a copy of the play, which he described laconically as "quite interesting," to the Brückners, so that they could become familiar with it: "Read through it, so you can give the scenery the proper mood."[58] The Brückners finished the scenery by the first week in December and sent the set to Meiningen. On December 13, Chronegk wrote that he was returning the scenery because part of it was peeling and some changes needed to be made.[59] All scenery was apparently sent on approval, because Chronegk also discussed scenery for *Jungfrau* and *The Merchant of Venice* that he was returning.

The final rehearsal was held on December 18,[60] and invited guests arrived in Meiningen the morning of the first festival performance. Voss and Ibsen traveled together from Munich.[61] The festival began December 21 with Echegaray's *Galeotto, Ghosts* was on the 22nd, and Voss's *Alexandra* came on the 23rd. Georg's difficulties in attracting an audience have already been mentioned; suffice it to say that he was forced to give the tickets away to fill the house.[62]

There must have been those in the audience who did not care for the piece, but they kept their opinions to themselves out of respect for Duke Georg. Hans von Bülow caused a scene, however. During the first act, he rose from his seat in the first balcony, and left with much clattering, saying loudly, "Disgusting—a piece for seamstresses!"[63]

Voss sat in Georg's box, as did Lindau and Ibsen. He reported that the audience generally reacted warmly, and when the final curtain came down, the house was silent for some moments. Then a solid wave of applause began, and Ibsen finally had to join the actors on stage to receive the audience's accolades.[64]

After the performance, Georg held a reception for the invited guests.[65] The Kaiser's granddaughter, Georg's daughter–in–law, was present, which surprised many of the other guests.

On the following day, Georg presented Ibsen with a medal—Ritter des Sächsisch–Ernestinischen Ordens erster Klasse mit dem Stern—in recognition of his contributions in the field of drama. Ibsen was very proud of the award, he mentioned in a letter to Ludwig Josephson, because it made him feel as if someone appreciated his efforts.[66] Georg wished to repeat the performance in Berlin, but was blocked by the censors. Franz Wallner, director at the Residenztheater, was able to gain a license for one performance under the stipulation that the performance would be a matinee and that all proceeds would go to charity. The play was given by the Residenztheater company on January 9, 1887.

Audience reaction was similar to that in Meiningen. There was silence at first, and then the storm of applause broke forth. Ibsen was called up repeatedly by the audience, and he appeared on the stage with tears of joy streaming down his face.[67]

There seemed to be no critical reaction to the Meiningen performance, but a performance in Berlin could not be ignored. By and large, the critics were confused by the play, objecting to it not on aesthetic grounds, but because it was too difficult to understand. They failed to see what the play had to offer in the way of a description of the human condition.[68]

The result of the two public performances was a demand for Ibsen's plays. *An Enemy of the People* and *Rosmersholm* were seen in Germany in 1887, and the Meininger repeated *Ghosts* in Dresden in November. *The Wild Duck* and *A Doll's House* appeared in 1888, and when the Freie Bühne opened in 1889, it was with a performance of *Ghosts.* Georg had truly helped Ibsen make his breakthrough in Germany.

Georg's interest and patronage extended to other playwrights of less renown than Ibsen. Some of the dramatists he introduced or fostered on the German stage subsequently enjoyed at least moderate success. Among them were such more or less noted figures as Richard Voss, Otto Ludwig, Björnstjerne Björnson, and Ernst von Wildenbruch. Others, such as Julius Minding, were forgotten almost as soon as their plays were dropped from the Meininger repertoire.

Richard Voss was one playwright to whom Georg became a patron and a friend. According to Witkowski, Voss's plays used "seeming psychological depth and outwardly modern expression" to portray "women of abnormal disposition" in a manner reminiscent of the French play of manners.[69] Because of the reputation of his play *Magda* (1875), Voss was invited to Meiningen as Georg's guest in 1884. Helene took an immediate liking to him, and invited him for another visit the same year.[70] On his second visit, he brought a play he was writing, *Alexandra* (published 1886). Helene asked him to read the play for Georg and her. Voss did so, feeling that they were being patronizing; he assumed Georg was not really interested in literature, since he was a Duke. The couple liked the play, however, and immediately accepted it for their theater.

The premiere was held in 1886, during the festival that included the premiere of Ibsen's *Ghosts.* Georg had requested a different last act, which Voss willingly wrote for the Meininger.[71]

Voss became one of Georg's close friends. He spent summers at Georg's house on the Königssee in Bavaria, and winters at Villa Carlotta, where he wrote his play *Schuldig.* [72] Helene even began calling him "Vössle."[73]

The relationship between Georg and Voss ended on a sour note, however. Voss had written a novel entitled *Ein Königsdrama,* about the last member of a degenerating royal family. He sent a copy of it to Georg, who returned a letter saying that his stage would no longer present the plays of a writer who could create such a tale. In spite of Voss's apology, Georg never removed his ban.[74] Voss's later role in the history of drama remained small.

Otto Ludwig was one of Georg's favorite writers because of his Thuringian background, but his play *Der Erbförster* appeared only twice in the Meininger tours. By 1900 the play had nearly been forgotten,[75] but when the Meininger presented it in Berlin in 1876, it was acclaimed by the critics. Frenzel called it the best thing the Meininger had done, praising them for the simplicity of their stage setting.[76] The scenic atmosphere seemed to perfectly match the intellectual qualities of the play. The actors seemed exactly suited to their parts.

The royal theater in Berlin immediately brought out its own version of *Erbförster.* Neither troupe enjoyed success with the piece. In Grube's opinion, there was not enough visual quality to draw a crowd, and the intellectual weight of the piece made it too deep for most audiences.[77] *Erbförster* was kept in the home repertoire at Meiningen, though, where Ludwig's other plays— *Die Makkabäer, Hans Frei, Torgauer Heide,* and *Die Pfarrrose* —were also added between 1890 and 1900.

Björnstjerne Björnson, the Norwegian playwright who anticipated Ibsen, was introduced to German audiences by the Meininger. *Between the Battles* was first presented in German in Meiningen on March 29, 1867.[78] The play was taken to Berlin in May, and eventually was performed 21 times on tour. Critics disliked it, as previously discussed, but it remained a mainstay at Meiningen, partially because its one-act length made it a good "filler." Helene was later to lament that no one remembered Georg's interest in Björnson. She pointed out that several of the Norwegian's plays first appeared in Meiningen.[79]

One of the authors for whom the Meininger's performances most clearly led to later popularity was Ernst von Wildenbruch. Wildenbruch had labored as a playwright for over ten years without having a single play performed. He had even participated in an 1878 Munich literary competition in which his play was not even suggested for presentation. Later critics were to wonder why Wildenbruch had never been noticed before, since his plays, which began appearing following the Franco–Prussian war, were full of national color and pride.[80]

It fell to Georg to see the value of Wildenbruch's work. On March 6, 1881, the Meininger became the first to stage a Wildenbruch play, *Die Karolinger.* Suddenly Wildenbruch became fashionable. Berlin's Viktoria Theater repeated the performance on October 26; two days later it was seen in Hamburg. He was acclaimed as the new Schiller, who would pull Germany out of the morass of nineteenth century drama. Within months, Wildenbruch no longer needed the Meininger, and Georg dropped his plays from the theater's repertoire.[81]

The idealist Julius Mosen (1803–67) often tried to intercede with theater directors in behalf of his friend Julius Minding, who is remembered for only one play, *Pope Sixtus V.* Again, Georg was the first to accept the play, which was performed in Meiningen on December 26, 1873.[82]

The Meininger took the play with them to Berlin in 1874, where it lasted only four evenings. The critics called it a weak work, undeserving of a place on the stage. Georg eliminated the play from both the home and traveling repertoires, and it was never performed again elsewhere. Minding later took his own life in New York.

Through his work with both major and minor dramatists, Georg had an influence on Germany's literary history, as well as on its theatrical progress. Just as his theater reforms grew out of the work of those who went before him, so also his patronage of struggling playwrights had its antecedents, at least in the history of the royal family of Saxe–Meiningen. After all, it was less than a hundred years earlier that his grandfather and namesake, Duke Georg I, had granted a promising but impoverished young writer named Schiller a title and helped him to launch a career in the nearby duchy of Weimar.

4

Theory and Practice

"My anger is and will be directed, as long as I live, against all frivolity in art."

Georg II, Duke of Sachsen–Meiningen [1]

Investigation of Duke Georg's dramaturgical concepts and the ways in which they were put into practice in his theater indicates that the artistic elements of Meininger productions did not develop accidentally, but that Georg guided his theater toward an ideal of harmony between text and staging. A sampling of critical opinion demonstrates, however, that few people understood the scope of Georg's work, and that the criticisms themselves were widely divergent.

One of the most common misconceptions about the Meininger was that they played only to impress their audiences, while ignoring artistic and literary considerations. There were few who considered Georg's work an attempt to combine textual fidelity with staging that could cause an audience to become totally caught up in a play. Some critics praised only the visual aspects of the Meininger performances; others, the troupe's representation of the spirit of the plays themselves. Opposing critics generally condemned the Meininger for the elaborateness of their staging.

Georg's Theater: The Stagecraft

While still in his mid-twenties, Georg had already developed definite ideas of what was aesthetically pleasing on the stage. For his 1850s production of Gluck's *Iphigenia* (discussed in chapter 1), for example, Georg followed a definite plan which he had devised for improving the artistic quality of the performances seen in Meiningen's theater.

In January 1864, 31 months before becoming Duke, Prince Georg wrote to his father's director, von Stein, outlining suggestions for an upcoming performance of Gounod's opera *Faust.* [2] The letter mentions many of the points that collectively were to become recognized as key components in Georg's conception of staging: attention to small detail, asymmetrical blocking, and realistically staged crowd scenes.

One of the difficulties involved with a discussion of Georg's theories is that he neither published a treatise on the theater nor formulated in one place an overall program for carrying out his ideas. From discussions he had with various people connected with his theater, however, it is possible to gain an overview of his technique. One such person was Paul Lindau, who compiled a collection of Georg's instructions on blocking, scenery, and mob scenes.[3] In each area Georg carefully noted details that added to the realistic effect he desired.

One of Georg's primary concerns, Lindau relates, was with the composition of the picture presented on the stage. He felt that the middle of the stage picture should never be in the middle of the stage, because the director would then be tempted to balance the groups appearing on the stage in a symmetrical fashion. To Georg the word "symmetry" was nearly synonymous with "boredom," since symmetry led to a quiet, static condition that was the antithesis of the constant state of flux represented by drama. Mobile scenery, such as trees or walls, was not to be placed at center stage, but on either side, far enough away from the wings to be seen by the entire audience. Actors, likewise, were directed never to stand directly in front of the prompt box, which at that time was situated in the lower center of the stage.

The entire middle area of the stage, approximately the width of the prompt box and reaching from the front of the stage to the backdrop, was made forbidden territory. An actor could enter that area only if crossing from one side to the other; he could not stop there. Actors were also cautioned to be aware of their distance from the prompt box, since Georg disliked seeing two actors equidistant from that clearly marked midpoint. By arranging the scenery so that smaller areas framing the action were formed on either side of the stage, Georg was able to discourage actors from standing in the middle.[4]

The special requirements of stage perspective often led to an incorrect relationship between actor and scenery. Georg realized that not all mistakes in this area could be avoided, especially when the stage perspective was designed to be quite deep.

Since actors did not diminish in size as they moved upstage as rapidly as the scenery, audiences frequently saw men as tall as trees, and houses whose doors reached only to an actor's knee and into whose second–story windows an actor could peer. According to Lindau's article, Georg directed that actors were to remain in front of deep streets and alleys, and never to stand near the backdrop. All props and scenery that were on the stage in areas where actors did stand were to be in approximately correct human scale.

If a play required a large building to appear near the front of the stage, it was more important to show part of a building with walls and columns extending past the top of the proscenium than to show the entire building from ground level to rooftop. An example of incorrect perspective was often found in the balcony scene of *Romeo and Juliet.* Georg believed it was better to have Juliet high above the stage than to have Romeo speaking beneath a balcony he could easily have reached, even without being especially athletic.

A second reason for keeping actors away from scenery was that any contact with two–dimensional scenery would cause it to move, thereby destroying the illusion. If an actor needed to touch a piece of scenery, such as a pillar, a rock, or a stone, that piece, Georg directed, should be made of solid materials so that it could support the actor without moving.

Mixing three–dimensional scenery with two–dimensional created new problems. It was necessary to pay close attention to the types of materials used and to the manner in which the scenery was painted so that it did not become immediately obvious that there were different types of scenery on stage. Additionally, if painted scenery included reproductions of three–dimensional props so as to give the illusion of a group of items, Georg insisted that more than one solid prop should be placed onstage. A flower garden from which a flower was picked, for example, should contain more than one real flower in front of a painted background of flowers.

In Georg's theater, all scenery was constructed before rehearsals began. The Duke believed, Lindau mentions, that it was much easier to create the proper mood among his actors if they were working with actual scenery from the very beginning. If, for some reason, a set could not be completed by the first rehearsal, at least all doors, carpets, benches and furniture were present and the boundaries of the finished set marked on the stage.[5]

The same applied to props and costumes. Actors were required to rehearse with props that were held, such as swords, so that they became familiar with the weight and balance of the pieces and could adjust their movements accordingly. Costumes, too, often required a change from usual body movements, and if a costume was not finished for rehearsal or was fragile, similar clothing was worn. All this was done so that in performance the actor no longer felt as if he were in a costume that had just been issued him, but rather in familiar, oft–worn clothing.

An added advantage of rehearsing with actual props was that Georg could help his actors avoid undesirable parallel lines. One of his general rules was that there was to be nothing parallel on his stage. Swords, lances, spears and the like were not permitted to point in the same direction. Through constant coaching the Duke made it second nature among his actors to point their weapons in different directions and always to make the distances between them slightly different.[6]

Lindau recalls that Georg considered it undesirable for an actor to stand parallel to the proscenium, or for two or more to face the audience directly. Actors were also instructed not to cross the stage in a line parallel to the stage front. Even when moving from stage front to stage back or the opposite, actors were told not to do so in a straight line but to move along a slight angle. Similarly, three or more actors were forbidden to stand in a straight line, and the distances between actors had to vary.

A related stage direction was that the actors should use different levels on the stage. They were never permitted to stand on a stairway with both feet on the same step. Likewise, if rocks or uneven ground were represented on the stage, Georg found it highly desirable for actors to put one foot on the rock or at a different elevation from the other foot.

The Meininger are associated perhaps most frequently with "mob scenes." That many have felt this to be the group's strongest point is due in no small measure to Georg's attitude toward minor roles and supernumeraries. He felt that small parts, often neglected by other directors, were so important as to demand extra attention. "Major parts carry themselves," Georg told the actor Karl Weiser, "a minor part must be carried by the actor."[7]

As much as he may have wanted to, however, Georg was not able to fill every role on the stage with a trained actor. When the troupe performed in Meiningen, Georg was able to use his own soldiers as extras,[8] but when on tour, Chronegk hired locals to fill in the ranks. Among those who tried out he found some with talent and a desire to follow his directions, but he also found those who had no talent and those who felt they had too much talent to follow directions. One of Chronegk's main tasks, therefore, was to sift through the available pool of extras until he found a sufficient number qualified to join the Meininger. These were not then left without guidance, but were placed under the leadership of a permanent "Meininger," whom they would follow during performances. The permanent actors always stood at the front of their small groups, so that the first line of "extras" that met the audience's eye was a group of experienced actors.

The group leaders, too, were not left to their own devices during performances. Whereas a playwright's directions for the mob might be simply "Shouts," "General astonishment," "Muttering," and the like, Georg wrote appropriate speaking parts for each of his group captains. These parts were memorized and rehearsed, so that the effect was the natural conversational pattern of a large group. The rehearsals were not rushed, and Georg paid close attention to each group leader's actions, his goal being that every member of the mob represent an individual *("Eigenexistenz"* is the term used to describe the desired effect). The Duke also tried to have as many types as possible represented on the stage—from excited to calm, old to young—so that the mob as a whole appeared to have formed itself at random.[9]

At most theaters the effect Georg was able to achieve would have been impossible, because most actors regarded a "bit part" as something distasteful that was never played by anyone other than a beginner. On Georg's stage, however, all members of the troupe, from the most famous to the newest, were required to take roles in the chorus. Max Grube was able to remember only one exception to the rule—Joseph Weilenbeck, who was blind.[10]

Grube further mentions two examples of experienced personnel being told to take bit parts. The first cited is that of himself. When he rejoined the Meiningen company after several years of experience elsewhere, his first role was that of a silent spectator in Shakespeare's *The Winter's Tale*.

The second incident involved Hans von Bülow's second wife, Marie Schanzer, who was engaged as an actress while her husband directed Meiningen's orchestra. In 1885 she refused to play walk–on parts, and her husband interceded in her behalf with Georg. Georg's response was to ask for their resignations, even though Bülow had made the Meiningen orchestra one of the continent's best.[11]

Georg's published regulations clearly spelled out the actors' obligation to play walk–on roles. Paragraph 17 of the official rules of the Meininger Hoftheater published in 1868 points out that even though some contracts mention a specialty *(Rollenfach)*, the theater direction could request that a different type of role be played in an emergency. In the 1880 revision of the rules, paragraphs 20 and 21 replace the original, and state that even though a specialty had been agreed to, if it was decided that the overall harmony of a production required it, another role, even that of a walk–on, could be assigned. Paragraphs 22 of the 1868 rules and 26 of the 1880 rules reiterate the requirement for all actors to play in crowd scenes. The statement is made that no one will be exempted from playing walk–on roles, but in the next sentence some exception is made for those who play leading roles.[12] Judging from the examples cited, the conclusion must be drawn that although Georg did not want his leading actors playing walk–on roles every day, he felt that the needs of the ensemble required all to take such roles when the production would be enhanced by their doing so.

The question arises whether there was a ranking system for actors at the Meiningen theater. Georg eliminated all titles among his actors, with the exception of honorary member *(Ehrenmitglied)* for those who were regular guest artists. He even went as far as doing away with Herr, Frau, and Fräulein and listing actors and actresses only by their full names.[13]

In contrast to Grube's report, though, that there were no specialties at Georg's theater,[14] stand reports by Kainz that he was "engaged strictly for leading roles,"[15] and by Nesper that for ten years he stood "in first place in the specialty of leading heroes."[16] Max Grube's own contracts stated in 1873 that he was hired only as an "actor," but listed him for 1874–75 as "an actor for character parts."[17]

The answer to the question concerning ranks among actors would seem to be that there was a hierarchical system, with unproven actors being hired without a specialty and with actors who showed a specific talent later receiving a classification. Once this was done, though, it was generally ignored by everyone, so that in actuality one was expected to play all types of parts.

Most of the Meininger actors seemed to accept the fact that they would have minor as well as major roles to play. Grube mentions two reasons why they felt this way. First, they knew that Georg watched every minor role as closely as he did the major parts, since he wanted everything on the stage to be harmonious. They were thus not passing up a chance to be seen by the director when they played minor roles. Second, the Meininger felt that they were part of an experiment that could change the theater, and that they owed it to the world to make their walk–on performances as convincing as possible.[18] The result of their labors is reflected in an anecdote told by Grube. When the actor Strassman of the Munich Court Theater was a guest in the Meiningen production of *Wilhelm Tell*, he was astonished at the uniformly high quality of acting among the bit players, and compared them all to the production's star. "What am I supposed to do?" was his question. "Everyone on the stage here could be Tell!"[19]

It is apparent from Lindau's report that Georg followed rules for forming an artistic "picture" with his mob scenes just as he did with the smaller groups already mentioned. He considered the most attractive feature of a large group the line formed by the members' heads, and he tried to keep that line from being uniform. He directed that, where possible, some of the group should kneel while others stood around them. If a group was gathered around a person or object, an irregular semicircle was to be formed (plate 31).

The extras were extensively rehearsed, because they always seemed to forget one or more of Georg's instructions. He continuously told them, Lindau relates, that they should move as soon as they became aware that they were standing in the same way as their neighbor. The Duke also forbade all from looking directly at the audience, although the eyes of those who were on stage for the first time were often irresistibly drawn toward the darkened theater.

Stage events that might be disturbing or distasteful to the audience, such as dragging off the wounded and dead, were hidden from direct view. This was not done by forming a wall of actors in front of the action, however, since that lent an unnatural appearance. The group that stood in front of the action was loosely formed, so that the audience could see some, but not too much, of what was happening at the rear of the stage.

Even Georg, with the entire company at his disposal, could not actually fill a stage with extras. The Berlin Court Theater tried to do so by using whole companies of soldiers, but succeeded only in making the stage look like a parade ground. Georg, as explained by Lindau, had a simpler, but much more effective technique. He arranged the groups of extras so that they extended past the drops and into the wings, so that no one in the audience, even those seated in the balconies, could see the point where the actors ended. This technique is illustrated in plate 32. The psychological effect was one of a group much larger than actually appeared on the stage.

The term "ensemble" is frequently used in conjunction with the Meininger. It often refers to the "mob scenes" and the way in which all members of the troupe played a variety of roles. It is also used, though, to refer to the quality of the Meininger acting and the *Zusammenspiel,* i.e., the harmonious and supportive interaction on stage during a performance. This ensemble quality was achieved partly through Georg's exclusion of "star" performances from his stage, but it was mainly a result of thorough rehearsal.

Meininger rehearsals lasted much longer than the rehearsals customary at other theaters at that time. For a new play, 20 to 25 rehearsals were held, beginning with a reading of the play to gain a general overview. Bit players, if they were not familiar with the play, were required to stay for the whole reading even though they had only a few words to deliver.[20] Individual scenes were then rehearsed, sometimes one scene for as long as two or three days. Following the scene rehearsals came rehearsals of entire acts, then a general rehearsal, and finally a dress rehearsal. The dress rehearsal differed from the general rehearsal only in that the costumes that were too fragile to be worn during all rehearsals replaced the substitute copies that had been in use; all previous rehearsals, even the scene rehearsals, had been held with props and costumes.

At rehearsals, the complete attention of all was required. There was a directive that there was to be no backstage talking loud enough to be heard by those reciting, and all laughing and joke–telling was forbidden. Those who were not in a scene were not permitted to eat, drink, or busy themselves with other activities, such as knitting, where they could be seen by the actors on stage.[21]

As pointed out in chapter 2, simple plays were chosen for performance in Meiningen so that more time could be spent preparing the pieces to be presented on each year's upcoming tour. Usually eight to twelve performances were given in Meiningen each month, which often left five afternoons and evenings as well as six mornings per week open for rehearsal. The afternoon rehearsals began at four or five o'clock and lasted as long as necessary, sometimes well past midnight. When rehearsals lasted that long, a break was taken for dinner, and the following morning's rehearsal was cancelled.[22]

Several actors have left records of the lengthy rehearsals. In letters to his parents, Kainz mentions a rehearsal of only two scenes of *The Robbers* that lasted from 4:30 p.m. until 11:00 p.m. and a dress rehearsal of the same play lasting from 5:30 p.m. until midnight.[23]

Another actor fell victim to the long rehearsals when he was to appear on stage with a lighted candle in act 1, scene 2 of Grillparzer's *Die Ahnfrau.* Since actual props were used during the rehearsals, he duly waited in the wings with burning candle while the first scene was rehearsed. When his cue finally came, he walked onto the stage only to hear the Duke's voice. "You have to walk on with a burning candle," Georg called, stopping the rehearsal. Only then did the actor notice that the rehearsal of scene one had lasted for so long that his candle had burned down completely and gone out.[24]

Georg set an example for his company by remaining present at the rehearsals for as long as his actors were there. He would call breaks as necessary—Amanda Lindner tells of being invited by Georg and his wife Helene to join them for tea and a light meal during a ten hour-long-dress rehearsal of Schiller's *Die Jungfrau von Orleans* [25] —but he never left before the rehearsal was over. Another actress tells of an evening in which the entire cast seemed especially worn down by the rehearsal's length. At 10:30—the rehearsal had begun at five—Georg arose from his customary spot in the balcony and told the cast that the late hour was no excuse for not putting forth their best effort. Saying that, as an example, he would stand during the rest of the rehearsal just as they did, he came down to the orchestra, and, leaning on his cane, directed the rehearsal to its conclusion.[26]

The Duke's presence at rehearsals brings up the question of what his role was there. Theater experts have said that Georg never directed.[27] Indeed, Georg did not direct in the usual sense. There was no traditional director's table and chair, because there was no promptbook.[28] When Georg arrived, he was often accompanied by his wife, Helene, and they took their places in the middle of the first balcony, which was darkened.

Before the actual rehearsal began, the supernumeraries were drilled in their parts. All who were not otherwise participating in the play took part in these drills, which were led on stage by Chronegk, the director.[29]

The actual rehearsal then began. Chronegk sat in one of the front rows of the orchestra, with a runner beside him to take his directions backstage. Seated at one side of the stage was the producer for the production, who acted as an assistant stage manager. The producer was always a member of the troupe who had been with the company for some time, and knew its quirks. Chronegk's role seemed to be one of seeing that Georg's wishes were carried out, since the Duke was the only one allowed to interrupt a rehearsal. This Georg did for the slightest infraction, from an incorrectly intonated word to two extras standing too near each other.[30]

Georg was a believer in the efficiency of the telegraph, and if he was away from Meiningen for any reason during rehearsals, he would send a constant stream of instructions and suggestions to Chronegk. When the Meininger were on tour, Georg, who stayed at home, would continue his barrage of telegrams.[31]

Since the Duke did not travel with his players, it could be expected that rehearsals while on tour were somewhat different than they were in Meiningen. One of the best descriptions of Chronegk's direction when away from home is given by Constantin Stanislavsky.[32] He relates that Chronegk was the best of friends with all members of the company when outside the theater. Once inside, however, he became a different person. He would sit in his usual place, in complete silence, waiting for the precise moment that rehearsal was scheduled. (In Meiningen, Georg at least stipulated that rehearsals would begin five minutes after they were scheduled.)[33]

> Then he would ring a large bell and declare in a quiet voice, *"Anfangen"* (Begin). Everything quieted down. The rehearsal would begin at once and continue until he rang his bell again. Then he would make his remarks in a dispassionate voice, ring the bell again, repeat the fatal *"Anfangen"* and the rehearsal would continue. (plate 33).[34]

Stanislavsky noted that there was a problem on the evening under discussion, because one of the leading actors was late. After a long pause, Chronegk finally declared that another actor was to play the part while the Meininger were in Moscow, while the tardy actor would be relegated to leading the extras in the rear. " *'Anfangen!'* And with the fateful sound of the bell, the rehearsal continued, with an understudy in the part of the actor who was late."[35]

Helene also made an important contribution to the Meiningen theater in her main role of drama coach. She studied roles with the members of the troupe who needed or desired her assistance, but her training went beyond correcting diction. She also read through the script with the actors and actresses and discussed with them the relationship of each individual character to the play as a whole.

Even one so talented as Josef Kainz, who, according to Helene, needed no coaching, turned to her for assistance, and she helped him in his role as the Prince of Homburg.[36] According to Kainz, the younger members of the troupe would come to her after each rehearsal, and each received the same degree of attention from her. Additionally, she concerned herself with the education of the young actors and actresses by discussing with them topics from outside the theater and recommending books to them.

Amanda Lindner, who came to the Meininger when only seventeen, became Helene's special charge. Helene spent considerable time coaching Lindner, who gives Georg's wife all the credit for her acting ability.[37] In the first year of her residence in Meiningen, 1886, she learned from Helene her parts for *Wallenstein, Tell, Julius Caesar, Ahnfrau, Twelfth Night,* and *Jungfrau von Orleans,* in which she had her greatest triumph. Helene spent much extra time with her preparing for the role, and Lindner relates that Georg was often present at the sessions, but only as a spectator.

Robert Prölss, who made an early study of the Meininger, mentions a different division of labor for drama coaching.[38] According to him, Chronegk studied the smaller roles at home with the actors, Helene was in charge of the main women's roles, and the leading men's roles were coached by Georg, Helene, and Chronegk together.

Helene was active on two other fronts as well. She was present at all auditions and helped choose new theater personnel. Lindner mentions auditioning before Helene, Georg, and Chronegk,[39] and Arthur Kraussneck auditioned before Helene and Georg.[40] Helene also assumed the responsibilities of keeping up with newly-written plays and theoretical literature and helping to revise older works for the Meiningen stage.[41] She exercised an influence on Georg in the area of repertoire, and the Meininger emphasis on Shakespeare may be in part attributable to Helene's English background.

Mention has been made of Georg's penchant for rehearsing with actual costumes and scenery. A glance at the Duke's design methods will further illustrate his desire for accuracy on the stage. Costumes were not left up to the individual; indeed, Georg had eliminated that practice in the 1850s with his "Crown Prince's wardrobe." The Duke himself designed new costumes for every production. The designs were first sketched in pencil and then filled in with pen and ink. When a new piece was going into production, each actor would find a sketch of his costume at his dressing table so that he and the costumer could see exactly what Georg's wishes were (see plates 34 – 41).[42]

In contrast to the costumes at other stages, which were often of a general nature and were chosen to approximate the dress of the play's period, Georg researched clothing styles through the centuries. Whereas most theaters purchased costume fabric from the firm of Katz located in Krefeld, Georg used material that was as close as possible in texture, color, and weight to the fabric that would have been used at the time of the play's setting. Some of the fabric came from Lyon and Genoa, and some was woven especially for the Meiningen theater.[43] Even the suits of armor were replicas of actual armor, and were manufactured by a Paris firm—Granget—in sizes designed to fit nineteenth–century actors. In Drews' opinion, the spectacle seen on the Meininger stage was costumed so accurately that the audiences could use the performances as a textbook of the history of clothing.[44]

Georg likewise designed his own sets. Just as with the costumes, he sketched his plans in pencil and filled them in with pen and ink. Often the Duke would make several such sketches before achieving the desired effect, as shown in the series of set designs for the prologue of *Die Jungfrau von Orleans* (plates 42–48). Sometimes his sketches would be devoid of people, such as those for *Jungfrau* or the closed set for *Miss Sara Sampson* (plate 49), and sometimes human figures would be sketched in to show the relationship between the actors and the set, as is the case with Georg's drawing for *Prinz Friedrich von Homburg* (plate 50). In these set designs, individualizing characteristics were never drawn on the people's faces, and often just the shape of the head was included.

When set designs were complete, they were sent to the Brückner brothers in Coburg. Max and Gotthold Brückner were the sons of the Coburg court theater painter, and both followed the same profession as their father. They produced their first scenery for the Meiningen theater in 1858, and in 1866 they produced the scenery for Haase's production of *The Merchant of Venice* at the Coburg court theater, which production seems to have set Georg on his path as a director. The Duke sent them ever–increasing orders for backdrops until they finally were able to open their own workshop in Coburg in 1872. Wagner became acquainted with their work through Georg's theater, and hired them as his painters in 1874. Through the Meininger theater and the Bayreuth opera, the fame of the Brückners spread throughout Germany, and eventually orders came from Russia and America as well.[45]

One of the major changes in scenery brought by the Brückners was the basic color. Much nineteenth century scenery had blue or lavender as its basic color. Although the architecture painted on the backdrop was generally accurately reproduced, a backdrop was, just as its name implies, merely a painted canvas in front of which action took place. The Brückners desired their backdrops to become an integral part of an overall stage design, and designed them so that the audience was unaware of the point at which three–dimensional scenery was replaced by a painted scene. They replaced pastel tones with a basic reddish–brown known as "cassel brown." The effect was to blend the backdrop easily into the overall stage picture through the shadows and reduced light at the rear of the stage. The actors no longer appeared as dark figures against a light backdrop, but as light figures against a darkened landscape.

The Brückners won Georg's immediate acceptance because their goals were the same as his. Their backdrops contained accurately painted details that agreed with the specific directions sent by Georg, as opposed to the broadly outlined forms that showed little detail seen on other stages. Brückner scenery was designed not to be eyecatching, but rather to become part of a harmonious whole. Georg valued their work most of all for that one point, and as early as 1875 made them his exclusive painters.

When Max Brückner asked Georg if he should subcontract some of the work for *Hermannsschlacht* because he was falling behind, Georg asked him to do all the work himself so that his name would appear on the Berlin program as sole painter. Georg's reason was that he had more confidence in Brückner: ". . . because I trust you more than any other painter."[46]

Georg did not lower his standards when it came to props, either. As Duke he owned many antiques, furniture, and other interior furnishings as well as weapons, and he never hesitated to take valuable pieces from his residence, his castles, or one of the duchy's museums for use on his stage. If he could not obtain an actual period piece, he would have a copy made of an original.[47]

Sometimes, however, Georg's penchant for historical accuracy seems to have gotten the better of him. In *Macbeth* the plates used in the banquet scene (act 3, scene 4) were thick slices of bread, cut lengthwise through a round loaf, because Georg had once read that it was a Scottish custom to eat from bread plates that were consumed with the meal.[48]

Grube testifies that the food and drink used on the Meininger stage were always as real as everything else, and recalls one time that realism ruined the play. The wine used in the drinking scene in *Othello* (act 2, scene 3) was from the Duke's wine cellar, and all the actors in the scene, including the "Gentlemen" who had no speaking part, became quite jolly in their toasting, with resultant changes in the script.[49]

A joke about the Meininger and the real food used on their stage was that the actors in *Hermannsschlacht* had gone on strike. Their reason was that they did not want to eat the gruel, which had been prepared according to an ancient Germanic recipe.[50]

Two plays presented in Berlin demonstrated the value placed on historical reproduction by Georg and the effect the illusionistic stage had on the audience. The Berlin advertisements for *Maria Stuart* boasted of the value of the props in a manner reminiscent of Kean's theater programs, saying that the cross worn by the heroine was an exact reproduction of the one actually worn by Mary Stuart, that the wooden steps used in the last act were the steps that "actually creaked beneath the queen's feet during her last steps," and that the British Museum's architectural drawings of Fotheringay Castle were used to design the sets.[51]

Such fidelity to detail did not extend to the use of actual "poison" candles as the instruments of murder in Albert Lindner's *Bluthochzeit;* the Meininger used scented candles to represent the poison. The scent, which drifted out into the audience, reportedly caused a Berlin banker to fear for his safety when he smelled it. Turning to his wife, he cried, "Come, Sarah, let's get out of here; otherwise they'll poison you, too."[52]

One of the necessary evils of a realistic style of production such as that of the Meininger was the curtain between scenes *(Zwischenvorhang)*. This curtain, first used by Devrient in Karlsruhe in 1859,[53] was a standard fixture of the nineteenth-century stage. Its use was necessary because of the extensive changes that needed to be made to the set between many of the scenes. Whereas scene changes on an open stage have the effect of disturbing the illusion but of providing a form of continuity, changes behind a curtain disturb the illusion while effectively dividing the play into many more acts. Many stages, including the Meininger, provided music for the audience while the curtain was down, which called even more attention to the change.

Georg regarded the curtain as distracting, but in many plays there was nothing to replace it. He attempted changing scenery on a darkened stage with the curtain up, but found that this worked effectively only in a limited number of cases.[54] In some plays, such as Moliére's *The Imaginary Invalid* and Shakespeare's *Twelfth Night,* sets were designed that required no changes during an act. When that was done, the curtain did not need to be dropped.

While Georg endured the curtain as a necessary evil, he placed some restrictions on the practice of an actor's responding to applause and calls from the audience. After a play's final curtain the entire cast reappeared, as was tradition, but individuals also often came back on stage after their exits to acknowledge applause.[55] Audiences of the period, it must be remembered, were used to "stars" appearing on stage and expected acknowledgments from their favorites in return for their applause. Most seemed not to regard such interruptions as a disturbance in the play's continuity. Georg made it clear, though, that there was to be no acknowledgment of applause during a scene.[56]

In his overall plan for pleasing the audience, even stage noises were considered worthy of Georg's attention. The Meininger used the same thunder, wind, and rain machines as other stages, but the stage hands became active participants in Georg's rehearsals. If the effect they created was not exactly what he wanted, he would stop the rehearsal and drill them until the sound produced was the desired one.[57]

If the sound of a large crowd had to be made, all acting personnel who were backstage assisted in creating the effect. When the sound of a band of soldiers talking in a high tower had to be produced, for example, everyone climbed into the flyloft and murmured, but the sound was lost in the scenery. Then it was tried from every corner of the stage, but without success. Someone finally suggested that all lie on their stomachs and murmur into the floor. It is no doubt a mark of the spirit of the troupe that no one laughed at the suggestion, and so it was tried. It worked. Georg was pleased and the rehearsal continued.[58]

The word *Rhabarber* (rhubarb) somehow became associated with the Meininger. It was said that the Meininger had discovered that when a group of people spoke this word behind the scene at normal conversational volume, the most realistic crowd noise possible was produced.

The most entertaining—and no doubt most fanciful—story of how the Meininger came to use *Rhabarber* is that Georg and Helene were watching a rehearsal of *Julius Caesar* when Helene began to feel ill. Since Georg supposedly did not allow breaks during rehearsals (see note 25 above, however), she sent a servant to fetch her rhubarb pills. In the meantime, Georg had halted the rehearsal to give some suggestions to the supernumeraries. Grabowsky (director until 1867) was on stage trying to arrange the crowd as Georg directed, but was having little success. The Duke grew more and more impatient. Finally Grabowsky told him that the chorus did not know what to say before Brutus began his speech.

Just at that moment the Duke bumped into the servant who had gone to fetch the pills and who was feeling his way back in the darkened balcony.

"Now what are you bringing?" the Duke queried.

"Rhubarb, as ordered, your majesty!"

Georg, who knew nothing of Helene's request, cried out half surprised, half angered, "Rhubarb?"

Grabowsky, who had been waiting for the speech Georg had prepared for the crowd, assumed that he had now been told, and the chorus began to repeat "Rhubarb."

Georg apparently liked the sound, and from that time forth, the story went, *Rhabarber* was a Meininger trademark.[59]

The Kiel theater historian Eugen Wolff sent out questionnaires about the history of this curious word.[60] From Max Grube came word that the Meininger had never used the word, at least never officially, although some of the younger actors at the theater might have said it as a joke. It was reported that when Georg desired a general crowd noise to come from backstage, he passed out newspapers to the cast and had each member read aloud from a different section, such as weather reports, obituaries, or sports.[61]

Georg's Theater: The Texts

That the word *Rhabarber* became associated with the Meininger is symptomatic of a general misunderstanding of Georg's priorities regarding the drama. Audiences came to think of the props, staging, and effects—those elements defined by some as outward direction[62] —as the essence of the work of Georg and the Meininger. Paul Lindau had mentioned in an 1878 review[63] that such dazzling effects were nice, in their place, but that he felt the drama itself deserved better attention.

In a letter to Lindau, Georg replied to the critic's accusation that he was ignoring the inward direction. Therein the Duke pointed out that it was not his intention to ignore the drama, although he could not ignore the framework in which it was presented. He also admitted that some of his effects might be considered excessive, but claimed that would be a value judgment. Coming to the center of the argument, Georg assured Lindau that the appearance of a production was never the most important thing to him; indeed, he was strongly opposed to such an emphasis.[64]

During an era in which the Royal Theater of Berlin presented *Die Räuber* in a version ending with "Hauptmann" delivering a sermon to the robbers about their misdeeds concluding with the message, "Go home, serve the state, become useful citizens,"[65] Georg, assisted by Helene, carefully compared editions of dramas with the originally published text in order to restore a play to a form as close to an author's original as possible, while retaining stagcability. The results of their labors appeared as a series of texts beginning in 1879.[66]

The Meininger version of *The Robbers* is a good example of the type of revisions Georg and Helene made. Schiller originally had the play published in 1781 at his own expense, anonymously, and with Frankfurt and Leipzig listed as places of publication. Its title was *Die Räuber, ein Schauspiel* (The Robbers, a Play), and this version is often referred to now as the *Literaturausgabe* (literary edition) or *Druckausgabe* (printed edition). During the printing of the first edition, Schiller sent a copy to the Mannheim book dealer Schwan, who refused to publish it but who showed it to the director of the Mannheim National Theater, Wolfgang Heribert von Dalberg. Dalberg immediately saw theatrical possibilities for the play, and asked Schiller to make it stageable. Schiller revised the play for Dalberg between August and October, 1781.

Dalberg took Schiller's stage version, but made several changes without telling the author. It was mid–December 1781 before Schiller discovered Dalberg's changes, which included such additions as Amalia's suicide. Although it was too late to prevent the unauthorized changes' inclusion in the Mannheim production, which opened January 13, 1782, Schiller undertook a further revision. In the meantime, a second, unauthorized edition was printed by Tobias Löffler of Mannheim in 1782.

Schiller's final revision, which appeared with the title *Die Räuber, ein Trauerspiel* (The Robbers, a Tragedy)[67] in February 1782, included many of the drastic changes Dalberg had insisted on. This edition became known as the *Mannheimer Bühnenbearbeitung* ("Mannhcim stage version").

The greatest change in the Mannheim edition was the time in which the play was set. Schiller's original said: "The location of the story is Germany. The time period is about two years." The new version said: "The location of the action is Germany. The play takes place during the time when 'everlasting peace' had been established in Germany." Instead of a play that seemed to breathe "eighteenth century," the world now had a drama about a robber band at the end of the fifteenth century. Schiller hastily made appropriate historical changes, and instead of Hermann telling Moor of Karl's joining the Prussian forces under Friedrich and going to fight the Austrians in Bohemia (act 2, scene 2), he tells Moor that Karl has joined the army of Mathias of Hungary, and has gone to Pest to help the Poles fight the Turks (act 2, scene 5).

Acts and scenes were changed in the Mannheim edition, and although five acts were retained, the number of scenes was greatly increased. Schiller's original had five scenes in the fourth act, while the new version had eighteen. Additionally, several long speeches were shortened or eliminated.

When Georg set about preparing *The Robbers* for the Meiningen stage, his first decision was to return the play to the original time, i.e., the eighteenth century. The Mannheim edition was so widely accepted that only twice before had the play been presented as other than a mediaeval drama: once in Leipzig in September 1782 and again in 1861 by Philipp Eduard Devrient in Karlsruhe.[68]

Having decided on the period of the play, Georg had to make a second important decision, namely, how much of Schiller's original to include. Schiller himself admitted that his original was not stageworthy (in the "supressed preface to *The Robbers* "). The most logical course seemed to be to take whatever poetic elements were stageworthy from the original, and replace all other segments of the play with variations that had proven successful on the stage. A reconstruction of the Meininger text shows that the play, as performed at Georg's theater, was composed of the following scenes:[69]

Meininger Act 1,	scene 1:	dI,	1
	scene 2:	dI,	2
	scene 3:	mI,	2
Act 2,	scene 1:	dII,	1
	scene 2:	dII,	2
	scene 3:	mII,	7
		dII,	3, ll.235–end
Act 3,	scene 1:	dIII,	1, ll.1–23
		mIII,	1
	scene 2:	mIII,	2–4
Act 4,	scene 1:	mIV,	1–9
	scene 2:	mIV,	10–11

```
                 dIV,  4,  ll.19–end
      scene 3:   dIV,  5,  ll.1–259
                 mIV,  16
                 dIV,  5,  ll.318–end
Act 5,  scene 1: dV,  1
        scene 2: dV,  2
```

Georg made some revisions in Schiller's text for the Meininger production of *Fiesco,* also.[70] The locale of act 1, scene 9, was moved from the interior of Fiesco's hall to a courtyard with orange trees. This meant that Fiesco could no longer watch the Moor's suspicious movements in the mirror, but it did enable the two to converse under more private circumstances.

All other major changes were made in act 5. The locale of the entire act was changed from the public square to the interior of a building next to the Thomas gate. Act 5, scene 1, was eliminated, either because of the shift in setting (Bulthaupt's opinion) or because Georg felt it was beneath Fiesco's station to ring Andreas's bell himself (Grube's view).

There were two versions of act 5, scene 8: one from the original text and a 1785 revision by Schiller for the Leipzig municipal theater. Georg combined the two versions. On the Meiningen stage, Bertha is not disguised as a boy, as she is in the original, but her monologue from the 1785 version is eliminated and the scene is not played in a subterranean vault.

Georg also changed the costumes mandated by Schiller. The Meininger costumes were rich and colorful to reflect the wealth of the city of Genoa in 1547; the black costumes Schiller mentions were not worn until some years later when introduced by Philip II of Spain.

Kleist's *Käthchen von Heilbronn,* as revised for the stage by Georg, serves as a third example of a production improved by his attention. The original text contained some passages considered unfit for nineteenth century morals. Franz von Holbein accordingly cut several scenes and rewrote others. Heinrich Laube later made a second revision that, while including some original parts changed by Holbein, was still quite different from Kleist's play.

Among the scenes restored to the play by Georg[71] were act 4, scene 4, showing Kunigunde before entering the grotto; act 5, scene 2, in which the Kaiser fondly remembers his evening with Gertraud and Käthchen's conception; act 5, scene 4, with Kunigunde in her "unassembled" form; and act 5, scene 5, when Count von Strahl meets Kunigunde before her make–up is completed. Georg also corrected the change Tieck had made in the play by having Theobald be Käthchen's assumed father. Tieck had made him her assumed grandfather, because he felt a father (Theobald) could more easily forgive a sexual indiscretion in his daughter (Gertraud) than in his wife. Georg also set the time of the play as the reign of Maximilian I (1493–1519), instead of leaving it as an undefined mediaeval time.

Some scholars, going against prevailing opinion, have considered the greatest legacy of the Meininger not their work in the areas of historicity or ensemble, but rather the restoration of Shakespeare and Schiller to the German stage.[72] Georg's leading principle in his Shakespeare and Schiller revivals was that of fidelity to the author's designs for a play. E. A. Stahl could think of only one instance when the Meininger were not faithful to the original spirit of a play. That was in the case of Shakespeare's *Taming of the Shrew,* which was adopted in Deinhardstein's version only because that edition had been used for many years in Meiningen and Georg did not want to start over from the beginning with the play's production.[73]

It would seem that Georg took as much pride in being certain of the poetic and dramatic correctness of the texts used at his theater as he did in seeing that the staging of a piece was appropriate down to the smallest detail. With an overview of the Duke's work in both "inward" and "outward" direction, it is apparent that neither one took precedence. His oft–mentioned love of harmony shows that his goal could only have been to present both text and staging as a unified and complementary whole. The term *Gesamtkunstwerk* is indelibly associated with Wagner, and yet it seems entirely appropriate to also use the word in describing Georg's craftsmanship.

All the elements discussed above were directed by Georg toward only one end. He never hoped to gain personal fame or wealth from his theater; he wanted only to return the drama to its proper place and stature. It was perhaps an oversimplification, but when Grube once asked Georg why he had undertaken all that he had in the theater, the Duke's reply was: "I was angry that Shakespeare was performed so poorly in Germany."[74]

Georg considered himself the playwright's servant. Acting only out of love for the theater, he created an illusionistic stage at which an audience could become totally involved in a play. The Duke felt that the artistic value of a play, not to mention whatever message the play's author intended to convey, could not be sensed by a dispassionate audience. For that one reason he created a spectacle that never failed to draw attention to the stage. By creating a mood that complemented a correct text, the Duke believed, he could most effectively reach his audiences. In summing up the attraction the Meininger held for the theatergoing public, Georg stated, "Our primary characteristic was that of creating the appropriate mood in the spectators."[75]

The Critics

There were some critics who recognized Georg's desire for harmony between a play and its presentation. Walter Bormann considered Georg's goal of presenting drama as a unity of text, spoken word, and spectacle to be an appropriate realization of the intentions of all playwrights.[76] Isolani pointed out that all Georg had done was directed toward eliminating any devisive or unharmonious elements from his productions, and that the form always took second place to the actual play on the Meininger stage.[77] Max Kurnik likewise saw in the Meininger productions complete congruity between content and form. He described Georg's motto as "perfect harmony of performances."[78] Hans Herrig pointed out that the Meininger satisfied what he considered to be the most important dramatic principle: that all details be subordinated to the work as a whole. He went so far as to say that at the Meiningen theater, "serious drama was taken seriously for the first time."[79]

It is not the purpose of this work to review fully the critics' appraisals of the Meininger.[80] A chronological sampling of critical reaction demonstrates that opinions of the Meininger varied widely in detail, as is the case with any artistic endeavor, but that the critiques generally addressed the same broad topics. The group received praise from some for those very things for which they were damned by others.

The Meininger opened in Berlin in 1874, and the great body of criticism began at that time.[81] Frenzel's comments on the opening night performance of *Julius Caesar* included praise for the elimination of the drop curtain during the first, second, and fifth acts.[82] He liked the costumes and the weapons, feeling that everything had an ancient character about it. The masses received his highest praise; he described them as nearly perfect. When Caesar was murdered, the crowd's reaction was unlike anything Frenzel had seen on stage before. One would have had to see it, the critic felt, to appreciate how finely crafted the acting was: " . . . to sense how powerful, how high, and how deep the effect of dramatic art can be."[83]

Frenzel's description of the Forum scene (act 3, scene 2) tells something of how many different actions were being performed on stage at once. Anthony was carried on the mob's shoulders as he read Caesar's will aloud; some attacked Caesar's hearse while others stormed the scene with lighted torches; in the midst of wild shouting, Cinna was murdered. Although Frenzel was impressed by the scene, he most politely wondered if there was not a bit too much happening at once: " . . . whether the noise could not be lowered by half a tone?"[84]

Paul Lindau, the most vocal of the Meininger's early critics, also praised the decorative elements.[85] He saw nothing anachronistic on the stage, and could not deny that the sets had an artistically correct appearance. The costumes, he thought, were also excellent, even though an occasional actor appeared to have difficulty with the weight of the clothing. The direction was, in Lindau's opinion, excellent.

Only in one area did Lindau feel he needed to offer criticism. That area was exaggeration: the troupe offered too much of a good thing. There was too much movement and too much shouting. He also felt that the supernumeraries had been drilled too much. Often they appeared to be puppets, he commented, all making the same movements.

Pope Sixtus V brought a shorter review from Frenzel, a longer one from Lindau. Frenzel limited his remarks to praising the set and arguing that a realistic set is more likely to draw an audience into a play than is a plain set with only a few representative furnishings.[86]

Lindau devoted much of his review to a discussion of Minding's play, mentioning its history and its constant failure on the stage.[87] Whereas the Meininger and Shakespeare worked together the first night, in Minding's play there were only the Meininger to carry the weight, and the effect was often comic. The liveliness on stage, so interesting in *Julius Caesar,* was totally out of place in such a dull play. Then, too, seeing the supernumeraries perform for a second time proved to Lindau how exaggerated their actions were. As he described it, whenever someone crossed the stage, at least five actors pointed at him and all the rest nudged each other. Things that would ordinarily barely be noticed caused astonished reactions from all present; if someone told an only moderately funny joke, all would double up in laughter.

Shakespeare's *Twelfth Night* opened May 20. Frenzel again had little to say about the performance. The set and costumes were exactly right for the piece, he maintained, and Georg had successfully eliminated the drop curtain. The play itself was typical Shakespeare, and carried with it lightness and joyfulness. Frenzel was glad to see it in almost its original form instead of in one of the revised versions often used in Germany.[88]

Lindau seemed to be in agreement with everything Georg did in Shakespeare's comedy.[89] He found the set superb and he especially liked seeing the play without the curtain's interruptions. He even discovered some new acting talent among the Meininger that evening, and, because there were no supernumeraries, had nothing negative to say about them.

Frenzel did not review Lindner's *Bluthochzeit,* the Meininger's next offering, but Lindau found the play to be the worst Meininger performance yet. He had read the text beforehand, since the play was not often performed. After watching the Meininger perform it, though, he felt as if he had read the wrong play. There was nothing of substance left in their performance, he wrote; instead, the evening was merely a series of well–constructed pictures. According to Lindau, the form of the presentation was so overpowering that the play's content was completely ignored by the audience. This criticism, which became one of the most often repeated, expresses a contradiction to Georg's principle of harmonious balance between content and form. It is now impossible to judge the validity of Lindau's claim. Audiences, however, seemed to disagree with him.

Lindau found the special effects expecially distasteful. Georg's directions called for actual gunfire backstage, and in the theater the gunfire was accompanied by clouds of gunsmoke. The smoke filled the house, and some in the audience began to cough. The smoke and coughing destroyed any artistic pleasure Lindau had had up to that point:

> Who could have felt anything akin to artistic enjoyment with this noisy, smoking, stinking nonsense in the midst of general coughing? I lack appreciation for this type of beauty, and if it is the stage's task to produce such feelings, then I consider every hour that I have devoted to this accursed institution to have been wasted.[90]

In fairness, Lindau reported that the audience did not share his disgust. Judging from the applause, everyone else loved the play. Actors were called back at the end of each scene, each act, and at the end of the play. Lindner was called out at the end of the second act. In short, everyone was called out except for the stagehands who fired the guns.

Once again, Frenzel had little to say with regard to Björnson's *Between the Battles*. He was glad to see Björnson represented on stage for the first time in Germany (apparently unaware of the earlier productions of Björnson in Meiningen), and felt that the piece was exactly right for the introductory part of a two play program.[91]

Lindau did not review any more of the 1874 Meininger productions. He turned that task over to M. von Szesiski, who expressed a concern with the text and dramatic value of Björnson's play.[92] It is in one act, and much of the background has to be gleaned from the very compressed action of the play. Szesiski felt that no one in the audience made the effort to understand the play. This happened for one reason: the stage was so richly decorated with all of the historical trappings everyone expected to see in a Norwegian house that the audience became involved with looking and forgot to listen.

Frenzel could not praise *The Imaginary Invalid* enough. In his opinion, the play proved to all doubters that the appeal of the Meininger did not lie solely in their decorations, because in Molière's play there was only one simple set. It was, he claimed, their best example of a harmonious work, one in which they lent body and color to the spirit put into the play by Molière.[93]

According to Frenzel, the audience could not stop applauding. The personnel played together so well that all who were present fell under the spell of the play's poetry. In summing up the season's accomplishments by the Meininger, Frenzel felt that the secret of their success was that they knew how to present Molière and Shakespeare, and that they were able to present a play just as its author had intended.

Szesiski also felt that the Meininger production of *The Imaginary Invalid* was the company's best because of the actors' strength in the area of comedy. He mentioned that the Meininger did not shy away from scenes that were considered vulgar by some, and praised Georg's version with only one exception. The weakest point of the whole play, in his opinion, was the last line, which had been completely changed by Georg (as discussed in chapter two).[94]

Hans Hopfen, a third Berlin critic, wrote a summary article about the 1874 Meininger visit to Berlin.[95] Hopfen felt that the drilling of the supernumeraries and the heavy emphasis placed on their role in the plays could be justified only if the goal of the production was to lower the level of acting to the least common denominator. He disliked the Meininger group scenes because they showed too much life and action. It would have been one thing, he claimed, if Shakespeare had written plays in which the mobs were the most important character, but it was quite another for so many things to be happening on stage at once. Such a plethora of interactions drew attention away from the main dialogue.

Hopfen applied a similar argument against Georg's set decorations. He felt that the Duke had devoted so much attention to every detail that things of little importance became as important to the audience as the main features of a play: "The stage has become a peep–show, a curiosity shop, a waxworks, a museum. This is no longer a tragedy, but a spectacle."[96]

He wanted to make it clear, Hopfen pointed out, that he did not consider Georg's attitudes worthless, just misdirected. The Meiningen stage had no great actors, and so all its energy was poured into things over which it had some control. All the Meininger needed were some talented actors, and then the troupe's good qualities—seriousness, energy, and patience—could work together to form a truly great theater.

In reviews of the 1874 Meininger tour, textual revisions, including elimination of the drop curtain in one play, accurate costuming, forceful, lively crowds, well–designed sets, and the ensemble were mentioned as positive qualities demonstrated by the Meininger. Negative points included exaggerated acting by the supernumeraries, too much sameness in the non-speaking roles, too much detail in the sets and props, distracting special effects, clumsy textual revisions, and lack of any acting strength. Already a trend had begun that was always to characterize critiques of the Meininger: praise and criticism of the same facets of their performances. The acting, reviews said, was good and bad, the costumes and sets enlightening and distracting, the supernumeraries delightful in their supporting roles and overpowering because they failed to support the main roles.

The following year the Meininger played in Vienna and Budapest in addition to Berlin. Critics in all three cities noted their appearances.[97] Without discussing each play or critic separately, a summary of the opinions voiced during that year can be made. The positive points mentioned were: (1) The Meininger productions seemed better polished than those at other stages because they produced fewer new pieces each year and rehearsed longer. (2) The mass scenes were well played, and helped build audience involvement with the play (mentioned three times). (3) The decorations—sets and props—were of uniformly high artistic quality (mentioned seven times). (4) Attention was paid by the director to the necessity of avoiding parallel lines on stage and of crossing the stage diagonally. (5) Unfamiliar plays were introduced *(Esther* and *The Learned Ladies)* (mentioned twice). (6) The talents of individual actors seemed improved over the previous year (twice). (7) The director had combined all stage elements into a unified whole that worked in harmony with the text of the play (twice). (8) Textual changes improved the play (especially Act V of *Fiesco)* (twice). (9) The costumes were even better than in the previous year, and the actors had obviously been trained in how to wear them (twice). (10) The director made use of different stage levels formed by rocks, etc., and of the scenery to group the action in small, defined areas. (11) The literary value of the plays became apparent through the scenic elements.

On the negative side, critics felt that the Meininger had erred in several areas: (1) The version of a play used was sometimes not the best available (twice). (2) The director's hand was too evident (twice). (3) The theater should not be an archaeological museum, and minor mistakes in scenery and costumes will probably go unnoticed by an audience. (4) Similarly, too much attention was paid to trivial decorative matters that distracted the audience (three times). (5) The Meininger were pedantic; they wanted everyone to know of their correctness by printing the history of the stage sets in the theater program (twice). (6) There was too much business on stage (twice). (7) A traveling theater faced many problems that could not be overcome, such as the differences in the stages and the temperaments of the local supernumeraries. (8) There were no outstanding acting talents among them.

Lindau added two small points to the list of negative comments in 1876: first, that he found the pauses too long when the drop curtain was down, and second, that the Meininger had eliminated animals from the stage in cases where they were necessary to the action of a play, such as in *Wilhelm Tell* (Georg's revision of *Tell* was discussed in chapter 2).[98]

Theodor Fontane made an occasional comment about the Meininger.[99] In 1877, for example, he pointed out that the Meininger were able to present Molière well because of their costumes. The historical design of the costumes was not responsible, he said, but the actors' familiarity with the costumes. By rehearsing in costume, they gave the appearance of having worn the clothes for years.

However, Fontane was not enthusiastic about at least one of the Meininger's special effects. Georg was especially proud of the appearance of Caesar's ghost in *Julius Caesar* (act 4, scene 3) but Fontane was singularly unimpressed. Of the special lighting effects, he wrote: "The appearance of Julius Caesar in Brutus's tent has the effect of a frightened schoolmaster who, clothed in a bathrobe, suddenly steps in front of a window illumined by the full moon . . . ."[100]

The critiques hardly changed over the years. Reviews from 1876 to 1887 mention the same points time and again.[101] The criticisms of the Meininger can be grouped into three main themes: (1) The Meininger had no talented actors, and the quality of their performances never rose above the mediocre. (2) The great attention devoted to historical correctness in costumes and props served only to catch the audience's eye and turn its attention away from the more important spoken word. (3) The supernumeraries were so thoroughly drilled in their parts that the stage business became too lively and the main roles appeared to be no more important than the walk–on roles.

On the positive side, the strong points mentioned by the critics can likewise be summarized under three headings: (1) The Meininger used texts that were faithful to the spirit originally set down by the author. (2) Their historically accurate props and costumes satisfied a basic need among the theater–going public to see reality embodied on the stage. (3) The Meininger formed an ensemble that always presented a crowd harmonious with the stage setting and the demands of the text.

Even as late as 1906, a reviewer commented that the excellent acting of the Meininger made up for any shortcomings in the play itself. "The acting," the writer said of the Meininger performance of Sudermann's *Johannisfeuer,* "in all roles, from the leading to the smallest, was so extraordinarily good that the performance totally complemented the play's content."[102]

It must be pointed out, however, that most critics, whether praising Georg's work or condemning it, failed to see the whole picture. Those who wrote of the Meininger dealt with one or more of the major topics mentioned above, but seldom with the total intent of a production.

The tone of the criticism became milder as years passed, demonstrating either that Georg accepted some of the suggestions offered to him, or that the critics gradually became more tolerant of the Meininger. It is significant that Paul Lindau, one of the Meininger's most vehement opponents in the 1870s, became director of the theater in 1895. The history of the Meininger indicates that they changed little over the years; the conclusion must be drawn that Lindau, at least, was finally convinced of the appropriateness of their methods.

Except for responding to Lindau's critique (see p. 91), Georg remained aloof from published criticism. At times he must have felt the criticism to be unfair, since he was being praised for his crowds and stage decoration at the same time he was being attacked because of them. His goal, as already mentioned, was to create a unified work of art, and his crowds and sets were part of his overall concept. Textual revision, mentioned favorably by the critics, was the other half of the Duke's comprehensive plan.

The lack of top talent—some would call it virtuoso talent— was necessary for the Meininger on two counts. The number of truly great actors and actresses is limited by nature, and small, provincial Meiningen had no hope of obtaining such people. Besides, Georg did not want a great talent working for him who would destroy the ensemble he worked so hard to create. He genuinely felt that a higher artistic level could be reached without self–serving artists. He also felt that art, in whatever form, demanded complete seriousness and devotion. This belief became the guiding principle in Georg's own life. It found expression in one of the Duke's most famous statements:

> Artists are nothing   only art is valuable; that is, an artist deserves support only if he advances art for the good of mankind. The other sort of artist, who approaches art frivously and uses it to befool people, deserves to be fought and rendered innocuous.[103]

These remarks on the value of art serve as appropriate commentary on the statements by Frenzel and Lindau that began the introduction to this book. To Frenzel's view that the secret of the Meininger's success lay in their presentation of the playwright's intentions, Georg would agree that his only objective in operating a theater had been to serve the spirit of every piece his troupe presented. To Lindau's contention that the Meininger were guilty of stressing the visual aspects to the detriment of the play itself, Georg could counter that he intended to present plays as complete works of art, and that he never knowingly did anything that would be disharmonious. Georg felt that he had successfully created a stage where the playwright reigned supreme. Such small details as jewelry and sound effects were designed to blend harmoniously with such larger concepts as set design and text revision. Georg hoped to create a unified, harmonious staging that would arouse an audience's interest while presenting the ideas contained in a play.

Georg's dramaturgy struck a responsive note, especially among German theatergoers. In spite of good or bad reviews, the Meininger were popular with their audiences. They popularized the theater as no stage before—not the Weimar court theater, the Prussian court theater, or Vienna's Burgtheater— had done. Georg's theater took drama to the world. The Meininger were the first to succeed as a traveling stage with high artistic standards.

In spite of the Meininger's popularity, though, the theater was the focus of attention, rather than the actors. People came to see an ensemble, not a star. The real star remained in the background. He was Georg. Without his artistic guidance and authoritarian rule, the Meininger would not have been the immense success they were.

Georg may have felt that the playwright was the most important figure on his stage, but in actuality Georg himself was most important. The period of the Meininger marks a watershed in the development of the theater. Before the Meininger, the director's name rarely appeared in print. With the Meininger, the director became an important figure at theaters, whose name was nearly always featured on playbills.

The natural outcome of Georg's philosophy was the perfection of "director's theater." No longer could stars determine what would be performed and how plays would be staged. The only way in which a production that could be called unified could be mounted was by having one person responsible for all concepts and production details from play selection to opening night. Other stages copied Georg's technical ideas, to be sure, but his greatest legacy was, for better or worse, the enthronement of the director as a central figure.

There were those who came after Georg who ruled by intellect, basing their work on an aesthetic system. Others ruled by force and threat, and seemed to be able only to copy work that had been done before, while not giving any consideration to the requirements of art. Some of them brought the so-called "Meiningerism" into existence—a loud, declamatory style of acting—and very nearly ruined the reputation of Georg and his theater.

Although Georg was the first of the new, strong directors, he was also the last of another type. World War I brought an end to all court theaters and Georg's death, just before the war's beginning, marked the practical end of that institution in Meiningen. Never again would there be a theater that was supported by a political ruler in Germany. Funds for the theater would never again be as plentiful, and directors would never again have quite the same degree of authority as Georg.

Plates

Plates 2–3.   Two of Georg's early drawings.

Plate 4.   Ellen Franz as Gretchen *(Faust)*, Imogene *(Cymbeline)*, and
Elisabeth *(Don Carlos)*.

Plate 5.   Ellen Franz, photograph of a watercolor by
            Lenbach, Ca. 1870.

Plate 6. Georg II, Duke of Saxe–Meiningen, and Helene, Baroness
Heldburg, on their 1873 honeymoon trip.

Plate 7. Ludwig Chronegk (1881).

Plate 8.   Duke Georg II in military uniform.

Plate 9. Ludwig Barnay of the Meininger company.

Plate 10. Joseph Kainz of the Meininger company.

Plate 11.   Amanda Lindner as Johanna in Schiller's *Die Jungfrau von Orleans.*

Plate 12.   Amanda Lindner in Schiller's *Jungfrau.*
           Drawing by C.W. Allers, 1890.

Plate 13. Amanda Lindner in Schiller's *Jungfrau.*
Drawing by C.W. Allers, 1890.

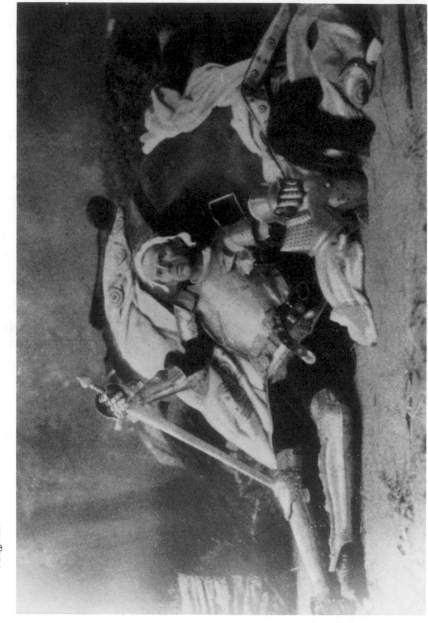

Plate 14. Max Grube, with stuffed horse, as Talbot in Schiller's *Jungfrau.*

Plate 15.   Duke Georg II at the close of his theater's tours (1890).

Plate 16.　Ludwig Chronegk at his retirement (1891).

Plates 17–19. Scenes from Christian Dietrich Grabbe's *Don Juan und Faust* at the Meiningen theater, March 6, 1896.

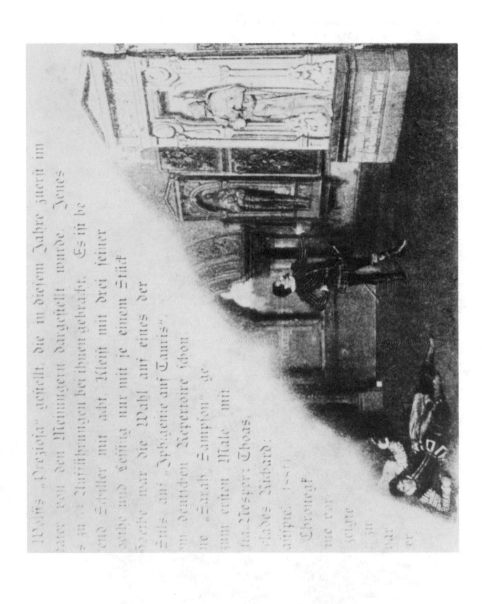

Plate 20. Duke Georg II and Baroness Helene on their 25th wedding anniversary, March 18, 1898.

Plate 21. Duke George II and Baroness Helene in 1898.

Plate 22. Group of former Meininger players assembled for the anniversary performance of the *The Merchant of Venice*, March 13, 1898, at the Meiningen Theater.

Plate 23.   Festival performance of Goethe's *Egmont*,
presented at the Meiningen Theater April 1, 1906, in
honor of Duke George's eightieth birthday.

Plate 24. Gottfried Keller's fragment *Therese* at the Meiningen
Theater, 1910.

Plate 25. Last known photograph of Duke Georg II and Baroness Helene.

Plate 26. Tomb in final scene of *Romeo and Juliet*,
Lyceum Theater, London, 1881.
Producer: Henry Irving. Designer: William Telbin.
Published in *the Illustrated London News* (1882).

Plate 27. Set for final scene of Romeo and Juliet, Meiningen Court Theater, 1897.
Sketch by Duke Georg II.

Plate 28. Georg's set design for Ibsen's *Pretenders*.

Plate 29. Costume design for Sigurd Ribbung in *Pretenders*.
Sketch by Duke Georg.

Plate 30. Duke Georg's sketch for the set of Ibsen's *Ghosts*.
(Theatermuseum Köln) (Cologne Theater Museum)

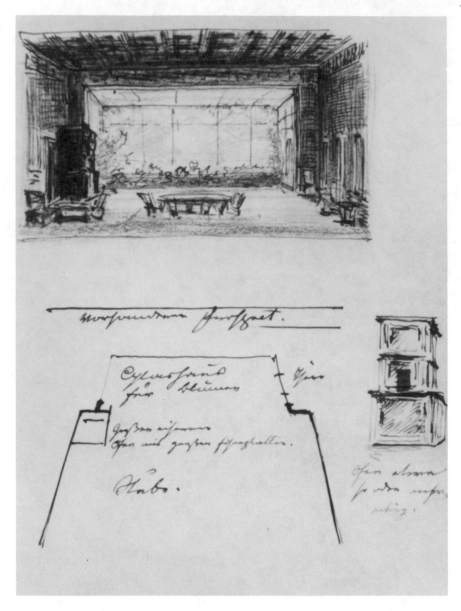

Plate 31. Duke Georg's sketch for the Forum scene in *Julius Caesar*.
The grouping of the crowd around a central figure, the line
formed by the heads, and the kneeling figures are points
Georg considered important.

Plate 32.   Duke Georg's design for Act V of *Fiesco*.
The groups extend past the edges of the set into the
wings, so that they seem to be more numerous.

Plate 33. Ludwig Chronegk, with bell, directing *Julius Caesar.*
Drawing by C.W. Allers, 1890.

Plate 34. Der alte Moor from Schiller's *Die Räuber*.
Costume design by Duke Georg.

Plate 35. Karl Moor from Schiller's *Die Räuber*.
Costume design by Duke Georg.

Plate 36. Hauptmann in Grillparzer's *Die Ahnfrau*.
Costume design by Duke Georg.

Plate 37.   Recruit in Schiller's *Wallensteins Lager.*
          Costume design by Duke Georg.

Plate 38.   Count Wetter vom Strahl in Kleist's *Das Käthchen von Heilbronn.*
Costume design by Duke Georg.

Plate 39. Thusnelda in Kleist's *Die Hermannsschlacht.*
Costume design by Duke Georg.

Plate 40. Duke Georg's costume design for Käthchen in Act V of *Das Käthchen von Heilbronn*.

Plate 41. Auguste Grevenberg of the Meininger theater as Käthchen in Act V of *Das Käthchen von Heilbronn*.
Comparison of plates 40 and 41 shows one of Duke Georg's designs as carried out by his wardrobe department.

Plates 42–47. Preliminary set designs, in chronological order, for the Prologue of Schiller's *Jungfrau von Orleans*. All sketches by Duke Georg.

Plate 48. Duke Georg's final set design for the Prologue of *Jungfrau von Orleans.*

Plate 49.   Duke Georg's set design for Act II of Lessing's *Miss Sara Sampson.*

Plate 50. Duke Georg's sketch for Act II of Kleist's *Prince Friedrich of Homburgh.*

Appendix A

Plays Presented at the Court Theater in Meiningen

Plays Presented in Selected Years Before and During the Meininger Tours (as Listed on Their Playbills)

Key to Abbreviations

C	comedy
D	drama
F	farce
T	tragedy

Fr.	translated from French
It.	translated from Italian
Sp.	translated from Spanish

Date	Play	Genre	Translation	Number of Acts	Author(s)
1867					
January					
1.	*Namenlos*	F		3	Kalisch and Pohl
3.	*Oedipus Rex¹*				
6.	*King Lear²*				
8.	*The Prisoners of the Czarina*	C	Fr.	2	
	Carlotta Patti	D		1	Salingré
13.	*Medea*	T		4	Grillparzer
16.	*Iphigenie auf Tauris*				
20.	*Emilia Galotti*				
22.	*Deborah*	Poetic D		4	Mosenthal
27.	*Othello*				
29.	*Die zärtlichen Verwandten*	C		3	Benedix
31.	*Der Goldbauer*	D		4	Birch-Pfeiffer
February					
3.	*Rosenmüller und Finke, oder Abgemacht*	C		5	Töpfer

Date	Play	Genre	Translation	Number of Acts	Author(s)
5.	*Der Attaché*	C		3	Meilhac
10.	*King Richard III*[3]				Shakespeare
12.	*Im Alter*	Domestic scenes		1	Bauernfeld
14.	*Mutter und Sohn*	D		5	Birch-Pfeiffer
14.	*Die Räuber*[4]				
17.	*Maria Stuart*				
19.	*Moritz Schnörche, oder eine unerlaubte*				
	Lieb	D		1	Moser
	Badekuren	C		1	Putlitz
	Hans und Hanne	Rustic pictures with music		1	Friedrich
24.	*Die zärtlichen Verwandten*				
26.	*Women's War*				
	"Indian March" from Meyerbeer's "African Woman"				
	Die Dienstboten	C		1	Benedix

March

Date	Play	Genre	Translation	Number of Acts	Author(s)
10.	*Julius Caesar*[5]				
12.	*Women's War*				
	Das Versprechen hinterm Herd				
14.	*Der Vetter*	C		3	Benedix
17.	*Der Königsleutnant*	C		4	Gutzkow
19.	*Mutter und Sohn*				
21.	*Ein Zündhölzchen zwischen zwei Feuer*	D		1	Hiltl
	Die Hochzeitrise	C		2	Benedix
24.	*Julius Caesar*[6]				
27.	*Spielt nicht mit dem Feuer*	C		3	Putlitz
29.	*Julius Caesar,* Act III				
	Between the Battles				

April

Date	Play	Genre	Translation	Number of Acts	Author(s)
2.	*Götz von Berlichingen*[7]				
4.	*Spielt nicht mit dem Feuer*				
7.	*Der politische Kanngiesser*	C		4	Holberg
11.	*Oedipus Rex*[8]				
14.	*Oedipus at Colonus*[9]				
15.	*Antigone*[10]				

October

Date	Play	Genre	Translation	Number of Acts	Author(s)
20.	*Romeo and Juliet*[11]				
22.	*Der Herr Studiosus*	character portrait		1	Birch-Pfeiffer

Date	Play	Genre	Trans-lation	Number of Acts	Author(s)
	Der galante Abbé	C	Fr.	2	Cossman
24.	*Die Anna–Lise*			5	Hersch
27.	*Donna Diana, oder Stolz und Liebe*	C		3	Moreto
29.	*Er muss auf's Land*	C		3	Friedrich
	Die Unglücklichen	C		1	Kotzebue
November					
1.	*Romeo and Juliet*				
3.	*Zopf und Schwert*	historical C		3	Gutzkow
5.	*Revanche*	C		2	Birch-Pfeiffer
	Ein gebildeter Hausknecht, oder verfehlte Prüfungen	F		1	Kalisch
10.	*Fiesco*				
12.	*Clavigo*				
14.	*Bürgerlich und Romantisch*	C		4	Bauernfeld
19.	*Die Valentine*			5	Freytag
25.	*Macbeth*[12]				
27.	*Das Schwert des Damokles*	D		1	Putlitz
	Fröhlich	musical quod-liebet		2	Schneider
29.	*Der arme Marquis*		Fr.	2	Bergen
	Er schreibt an seine Frau	C		1	Wagner
December					
1.	*Macbeth*				
3.	*Die Piket-Parthie*	C	Fr.	1	
	Der verwunschte Prinz	D		3	Plotz
8.	*The Doctor of his Honor*			3	Calderon[13]
10.	*Eine Frau, die in Paris war*	C		3	Moser
	Tannhäuser	Comic inter-mezzo			Kalisch
10.	*Der arme Marquis*				
	Tannhäuser[14]				
15.	*Eine Frau, die in Paris war*				
	Hans und Hanne				
17.	*King John*[15]				
19.	*Clavigo*				
21.	*King John*				
22.	*Pech–Schulze*	F with music		3	Salingré
26.	*Einer von unsere Leut!*	F with music		3	Kalisch
29.	*Between the Battles*				
	Eine Frau, die in Paris war				

Date	Play	Genre	Translation	Number of Acts	Author(s)
1868 January					
1.	Die Anna–Lise				
5.	King Richard II[16]				
7.	Revanche				
	Wer isst mit?	Vaudeville–F		1	Friedrich
9.	Die Hochzeitsreise	C		2	Benedix
	Il baccio	D		1	Rosen
12.	King Richard II[17]				
14.	Die Gustel von Blasewitz	Dramatic anecdote		1	Schlesinger
	Der Präsident	C		1	W. v. H.
	Englisch	C		1	Görner
19.	King Henry IV (Part I)[18]				
21.	Revanche				
	Der Präsident	C		1	Kläger
25.	King Richard II				
26.	A Midsummer Night's Dream				
28.	Er ist nicht eifersüchtig	C		1	Elz
	Am Clavier	C		1	Grandjean
	Die Herren von der Livrée	F with music		1	Jacobsohn
30.	Der Herr Studiosus				
	Die Soldatenbraut	Monologue			Vogelmann
	Guten Morgen Herr Fischer	F with music		1	Friedrich
February					
2.	King Richard III				
5.	Zolky, der alte Student	Dramolet		2	Maltitz
	Der Pariser Taugenichts	C	Fr.	4	
9.	King Lear[19]				
11.	Hermann und Dorothea	Idyllic family portrait		4	Töpfer
13.	Romeo and Juliet[20]				
	Der arme Poet			1	Kotzebue
	Lohengrin				
16.	Midsummer Night's Dream				
17.	Romeo and Juliet				
19.	Die Gustel von Blasewitz				
	Der Präsident				
	Englisch				
23.	Marriage of Figaro	C		5	Beaumarchis[21]

Date	Play	Genre	Trans-lation	Number of Acts	Author(s)
27.	*Marriage of Figaro*				
March					
1.	*King Henry IV (Part I)*				
3.	*Vor hundert Frauen*	C		4	Raupach
8.	*Das Käthchen von Heilbronn*				
11.	*Cymbeline*[22]				
13.	*Man sucht einen Erzieher*	C		2	Bahn
	Die Verlobung bei der Laterne	Operetta	Fr.		Offenbach
15.	*Don Carlos*				
16.	*Vor hundert Frauen*				
18.	*Cymbeline*				
20.	*Der Winkelschreiber*	C		4	Adolphi
22.	*Ein Arzt*	C		1	Hesse
	Die beiden Klingsberge	C		4	Kotzebue
24.	*Sie ist wahnsinnig*		Fr.	2	Schneider
	Die Piquet-Parthie	C	Fr.	1	
25.	*Zopf und Schwert*				
27.	*Feuer in der Mädchenschule*	C		1	Förster
	Frauenkampf	C		3	Olsers
29.	*Der Königsleutnant*				
31.	*Der Winkelschreiber*				
April					
2.	*Macbeth.*				
5.	*Er ist nicht eifersuchtig*	C		1	Ely
	Ehrziehungs-Resultate, oder Guter und schlechter Ton	C		2	Blum
12.	*Orestia*				Aeschylus[23]
October					
18.	*Die Nibelungen*	T		5	Hebbel
20.	*König Renés Tochter*	Lyrical D		1	Hertz
	Ein kleiner Dämon	C		3	Bahn
22.	*Das Tagebuch*	C		2	Bauernfeld
	Bädeker	D mit Gesang		1	Belly
25.	*Much Ado About Nothing*				
27.	*Ein delikater Auftrag*	C		1	Ascher
	Schwarzer Peter	D		1	Görner
	Der Kurmärker und die Picarde	Genre picture		1	Schneider
30.	*Kabale und Liebe*				
November					
1.	*Hamlet.*				
3.	*Die Bekenntnisse*	C		3	Bauernfeld

Date	Play	Genre	Trans-lation	Number of Acts	Author(s)
5.	*Die Curiatier*	D	Fr.	1	Helm
	Nach Sonnenuntergang	C		2	Lotz
	Zwei von der Nadel	D with music		1	Wilken
8.	*Cromwell's Ende*	T		5	Raupach
10.	*Die Räuber*				
15.	*Ludwig XI*	D		5	Delavegne
17.	*Er ist nicht eifersüchtig*				
	Der Erbfehler	C		1	
	Doctor Peschke, oder kleine Herren	C with music		1	Kalisch
20.	*Valerie*	C		3	Scribe and Melisville
	Ein gebildeter Hausknecht	Vaude-ville		1	Kalich
23.	*Die Waise von Lowood*	C		4	Birch-Pfeiffer
23.	*Much Ado About Nothing*[24]				
25.	*Am Clavier*	C	Fr.	1	Grandjean
	Badekuren	C		1	Putlitz
	Der Präsident	C		1	Kläger
27.	*Ein schlechter Mensch*	C		3	Rosen
29.	*Die Waise von Lowood*				
December					
1.	*Die Jäger*	Rustic Portrait		5	Iffland
3.	*Torquatto Tasso*				
6.	*Egmont*				
8.	*Ein schlechter Mensch*	C		3	Rosen
10.	*Der 24. Februar*	T		1	Werner
	Er experimentirt	C		1	Hollpein
	Rezept gegen Schwiegermutter	C		1	
13.	*Mutter und Sohn*				
17.	*Die Braut von Messina*[25]				
20.	*Ich bleibe ledig*	C.	It.	3	Blum
22.	*Das Tagebuch*	C		2	Bauernfeld
	Rezept gegen Schwiegermutter				
26.	*Der Vater der Debütantin oder Doch durchgesetzt*	C	Fr.	5	Bayard
27.	*The Marriage of Figaro*				
29.	*The Prisoners of the Czarina*				
	Ein gebildeter Hausknecht	Vaude-ville		1	Kalisch

Date	Play	Genre	Trans-lation	Number of Acts	Author(s)

1872
October

15. *Ein Schützling*		C		3	J. L. Klein
20. *Maria Magdalene*					
22. *Jugendliebe*		C		1	Wilbrandt
The Miser		C		5	Molière
24. *Kabale und Liebe*					
27. *Twelfth Night*[26]					
29. *Das Stiftungsfest*		D	.	3	Moser

November

3. *Don Carlos*					
5. *Das Tagebuch*		C		2	Bauernfeld
Doctor Peschke					
8. *Das Stiftungsfest*					
10. *Ein geadelter Kaufmann*		C		5	Görner
12. *The Glass of Water*		C		5	Scribe
14. *Much Ado about Nothing*					
17. *Wilhelm Tell*					
19. *Miss Sara Sampson*					
23. *Bürgerlich und Romantisch*		C		4	Bauernfeld
25. *Im Vorzimmer Seiner Excellenz*		Portrait		1	Hahn
Der verwunschene Prinz		D		3	Plötz
28. *Ein geadelter Kaufmann*					

December

1. *Hamlet*[27]					
3. *Maria Magdalene*					
5. *Gegenüber*		C		3	Benedix
Unter dem Siegel der Verschwiegenheit		C		1	Berg
8. *Twelfth Night*					
10. *Tartuffe*					
12. *Adrienne Lecouvreur*		D		5	Scribe[28]
15. *Gegenüber*					
Bädeker					
17. *Macbeth*[29]					
19. *Maria Stuart*					
22. *Othello*					
26. *Das Stiftungsfest*					
Theater-Geschichten					
29. *Ein geadelter Kaufmann*					

1873
January

1. *Berliner Kinder*		C		4	Salingré
3. *Figaro's Hochzeit*[30]					
5. *Philippine Welser*		historical			
		D		5	Oskar v. Redwitz

Date	Play	Genre	Translation	Number of Acts	Author(s)
7.	*The Imaginary Invalid*				
	Das Versprechen hinter'm Herd	Genre picture		1	Baumann
12.	*A Midsummer Night's Dream*[31]				
14.	*Tartuffe*				
16.	*Ein Kind des Glücks*		D	5	Birch-Pfeiffer
19.	*Romeo and Juliet*				
21.	*Lessing in Camenz*	Portrait		1	Wolmuth
	Unerreichbar		C	1	Wilbrandt
	Ein weisser Othello		D	1	Friedrich
23.	*Die Benefiz-Vorstellung*		C	1	Hell
	Herr Hampelmann sucht ein Logis		C	5	Malz
26.	*Wera, oder Unlösliche Bande*	Portrait		4	Berger
30.	*Egmont*				
February					
2.	*The Merchant of Venice*				
4.	*Der Pfarrer von Kirchfeld*		D	4	Gruber
6.	*Der beste Ton*		C	4	Toepfer
9.	*Unerreichbar*				
	Gegenüber				
11.	*Der Störchenfried*		C	4	Benedix
16.	*Wilhelm Tell*				
17.	Molière Celebration	Prologue			Dingelstedt
	The Learned Ladies				
19.	*Romeo and Juliet*				
21.	*Graf Esser*	historical	D	5	Laube
23.	*Faust*				
26.	*Preciosa*				
March					
2.	*The Merchant of Venice*				
4.	*Wéra*				
6.	*Twelfth Night*				
9.	*Macbeth*				
11.	*Maria Stuart*				
13.	*The Taming of the Shrew*[32]				
16.	*Don Carlos*				
18.	*Das Stiftungsfest*				
20.	*Sappho*				
October					
16.	*Gute Nacht, Hänschen!*		C	5	Müller
19.	*Die Jäger*				
21.	*Moderne Jugend*		C	3	Bauernfeld
	Alter schützt für Thorheit nicht		C	1	Wehl

Date	Play	Genre	Trans-lation	Number of Acts	Author(s)
23.	*Unerreichbar*				
	Epidemisch	D		4	Schweitzer
26.	*Die Karlsschüler*	D		5	Laube
28.	*Jugendliebe*	C		1	Wilbrandt
	Die Vorleserin	D		2	Bagard
30.	*Der Ball zu Ellerbrunn*	C		3	Blum

November

2.	*Die Maler*	C		3	Wilbrandt
4.	*Splitter und Balken*	C		1	Moser
	Deutsches Strafrecht	D		3	Girndt
9.	*Julius Caesar*				
11.	*Eine Tasse Thee*	C	Fr.	1	Neumann
	Epidemisch				
13.	*Die Maler*				
16.	*Die Mönche, oder Carabinien in*				
	Carmeliter-Kloster	C		3	Tenelli
18.	*Fairy Hands*	C		5	Scribe
20.	*Gute Nacht, Hänschen!*				
22.	*Der Erbförster*				
25.	*Ein Lustspiel*	C		4	Benedix
30.	*Die Räuber*				

December

2.	*Der Vater*	C		3	Bauernfeld
	Hermann und Dorothea	Vocal drama		1	Kalisch and Weirauch
4.	*Deutsches Strafrecht*				
	Alter schützt für Thorheit nicht				
7.	*Die Verschwörung der Frauen, oder Die*				
	Preussin in Breslau	historical D		5	Müller
9.	*Ein Lustspiel*				
14.	*Dorf und Stadt*	D		5	Birch–Pfeiffer
15.	*Der Fabrikant*	D		3	Souvestre
	Hans und Hanne				
17.	*Götz von Berlichingen*				
21.	*Die Räuber*				
23.	*The Imaginary Invalid*				
26.	*Pope Sixtus V*				
30.	*Twelfth Night*				

1874
January

1.	*Fairy Hands*				

Date	Play	Genre	Trans-lation	Number of Acts	Author(s)
4.	*Egmont*				
6.	*Eine Tasse Thee*				
	Epidemisch				
8.	*Das Lügen*	C		3	Benedix
11.	*Verschwörung der Frauen*				
15.	*Emilia Galotti*				
18.	*Romeo and Juliet*				
20.	*Das Lügen*				
22.	*Badekuren*	C		1	Putlitz
	Feuer in der Mädchenschule	C		1	Förster
	Aurora in Oel	C with music		1	Kalisch
25.	*Pagenstreiche*	F		5	Kotzebue
29.	*Die Vorleserin*				
	The Learned Ladies				

February

1.	*The Merchant of Venice*[33]				
3.	*Minna von Barnhelm*				
5.	*Dorf und Stadt*				
8.	*Macbeth*				
12.	*Blitzableiter*	C		1	Gensichen
	Ein Engel	D		3	Rosen
15.	*Twelfth Night*				
19.	*Mit der Feder*				
	Schwarzer Peter				
	Der gerade Weg der beste!	C		1	Kotzebue
22.	*Pope Sixtus V*				
24.	*Romeo and Juliet*				
26.	*Egmont*				

March

3.	*Bluthochzeit*				
5.	*Wilhelm Tell*				
8.	*Julius Caesar*				
10.	*The Taming of the Shrew*				
15.	*Macbeth*				
17.	*The Imaginary Invalid*				
19.	*The Learned Ladies*				
22.	*The Merchant of Venice*				
24.	*Maria Stuart*				
26.	*Die Tochter Belials, oder Die Scheinheiligen*	C		5	Kneisel
29.	*Twelfth Night*				

April

6.	*Pope Sixtus V*				

Date	Play	Genre	Trans-lation	Number of Acts	Author(s)
9.	*Julius Caesar*				
12.	*Bluthochzeit*				
15.	*Between the Battles*				
	Die Vorleserin				

November
1.	*Minna von Barnhelm*				
3.	*Philippine Welser*	historical D		5	Redwitz
5.	*Epidemisch*				
9.	*The Merchant of Venice*				
10.	*Die Tochter Belials*				
12.	*Othello*				
15.	*Julius Caesar*				
17.	*The Learned Ladies*				
20.	*Hamlet*				
24.	*Die Jäger*				
24.	*Das Lügen*[34]				
26.	*Die Jäger*				
29.	*Bluthochzeit*				

December
1.	*Ich verheirathe meine Mutter*	C		1	Günther
	Was ist eine Plauderei?	Mono-logue		1	Gensichen
	Irren ist menschlich	C		1	Schmidt-Cabanis
3.	*Clavigo*				
6.	*Philippine Welser*				
8.	*Das Stiftungsfest*				
10.	*Ich verheirathe meine Mutter*				
	Was ist eine Plauderei?				
	Irren ist menschlich				
13.	*Othello*				
17.	*Fiesco*[35]				
20.	*Fiesco*				
22.	*Die Jäger*				
26.	*Wilhelm Tell*				
27.	*Don Carlos*				
29.	*Ein Lustspiel*				

1875
January
2.	*The Learned Ladies*				
3.	*Much Ado About Nothing*				
5.	*Kabale und Liebe*				
7.	*Sappho*				

Date	Play	Genre	Trans-lation	Number of Acts	Author(s)
10.	*Ultimo*	C		5	Moser
12.	*Die Grille*	Rustic Portrait		5	Birch–Pfeiffer
14.	*Die Karlsschüler*				
17.	*Die Waise von Lowood*	D		4	Birch–Pfeiffer
19.	*Emilia Galotti*				
21.	*Mit der Feder*				
	Feuer in der Mädchenschule				
	Rothe Haare				
24.	*Unter Maria Theresia*	Portrait		5	Schwartz
26.	*Die Geschwister*	D		1	Goethe
	Im Judenbacher Dorfwirtshaus, im Jahre 1530	Pageant		1	
28.	*Maria Stuart*				
31.	*Ultimo*				

February

2.	*Die Waise von Lowood*				
5.	*Fiesco*				
7.	*Die Grille*				
11.	*Die Geschwister*				
	Judenbacher Dorfwirtshaus				
	Rothe Haare				
14.	*Romeo and Juliet*				
18.	*Epidemisch*				
21.	*Marga*	D		5	Heigel
23.	*Esther*				
	Ein Wort an den Minister	Genre picture		1	Langer
25.	*Ultimo*				
28.	*The Merchant of Venice*				

March

2.	*Unter Maria Theresia*				
7.	*Esther*				
	The Learned Ladies				
10.	*Die Hermannsschlacht*				
14.	*Die Hermannsschlacht*				
17.	*Julius Caesar*				
21.	*Die Hermannsschlacht*				
23.	Prologue with tableaux vivantes[36]				
	Elfrida von Monte–Salerno	D		5	Conrad
28.	Repeat of 23				
29.	*Fiesco*				

Date	Play	Genre	Trans- lation	Number of Acts	Author(s)
April					
2.	*Die Hermannsschlacht*[37]				
4.	*The Merchant of Venice*				
December					
5.	*Die Sirene*	C		4	Mosenthal
7.	*Twelfth Night*				
9.	*Ultimo*				
12.	*Bluthochzeit*				
17.	*Esther*[38]				
	Vom Stamm der Asra	C		1	Dohm
19.	*Erbförster*				
21.	*Das Gefängnis*	C		4	Benedix
26.	*Romeo and Juliet*				
27.	*Hamlet*				
1876					
January					
1.	*Wilhelm Tell*				
2.	*Esther*				
	The Imaginary Invalid				
4.	*Ein geadelter Kaufmann*				
9.	*Erbförster*				
13.	*Das Lügen*				
16.	*Julius Caesar*				
18.	*Das Gefängnis*				
23.	*The Merchant of Venice*				
25.	*The Learned Ladies*				
30.	*Pretenders*[39]				
February					
1.	*Die Tochter Belials*				
3.	*Epidemisch*				
6.	*Der Veilchenfresser*	C		4	Moser
9.	*Die Waise von Lowood*				
11.	*Judenbacher Dorfwirtshaus*				
	Dir wie mir				
	Vom Stamm der Asra				
13.	*Hermannsschlacht*				
17.	*Ein geadelter Kaufmann*				
20.	*Fiesco*				
22.	*Feuer in der Mädchenschule*				
	Was ist eine Plauderei?				
	Ein Wort an den Minister				
24.	*The Merchant of Venice*				
27.	*Graf Esser*				
29.	*Der Veilchenfresser*				

Date	Play	Genre	Translation	Number of Acts	Author(s)
March					
5.	*Käthchen*				
8.	*Käthchen*				
10.	*Ultimo*				
12.	*Hermannsschlacht*				
16.	*Graf Essex*	T		5	Laube
19.	*Macbeth*				
21.	*Das Stiftungsfest*				
23.	*Maria Mancini*	T		5	Moisky
26.	*Pretenders*				
28.	*Erbförster*				
April					
2.	*Wilhem Tell* [40]				
5.	*Pretenders*				
9.	*Macbeth*				
16.	*Käthchen*				
18.	*Wilhelm Tell*				
December					
13.	*Minna von Barnhelm*				
17.	*The Winter's Tale*				
19.	*Sie hat ihr Herz entdeckt*	L		1	Königswinter
	Feuer in der Mädchenschule				
	Hermann und Dorothea				
21.	*Romeo and Juliet*				
23.	*The Merchant of Venice*				
26.	*Julius Caesar*				
27.	*Grossstädtisch*	D		4	Schweitzer
31.	*Ultimo*	C		5	Moser
1877					
January					
1.	*Die Anna–Lise*				
3.	*Jugendliebe*	C		1	Wilbrandt
	Die Hochzeitsreise	C		2	Benedix
	Er ist nicht eifersüchtig	C		1	Elz
7.	*Käthchen*				
11.	*Leone*	D mit Gesang		3	Holtei
14.	*Wilhelm Tell*				
16.	*Twelfth Night*				
18.	*Der Sonnwendhof*	D		5	Mosenthal
23.	*Anna–Lise*				
25.	*Hamlet*				
28.	*Macbeth*				

Date	Play	Genre	Trans-lation	Number of Acts	Author(s)
30. *Grossstädtisch*					
February					
1. *Der Veilchenfresser*					
4. *Egmont*					
6. *Maria Stuart*					
11. *Die Ahnfrau*					
13. *The Taming of the Shrew*					
15. *Kabale und Liebe*					
18. *Fiesco*					
20. *Sappho*					
23. *Twelfth Night*					
25. *Julius Caesar*					
27. *Das bemooste Haupt*					
March					
1. *Er muss auf's Land*	C		3	Friedrich
4. *Die Bluthochzeit*					
6. *Egmont*					
9. *Esther*					
The Imaginary Invalid	Burlesque Doctoral Commencement Ceremony for Aryan				
11. *Julius Casear*					
13. *Die Versucherin*	C		1	Moser
Die Schwäbin	C		1	Castelli
Ein Stündchen auf dem Comptoir.	F with music		1	Haber
18. *Hermannsschlacht*					
21. *Zopf und Schwert*					
23. *Bürgerlich und Romantisch*					
25. *Hermannsschlacht*					
27. *Die Jäger*					
April					
2. *Käthchen*[41]					
4. *Das bemooste Haupt*					
6. *Noontime with Molière*					
The Learned Ladies					
8. *Fiesco*					
10. *Lumparivagabundus, oder das liederische Kleeblatt*	F with music		3	Nestroy
12. *Der Sonnwendhof*					
15. *Wilhelm Tell*					

Date	Play	Genre	Translation	Number of Acts	Author(s)
December					
9.	The Merchant of Venice				
11.	Sie hat ihr Herz entdeckt	C		1	Königswinter
	Der Strike der Schmiede	Dramatic scene			Coppea
	Feuer in der Mädchenschule				
13.	Leonore				
16.	Minna von Barnhelm				
17.	Macbeth [42]				
19.	Die Räuber				
21.	Clavigo				
23.	Hamlet				
25.	Concert of the Meininger Orchestra [43]				
26.	Bluthochzeit.				
27.	Der Rechnungsrath und seine Töchter	C		3	Feldman
	Ein Stündchen auf dem Comptoir	F		1	Haber
30.	Lumparivagabundus				
1878					
January					
1.	Euphrosyne	D		1	Gensichen
	Sperling und Sperber	D		1	Görner
	Hasen in der Hasenheide, oder alle fürchten sich	F		1	Angely
3.	Ahnfrau				
6.	Egmont				
8.	Der Veilchenfresser				
10.	Der Sonnwendhof				
13.	Ahnfrau				
15.	Ein geadelter Kaufmann				
20.	Die Räuber				
22.	Between the Battles				
	Die Versucherin				
	Hasen in der Hasenheide				
24.	Lorbeeerbaum und Bettelstaub [44]	D		3	Holtei
27.	Julius Caesar				
29.	Graf Effer				
February					
3.	Tartuffe				
	Der zerbrochene Krug				
5.	Das Stiftungsfest				
8.	Romeo and Juliet				
12.	Die Räuber				
14.	Eine Tasse Thee				
	Immer zu Hause	C		1	Grandjean

Date	Play	Genre	Trans-lation	Number of Acts	Author(s)
	17. *Käthchen*				
	19. *Der Hypochonder*	C		4	Moser
	22. *Philippine Welser*				
	24. *Fiesco*				
	26. *The Learned Ladies*				
	Immer zu Hause				
March					
	3. *The Winter's Tale*				
	5. *Der Hypochonder*				
	7. *Das bemooste Haupt*				
	10. *Caesar Borgia*	T		5	Grua
	17. *The Winter's Tale*				
	19. *Adelaide*				
	Er ist nicht eifersüchtig				
	Rothe Haare				
	21. *Hasemanns Töchter*[45]	D		4	L'Arronge
	24. *Hasemanns Töchter*				
	28. *Prinz von Homburg*				
	31. *Die Räuber*				
April					
	2. *The Winter's Tale*[46]				
	4. *Ahnfrau*				
	7. *Prinz von Homburg*				
	9. *Twelfth Night*				
	11. *Wilhelm Tell*				
	14. *The Winter's Tale*				
1880					
December					
	22. *The Taming of the Shrew*				
	26. *The Winter's Tale*				
	27. *Adrienne Lecouvreur*				
	29. *Wohlthätige Frauen*	C		4	L'Arronge
1881					
January					
	1. *Die Räuber*				
	2. *Mein Leopold*	D with music		3	L'Arronge
	4. *Ahnfrau*				
	6. *Fairy Hands*				
	9. *Don Carlos*				
	13. *Esther*				
	Wallensteins Lager				
	18. *The Merchant of Venice*				
	20. *Doctor Klaus*	C		5	L'Arronge

Date	Play	Genre	Trans- lation	Number of Acts	Author(s)
	23. *Hasemanns Töchter*				
	25. *Die Waise von Lowood*				
	27. *Im Vorzimmer Seiner Excellenz*				
	The Learned Ladies				
	30. *Der Verschwender*	Fairy Tale		3	Raimund
February					
	3. *Einer muss heirathen*	Musical declama- tory			
	Hasen in der Hasenheide	Inter- mezzo			
	6. *Julius Caesar*				
	9. *The Winter's Tale*				
	11. *Wilhelm Tell*				
	13. *Iphigenie auf Tauris*				
	16. *Emilia Galotti*				
	17. *Feuer in der Mädchenschule*				
	Epidemisch				
	20. *Hermannsschlacht*				
	22. *Fiesco*				
	24. *Wenn Frauen weinen*	C	Fr.	1	Winterfeld
	Was ist eine Plauderei?				
	Monsieur Hercules	D		1	Belly
	27. *Hamlet*				
March					
	3. *Die Räuber*				
	6. *Die Karolinger*				
	10. *Käthchen*				
	15. *Das war ich*	C		1	Hutt
	Monsieur Hercules				
	Die Dienstboten	C		1	Benedix
	17. *Die Copisten*	C		1	Bulthaupt
	Wallensteins Lager				
	20. *Julius Caesar*				
	23. *Das Stiftungsfest*				
	27. *Preciosa*				
	29. *Die Copisten*				
	The Imaginary Invalid				
April					
	3. *Die Geschwister*				
	Esther				
	5. *Twelfth Night*				
	7. *Preciosa*				

Date	Play	Genre	Translation	Number of Acts	Author(s)
10.	The Winter's Tale				
13.	Wilhelm Tell				
1883					
January					
4.	Maria Stuart				
7.	Minna von Barnhelm				
9.	Donna Diana				
11.	Im Vorzimmer seiner Excellenz				
	Ein ungeschliffener Diamant	F		1	Bergen
	Der Kurmärker und die Picarde	Portrait		1	Schneider
14.	Wallensteins Lager				
	Die Piccolomini				
16.	Wallensteins Tod				
18.	Wilhelm Tell				
21.	Much Ado About Nothing				
25.	Donna Diana				
28.	Die Hexe	T		5	Fitger
30.	Die zärtlichen Verwandten				
February					
1.	Reif-Reiflingen	D		5	Moser
4.	Egmont				
6.	Gringoire	Portrait		1	de Bauville
	Rezept gegen Schwiegemütter	C	Sp.	1	
	Das Versprechen hinterm Herd				
8.	Die zärtlichen Verwandten				
11.	Der Herrgottschnitzer von Ammergau				
13.	Esther				
	Hochzeitsreise	C		2	Benedix
15.	Johannistrieb	D		4	Lindau
18.	Preciosa				
20.	Hamlet				
22.	Herrgottschnitzer				
25.	Ahnfrau				
27.	Hexe				
March					
1.	Nathan der Weise				
4.	Wallensteins Tod				
6.	Aschenbrödel	C		4	Benedix
8.	Katharina Howard	T		5	Gottschall
12.	Julius Caesar				
13.	Die Räuber				
15.	Fiesco				
18.	Der Posten der Frau	C		5	Francois
20.	The Winter's Tale				
25.	Wallenstein Trilogy				

Sources

January 1867–April 1877—Personal examination of playbills at the Cologne theater museum.

December 1877–April 1878—George Bourlier, *Almanach des Herz. S.–Meiningen'schen Hoftheaters. Saison 1877-1878* (Meiningen: H. Marbach, 1878).

December 1880–April 1881—George Bourlier, *Almanach des Herzogl. Sachsen–Meiningen'schen Hoftheaters. Saison 1880-81* (Meiningen: H. Marbach, 1881).

January 1883–March 1883—Julie Braun, *Almanach des herzogichen Sachsen–Meiningen'schen Hoftheaters. Saison 1883* (Meiningen: Dr. H. Marbach, 1883).

Appendix B

Plays Performed on the Meininger Tours (1874–1890)

Play	1874	1875	1876	1877	1878	1879	1880	1881	1882	1883	1884	1885	1886	1887	1888	1889	1890	TOTAL
Ahnfrau					9	11	7	3	6	14	12	9	1		6	1		79
Alexandra														5				5
Between the Battles	4	4		5		1	2									5		21
Bluthochzeit	9	7	5	14	8	8	11	9	4							5	13	85
Braut von Messina												8	3					11
Erbförster			2															2
Esther		14	10	9	3	8	12	6	2	4	3					3		74
Frau Lucrezia																	2	2
Galeotto														7				7
Ghosts														1		1		2
Hermannsschlacht		28		13		11	9	2	3	10	11					7	7	101
Herrgottschnitzer														11				11
Hexe										19	25	5				7		56
Imaginary Invalid	4	7	10	9	3	8	12	6	2	4	11					2	2	83
Iphigenia									5	1		5				4	2	14
Jäger			2															2
Julius Caesar	22	21	9	19	15	22	18	32	23	18	24	21	12	23	14	19	11	330
Jungfrau von Orleans			10	10	40	13	14							109	40	25	20	194
Käthchen von Heilbronn		11	28	5		2	2	5		3	3		6			3		83
Learned Ladies			5									6	6				3	29
Lydia								2			10	6	6					25
Macbeth			5	5													1	10
Maria Stuart											21	18	9	19	22			89
Marino Faliero													5	7	7			19
Merchant of Venice	2	3		5									11	19	23	15	11	94
Miss Sara Sampson											7							7
Piccolomini									37	28	7	21	7	11	18	10	7	161
Pope Sixtus V	4								37		22							4
Preciosa				21	16	8										9		54
Pretenders			7															7
Prince of Homburg					17	11	6	4						1		7		38
Robbers					31	20	10	7				15		19	7	5		104
Rosen von Tyburn														2	5	2		5
s'Nullerl																		2
Taming of the Shrew	6						11					9	6	2	4	4		21
Twelfth Night		5	11	11	9	5	12	10	5	9	12		4	2		7	3	132
Verschwörung des Fiesco		32	8	19	11	7	17	14	10	11	8	21	7	11	11	10	8	152
Wallensteins Lager									37	28	22	21	7	8	18	7	7	176
Wallensteins Tod								15	13	27	16	17	7	14	15	10	7	140
Wilhelm Tell			21		8	27	23	22	21	14	12	24						223
Winter's Tale					50	29	18	18		27		19	8		21			233
TOTAL	51	132	116	145	187	174	171	197	221	235	233	200	102	242	209	171	102	2887

Appendix C

Text of Gerhart Hauptmann's 1932 Letter About the Meininger

Gerhart Hauptmann's letter to the *Berliner Börsen–Courier,* No. 533, 13 November 1932, describing his reaction to the Meininger:

"Julius Caesar" followed "Wallenstein." Here everything was majestic, filled with awe, terror, and presentiments of death. Everything proceeded oppressively, as if threatened by severe weather. Even by light of day, this Brutus, this Cassius, this Calpurnia, this Caesar walked as damned spirits in a world that showed all reality as if dissolved into fate and only fate. There was nothing banal here, only mysterious. No, but then the murder takes place in the Capitol. That was a magnificent, an inevitable reality. It was not one murder; it was a hundred murders at once. It was murder, one sensed, committed with thunderbolts, the detonations of which, it seemed, must shake the earth.

Murder, murder, and murder again! Macbeth, great in cowardice, noble in cowardice, was the final production. The high point was the appearance of Banquo's ghost. How could this intensification of murderous rage, of murderous madness have such a purifying, cleansing, enlivening, ennobling effect on me, lifting my soul to sublime heights? I think because it permanently lifted my mind above the flat and the dead, above the ugly and the common of my everyday existence and opened it up to higher insights, to higher experiences, and did it to such a degree, that my common needs and my common surroundings no longer overshadowed me with their power as strongly as they had before.

Appendix D

Correspondence Concerning the Meininger Production of Ibsen's *Ghosts*

Ibsen's letter to Georg forms pages 1 and 2 of the folded sheet referred to on p. 72:

Munich, November 13, 1886

Most gracious Duke,

I was very happy to receive the news from your majesty about the upcoming production of my play "Ghosts."

May I be permitted to offer my deepest appreciation to your majesty and to your noble wife for the gracious invitation. I shall certainly be in Meiningen in time for the presentation.

The interior arrangement of Norwegian country houses generally exhibits no distinctly national character. The living rooms of the oldest private houses of this type are sometimes covered with dark, colorful wallpaper. Below, the walls are covered with simple wainscoting. The ceiling, doors, and window frames are finished in similar style. The stoves are large, bulky, and usually of cast iron. The furniture is often in the style of the first French Empire, but the colors are generally darker.

I have imagined the living room of Mrs. Alving's house to be much as I have described it here. If the appropriate officials of the court theater desire further information, I am ready to help at any time.

With most respectful gratitude,
Henrik Ibsen

Page 3 of the sheet is Georg's set design, based on Ibsen's suggestions (see plate 30). Page 4 is occupied by Georg's instructions to his set painters, the Brückner brothers:

I request that you, my dear professors, construct a closed room for Ibsen's play "Ghosts," according to the instructions in this letter and with the help of my sketch.

"Ghosts" will be sent to you by Chronegk. You will see from that how the room must be made with respect to the doors and windows. To the rear is a conservatory for flowers. It would be best if the flowers were *real* (Georg's emphasis); through the windows one sees a

Norwegian landscape, for which I will use a backdrop from Wilhelm Tell. The rehearsals for this play begin on December 3.

15 November 1886

Respectfully,
Georg

(Original is among Duke Georg's papers at the Cologne Theater Museum.)

Appendix E

Prince Georg's 1864 Letter Concerning Gounod's *Faust*

Prince Georg's letter of January 1864 to Carl von Stein concerning Gounod's *Faust* (letter reprinted in Max Grube, *Geschichte der Meininger* [Stuttgart: Deutsche Verlags–Anstalt, 1926], pp. 27–29):

Permit me to make some observations regarding the opera *Faust,* which should be passed on to the producer:

1. Margarethe's appearance in act one: Her left arm now rests on a small table with thin legs. From a distance, it appears as if her arm is floating in the air. It would be good to cover this table with the dark blue tablecloth that I placed in the wardrobe. The scene would be improved thereby.

2. Act two: It is unfortunate that in the performances of the scene at the city gate, the playful sitting on tables by some of the young men, as the producer had wanted in the final rehearsal, is missing. If it were included, the group to the audience's left would be more lively.

3. Margarethe's first appearance: It would make her appear more maidenlike if Margarethe did not stand near Faust, but instead went across the set without stopping. Faust should walk backwards in front of her, after eluding her almost to the wings.

4. Scene with the jewelry box: A more beautiful box, and a removable mirror inside, ladies' jewelry instead of a golden men's neck chain. There is one in the wardrobe.

5. Moonlight: This might begin at the moment when Mephisto commands nature to breathe lust. If I remember correctly, in Berlin a magical moonlight spilled over the countryside at that moment. If there are blue silk lampshades here, they should be used on the lamps in order to produce a blue shimmer, which must also be visible at the stage rear.

I think the garden scene would be much improved if Margarethe's house were one soffit further to the rear, and the moonlight came from the other direction. That way it would illuminate more than just the side of the house, and Margarethe's face would not always be in the shadow.

6. The arrangement of the army scene is, at least in my opinion, horrid. The much–discussed goose step looks out of place.

I think it should be possible to change this scene to an effective one. One has to discard the view that the soldiers who sing the soldiers' chorus are soldiers in today's meaning.

Put sixteen local soldiers in the brown soldiers' outfits (from Wallenstein) and the singers in medieval soldiers' uniforms of different styles, using chain mail, and visorless and spiked helmets. Put three large non–commissioned officers in three suits of armor from the wardrobe. One of these knights should look like Dr. Locher in "Götz."

At the beginning of the scene, before the warriors appear, let the children and women run around the stage, on and off, to express their happy anticipation.

Then the singing warriors appear. Women and children run in front of them and form large, tight groups on both sides of the stage. The singing warriors march in tempo, not in straight rows, but in clumps, with joyful gestures, that is, with waving of their weapons and, here and there, waving their hats. This mass, which the three knights join, steps to the right side of the stage and presses together, so that one can see past it on the left. After this group has situated itself, the sixteen soldiers march in. Their leader remains standing at the wing, and orders "Halt; eyes front!" (softly) when the last file reaches that point.

These troops are in two parts. They must arrange themselves as they march in so that the left line is somewhat further to the rear than the right. After the soldiers, who have come on with lances on their shoulders, have stopped, they rest their lances on the stage and move, relaxing their posture somewhat.

In this fashion the scene would be brilliant. There is no doubt it could be done, especially since today is only choir rehearsal. The singing warriors would be given battle axes and maces and the like. Weapons such as two-handed swords can be obtained from the Henneberg Association, also crossbows and spears.

The producer should lead the entrance from behind the scene; it would be best if he were clothed as a knight à la Götz.

The soldiers could stand in the hall in front of the wardrobe before the scene begins, and would best march off stage right, while the singing warriors walk off stage left.

7. Church scene: Mephisto probably does not need to stand next to the harmonium in order to sing; he might also be able to bring his song forth if the harmonium were opposite him.

If that were done, the suppliants would be able to turn to the side opposite the altar where Margarethe is kneeling. They can then always look at the conductor by turning their heads. They would have to enter from the opposite side, and possibly kneel further to the rear. The backdrop in this scene is also too brightly illuminated. Only sufficient light is needed to see Margarethe's facial features. If it is dim at the rear, so much the better. If the praying congregation is arranged as I suggest, it would not see her noticable gestures, and would not be aware that she had fainted. She could then lie there unattended, which would make things more dramatic.

8. Jail scene: A flat mattress covered with straw would look better than a wooden cot. The mattress can be dragged out—even if the straw remains there, it will not disturb the final scene, the apotheosis, which will not be successful with our actors, anyway.

9. The apotheosis: The group at the rear may be too symmetrical. One cannot see the angel's wings, because they are white; if they were painted darkly in rainbow colors, they would stand out from the background.

Appendix F

Series Titles of the "Meininger Editions"

The thirty volumes of plays that had been especially revised had a uniform title, but two publishers:

> *Repertoire des herzoglich Meiningen'schen Hoftheaters, officielle Ausgabe nach dem Scenarium des Herzogl. Sachsen-Meiningen'schen Hoftheaters bearbeitet.* Dresden: Hof-Verlagsbuchhandlung, 1879 ff.; Leipzig: Friedrich Conrad, n.d.

The titles of the plays that were included in the series, with the volume numbers, were:

1. Björnson, *Zwischen den Schlachten* (Between the Battles)
2. Kleist, *Die Hermannsschlacht*
3. Kleist, *Das Käthchen von Heilbronn*
4. Kleist, *Prinz Friedrich von Homburg*
5. Molière, *Die gelehrten Frauen* (The Learned Ladies)
6. Molière, *Der eingebildete Kranke* (The Imaginary Invalid)
7. Schiller, *Fiesco*
8. Schiller, *Die Räuber* (The Robbers)
9. Schiller, *Wilhelm Tell*
10. Shakespeare, *Julius Cäsar* (Julius Caesar)
11. Shakespeare, *Der Kaufmann von Venedig* (The Merchant of Venice)
12. Shakespeare, *Was Ihr wollt* (Twelfth Night)
13. Shakespeare, *Das Wintermärchen* (The Winter's Tale)
14. Goethe, *Iphigenie* (Iphigenia)
15. Wolff, *Preciosa*
16. Schiller, *Wallensteins Lager—Piccolomini* (Wallenstein's Camp—The Piccolomini)
17. Schiller, *Wallensteins Tod* (Wallenstein's Death)
18. Goethe, *Clavigo*
19. Iffland, *Die Jäger* (The Hunters)
20. Schiller, *Die Jungfrau von Orleans* (The Maid of Orleans)
21–22. Fitger, *Die Hexe* (The Witch)
23. Lessing, *Miss Sara Sampson*
24. Schiller, *Maria Stuart*
25–26. Lord Byron, *Marino Faliero*

27. Schiller, *Braut von Messina* (The Bride of Messina)
28. Shakespeare, *Die Widerspänstige Zähmung* (The Taming of the Shrew)
29–30. Lindner, *Die Bluthochzeit* (Blood Wedding)

Notes

Introduction

1. "Nicht der Schneider oder der Decorationsmaler, nicht das vielberufene Kostümbuch unseres gelehrten Professors Weiss: dass sie uns das Schauspiel des Dichters voll, rund und ganz geben: das ist das Geheimnis der Meininger" (Karl Frenzel, *Berliner Dramaturgie* [Hannover: Carl Rümpler, 1877] 2: 130). All non–English material referred to in this volume has been translated by the author.

2. ". . . diese Uebertreibung in der Pflege des Aeusserlichen, wenn sie allgemein gehandhabt würde, wäre ein Verderb für die Bühne. Die Form, welche uns gezeigt wird, ist so berückend für das Auge, dass man nach dem Gehalt gar nicht mehr fragt. Für diese Art von Schönheit fehlt mir der Sinn" (Paul Lindau, "Aus der Hauptstadt. Dramatische Aufführungen. Vorstellung für die 'Berliner Presse'—Gäste—Die Meininger," *Die Gegenwart,* 5, No. 22 [30 May 1874]: 350–51).

Chapter 1

1. Suffering from translation, the handwritten dedication reads:

> "There are many opinions—
> but only one Meiningen.
> No matter how many have crossed my path,
> I know only one Duke."

This inscription was penned by Wagner on March 12, 1877, in volume one of his *Gesammelte Schriften und Dichtungen* (Leipzig: E. W. Fritsch, 1871–73), now in the music history department of the Meiningen state museum. Reported in Herta Oesterheld, "Dokumente zur Musikgeschichte Meiningens—6 Briefe von Richard und Cosima Wagner an Georg II.," *Neue Beiträge zur Regerforschung und Musikgeschichte Meiningens,* Südthüringer Forschungen, 5, No. 6 (Meiningen: Staatliche Museen Meiningen, 1970): 84.

2. William James Henderson, *Richard Wagner: His Life and His Dramas* (New York: G. P. Putnam's Sons, n.d.), pp. 178–79.

3. "Bestimmen wir daher, dass das Operntheater ein Kunstinstitut sein soll, welches zur Veredelung des öffentlichen Geschmackes, durch unausgesetzt gute und korrekte Aufführungen musikalisch–dramatischer Werke beizutragen hat" (Richard Wagner, "Das Weiner Hof–Opern Theater," *Gesammelte Schriften und Dichtungen,* 3rd ed. [Leipzig: E. W. Fritsch, 1898], 7: 281).

4. Titles included *Die Gunst des Fürsten,* performed in May 1776; *Der Hausvater,* August 12, 1776; *Der Postzug,* November 1777; *Die Schottländerin, oder das Kaffeehaus,* August 10, 1778; and *Julius von Tarent,* 1780. Some of the plays bore the imprint, "Zu finden in der Hofbuchdruckerei." They have since been destroyed. Max Grube, *Geschichte der Meininger* (Stuttgart: Deutsche Verlags–Anstalt, 1926), p. 23.

5. Grube mentions two excerpts from Duke Karl's journal describing visits by Goethe in 1775 *(Geschichte,* p. 23).

6. "Even his (Georg II) grandfather, Duke Georg I, liked to participate in amateur theatricals at the ducal palaces." Heinrich Stümcke, "Herzog Georg II. von Sachsen–Meiningen und das Theater," *Die Persönlichkeit* 1, no. 8 (August 1914): 556.

7. Schiller's flight from Württemberg ended 1782 in Meiningen, where he met the court librarian W. F. H. Reinwald, his future brother–in–law. He first met Duke Georg five years later, and attended a comedy performance at his theater. In 1789, he asked Georg to grant him a title, which he desired for his fiancée's sake. On January 2, 1790, Georg made Schiller a Privy Councillor *(Hofrat)* of the court of Saxe–Meiningen.

   Jean Paul married in 1801 and settled in Meiningen. For the next two years, Georg served as the author's patron.

8. Luise Elenore, Princess of Hohenlohe–Langenburg.

9. When Bernhard turned 21, he was given the title of Duke Bernhard II. In 1825 he married Marie, Princess of Hesse–Cassel (1804–1888). His sister Adelheid married William, Duke of Clarence, making Georg II a nephew of the later King William IV of England.

10. M. Grube, *Geschichte,* p. 24.

11. M. Grube, *Geschichte,* p. 25; Jsidor Landau, "Meiningen," *Die deutsche Bühne* 1, no. 19 (Dec. 1909): 326–28. Bernhard was never satisfied with the amount of money the directors took in. Böhmly was the only one to have his contract renewed for a second year.

12. Stümcke, "Herzog Georg," p. 559.

13. Paul Lindau, "Vergangene Zeiten," *Neue Freie Presse* (Vienna), No. 14, 232 (8 April 1904), p. 1.

14. Ibid., p. 2.

15. Alfred Klaar, "Herzog Georg von Meiningen," *Jahrbuch der deutschen Shakespeare Gesellschaft,* 51 (1915): 194. Perhaps Klaar is punning when he says that Bernhard's plays " *. . . seinen braven Untertanen auf's beste gefielen. "* Besides today's meaning of "obedient," *brav* was also formerly used as its English cognate meaning "fearless in the face of adversity."

16. Otto von Kurnatowski, *Georg II., Herzog von Sachsen–Meiningen und Hildburghausen* (Hildburghausen: F. W. Gadow und Sohn, 1914), p. 8.

17. Wilhelm Greiner, *Georg von Meiningen und die Freifrau,* Grüne Herzbücherei (Gotha: Englehard–Keyher, 1939), p. 10.

18. Ernst Koch, "Herzog Georg II. von Saxe–Meiningen," *Deutsches Fürstenbuch,* ed. Anton Ohorn (Leipzig: Rengerische Buchhandlung, Gebhardt & Wilisch, 1889–90), p. 180.

19. Charles Waldstein, "The Court Theatre of Meiningen," *Harper's New Monthly Magazine,* 82 (1891): 747.

20. Max Grube, "Georg II. als Landschafter," *Thüringen* 2, no. 1 (April 1926): 6.

21. Herbert Eulenberg, "Der Theaterherzog: 1826–1914," in *Der Guckkasten* (Stuttgart: J. Engelhorns Nachfolger, 1922), p. 245.

22. M. Grube, *Geschichte,* p. 6.

23. Greiner, *Georg,* p. 8.

24. Aloys Prasch, "Erinnerungen eines ehemaligen Meiningers," *Bühne und Welt* 1, No. 15 (June 1899): 693.

25. Carl, Freiherr von Stein, *Die Kunst in Meiningen unter Herzog Georg II.* (Meiningen: Karl Keyssner, 1909), p. 6.

26. Kurnatowski, *Georg,* p. 10.

27. Th. Hemsen, "Herzog Georg II. von Meiningen," *Der neue Weg* 55, no. 7 (1 April 1926): 125–26.

28. Kurnatowski, *Georg,* p. 10.

29. Stein, *Kunst,* pp. 6–7.

30. See Karl W. T. Frenzel, *Die Wandgemälde Wilhelm von Kaulbachs im Treppenhaus des neuen Museums in Berlin* (Berlin: Schauer, 1870) (10 vol.) for a reproduction of this work. For a discussion of the murals, see Max Schasler, *Die Wandgemälde im Treppenhaus des neuen Museums zu Berlin* (Berlin: Allgemeine deutsche Verlagsanstalt, 1854) and Wilhelm Stoever, *Wilhelm von Kaulbachs Bilderkreis der Weltgeschichte im Treppenhaus des Berliner Neuen Museums* (Steglitz–Berlin: Verlag der Kaulbachstiche, n.d.).

31. These reports had even grown into a legend during Georg's lifetime. Prasch relates the following tale as an example of a story in common circulation that had no basis in fact:

> One day a young man came to the famous painter Peter Cornelius, asked the master painter to look at some sketches, then tell him bluntly whether he considered him sufficiently talented to take up painting as a profession. Peter Cornelius judged the young man's work with an expert eye. His interest was reflected in his countenance, and he accepted the young man as a pupil.
> The young man who had come to the master under the guise of becoming an artist himself, and who had won the master's approval solely on the basis of the drawings he presented was none other than Crown Prince Georg II of Saxe–Meiningen. Only years afterwards did Peter Cornelius discover from another source who his favorite pupil had been (Prasch, *Erinnerungen,* p. 692).

32. The fate of this painting could not be ascertained. It is not included in Müller's 1962 catalog of the Meiningen Theater Museum and Archive. See Johannes Müller, "Das Meininger

Theatermuseum und sein Archiv," *Kleine Schriften der Gesellschaft für Theatergeschichte,* No. 18 (Berlin: Selbstverlag der Gesellschaft für Theatergeschichte, 1962), pp. 57–62. It is known, however, that some of the figures in this painting were only sketched in by Georg, and Kaulbach then completed them (Prasch, *Erinnerungen,* p. 693).

33. Kurnatowski, *Georg,* pp. 12–13.

34. Waldstein, "Court Theatre," p. 748.

35. Greiner, *Georg,* p. 13.

36. Described in *The Oxford Companion to the Theatre,* ed. Phyllis Hartnoll, 3rd ed. (London: Oxford University Press, 1967), p. 630.

37. Waldstein, "Court Theatre," p. 748.

38. Lindau, "Zeiten," p. 3.

39. Greiner, *Georg,* p. 13.

40. Eduard Devrient, *Geschichte der deutschen Schauspielkunst* (Berlin, 1905; neubearbeitet als *Illustrierte deutsche Theatergeschichte,* W. Stuhlfeld, ed. [Zurich: Eigenbrödler, 1929]), p. 447.

41. Kurnatowski, *Georg,* p. 29.

42. Koch, "Herzog Georg," p. 182.

43. Christian Mühlfeld, "Georg II. und die Musik," *Thüringen, eine Monatsschrift für alte und neue Kultur* 2, no. 1 (April 1926): 9–10.

44. Kurnatowski, *Georg,* p. 74.

45. Mühlfeld, "Georg," p. 10.

46. Letter to Bernhard Müller quoted in Mühlfeld, "Georg," pp. 8–9.

47. "Der Meininger," *Die Zukunft* 88 (1914): 13.

48. Greiner, *Georg,* pp. 16–17.

49. Dated December 21, 1866. Quoted in *Meininger Kunst,* "Die Wartburgstimmen," eds. (Hildburghausen & Leipzig: Thüringische Verlags–Anstalt, 1906), p. 12.

50. Dated December 22, 1866. Quoted in *Meininger Kunst,* p. 12.

51. Georg's wish was not immediately fulfilled, but in the meantime he fought in the Franco–Prussian war as a Prussian and Saxon general and commander of the 32nd and 95th Infantry Regiments. After war's end he was present at Versailles and had the satisfaction of joining in the first *"Hoch!"* for the new German Kaiser (Greiner, *Georg,* pp. 18–19).

52. Stein, *Kunst,* p. 25.

53. The *Tonkünstlerversammlung* was the annual convention and music festival of the Allgemeiner deutscher Musikverein. The aims of the AdM were to provide a stimulus for new composition and an opportunity for all musicians to perform. Its annual meeting, the high point of the year for the German musical world, served to bring to performance the best of both old and new music.

54. Greiner, *Georg,* p. 33.

55. Stümcke, "Herzog Georg," p. 559.

56. "Aus dem Werdegang des Meininger Hoftheaters unter Herzog Georg II.," in *Festschrift zur Feier des 100. Geburtstages Herzog Georg II. von Sachsen–Meiningen* (Meiningen: n.p., 1926), unpaginated.

57. Prasch, "Erinnerungen," p. 694.

58. Greiner, *Georg,* p. 49.

59. "Aus dem Werdegang," n. pag.

60. Artur Wolff, "Der Theaterherzog," *Die deutsche Bühne* 18, no. 19 (December 1926): 324.

61. Paul Lindau, "Helene Freifrau von Heldburg," *Die deutsche Bühne* 1, no. 19 (December 1909): 324.

62. Prasch, "Erinnerungen," p. 694.

63. Quoted in "Aus dem Werdegang."

64. Wendell Cole, however, identifies the rival actress as Marie Berg. Wendell Cole, ed., *Max Grube's "The Story of the Meininger,"* trans. Ann Marie Koller (Coral Gables, Florida: University of Miami Press, 1963), p. xvi.

    The tale that follows demonstrates the depth of mistrust that had grown up between father and son. The story is corroborated by two sources that appeared as reminiscences during the celebration of Georg's centennial: Wolff, pp. 78–79, and Erich Nippold, "Herzog Georg von Saxe–Meiningen," *Pflüger: Thüringer Heimatblätter* 3 (1926): 152–53.

65. Nippold, "Herzog Georg," p. 154.

66. Prasch, "Erinnerungen," p. 695.

67. Lindau, "Helene," p. 324.

Chapter 2

1.   Es gibt kein schöner Leben
           Als "Statisten"–Leben,
           Wie es Chronegk und der Herzog schuf.
           Stets "Heil Caesar" rufen,
           Plastisch stehn auf Stufen,
           Ist ein hoher, herrlicher Beruf!

    Karl Grube, *Die Meininger,* Das Theater, vol. 9 (Berlin & Leipzig: Schuster & Loeffler, 1904), p. 9.

2. An excellent general discussion of nineteenth–century theater history is found in Oscar C. Brockett, *The Theatre,* 3rd ed. (New York: Holt Rinehart & Winston, 1974), pp. 266–327. Brockett's outline is followed in this section.

3. Julius Bab, *Das Theater der Gegenwart* (Leipzig: J. J. Weber, 1928), p. 8. Bab fails to give other particulars of the performance, such as place and specific date.

4. Max Grube, *Geschichte der Meininger* (Stuttgart, Berlin, & Leipzig: Deutsche Verlags–Anstalt, 1926), p. 19.

5. Bab, *Gegenwart,* pp. 9–10.

6. Paul Schlenther, *Botho von Hülsen und seine Leute* (Berlin: Internationale Buchhandlung J. Gerstmann, 1883), p. 17. The "rustic, romantic style" was, in the German, *"Paul–und–Virginien Stil,"* referring to the 1787 novel by Bernardin de Saint–Pierre.

7. Bab, *Gegenwart,* pp. 11–12.

8. The playbill for the opening night of *King John* clearly outlined Kemble's intent:

    > This present Monday, January 19, 1824, will be revived Shakespeare's Tragedy of King John with an attention to Costume never equalled on the English Stage. Every Character will appear in the precise HABIT OF THE PERIOD, the whole of the Dresses and Decoration being executed from indisputable Authorities, such as Monumental Effigies, Seals, Illumined Mss., &c.

    Quoted in W. Moelwyn Merchant, "On Looking at *The Merchant of Venice,"* in *Essays on Nineteenth Century British Theatre,* ed. Kenneth Richards and Peter Thompson (London: Methuen & Co., Ltd., 1971), p. 172.

9. Three French playwrights must be mentioned in a discussion of the new realism in the mid–nineteenth century. Eugène Scribe (1791–1861) perfected the "well–made" play, whose elements are a clear exposition of situation, careful preparation for future events, unexpected but logical reversals, continuous and increasing suspense, and a logical resolution. Such a pattern was attractive to realists because of its exposition and logical progression. Alexandre Dumas *fils* (1824–1895) and Emile Augier (1820–1889) applied the realistic mode to their choice of subject matter and characterization by consistently directing attention to contemporary social problems.

10. Oscar C. Brockett, *History of the Theatre,* 2nd ed. (Boston: Allyn and Bacon, 1974), p. 335.

11. Friedrich Haase, *Was ich erlebte, 1846–1896* (Berlin, Leipzig, Vienna, & Stuttgart: Richard Bong, 1897), pp. 162–64.

12. Ibid., p. 165.

13. Ibid., p. 166.

14. Titles given to the leaders of a German theater are often confusing. Von Stein's title was *Intendant.* According to Gerhard Wahrig, *Deutsches Wörterbuch* (Gütersloh: Bertelsmann, 1975), *Direktor* = "Leiter, Vorsteher;" *Intendant* = "Leiter eines Theaters;" *Regisseur* = "Derjenige, der die künstlerische Gestaltung eines Dramas für die Aufführung auf der Bühne und die Leitung der Schauspieler bei den Proben führt." Stein's tasks seem to have been to manage finances, acquire all things needed by the company, and oversee the actual performances. Grabowsky was in charge of scenery and costume preparation, and of rehearsals.

15. Grabowsky's title was *Oberregisseur.* Siegward Friedmann, "Das erste Gastspiel in Meiningen," *Die deutsche Bühne* 1, no. 19 (December 1909): 330.

16. The Meininger Hoftheater was the first stage to use Wilbrandt's versions. Adolf Wilbrandt, trans., "Vorwort," *Sophokles' und Euripedes' ausgewählte Dramen, mit Rücksicht auf die*

Bühne übertragen (Nördlingen: C. H. Beck, 1866), 1: ix–x.

As an historical aside, the first Greek tragedy presented in America was *Oedipus Rex,* done at Harvard on May 14–20, 1881. The Harvard production reflected the same attitude toward historical costuming as that found in Meiningen. The costumes were designed by F. D. Millet, "who had made a prolonged study of costume from the historical and artistic points of view. Each dress was the subject of detailed consideration, with regard to historical accuracy, the figure of its wearer, the appropriateness to the station he was supposed to occupy, and even the color–composition of the scenes in which he took part." Henry Norman, *An Account of the Greek Play* (Boston: James R. Osgood & Co., 1882), pp. 51–52.

17. Paul Lindau, "Vergangene Zeiten," *Neue Freie Presse* (Vienna), No. 14232 (8 April 1904): 5. Lindau's memoirs are invaluable for a history of the Meininger. He became a close friend of Duke Georg during the 1880s, and recorded many facts about the Meininger, as told him by the Duke, not found in other sources available today.

18. "Aus dem Werdegang des Meininger Hoftheaters unter Herzog Georg II." in *Festschrift zur Feier des 100. Geburtstages Herzog Georg II. von Sachsen–Meiningen* (Meiningen: n. p., 1926), unpaginated.

19. "Aus dem Werdegang," unpaginated.

20. A detailed listing of the plays performed by the Hoftheater in Meiningen may be found in the Appendix. Compiled from theater bills stored at the Cologne Theater Museum, the listing comprises the years 1867–68 and 1872–77. Previously compiled listings for the years 1877–78, 1880–81, and 1883 are also included.

21. Wilhelm Oechelhäuser, "Die Shakespeare Aufführungen in Meiningen," *Jahrbuch der deutschen Shakespeare-Gesellschaft* 3 (1868): 383–96. This report was the first widely-circulated article calling attention to the theater reforms going on at the Meininger Hoftheater.

22. Erich von Possart, *Erstrebtes und Erlebtes: Erinnerungen aus meiner Bühnentätigkeit,* 2nd ed. (Berlin: Ernst Siegfried Mittler & Sohn, 1916), p. 234.

23. Ibid.

24. Ibid., pp. 240–41.

25. Lindau, "Zeiten," p. 4.

26.
Die Hofschranzen, die steh'n noch tiefer
Im Schöpfungsrange als die Affen;
Sie sind das schlimmste Ungeziefer,
Das Gott in seinem Zorn erschaffen.

(Lindau, "Zeiten," p. 4.)

27. "Aus dem Werdegang," unpaginated.

28. The absence of drama criticism in Meiningen grew out of a review of the first performance of *Julius Cäsar* under Georg's direction in 1866. The official newspaper published a rather indifferent discussion of the play, written by the wife of a local officer. In her review, she wrote of the scene in which Mark Anthony delivers his famous speech to the Romans from the pulpit of the Forum (act 3, scene 2). She mistook the pulpit for a fountain, however, and wrote, "The 'fountain scene' was well done." (Die Szene am Brunnen war sehr gelungen.)

After reading the review, Georg berated the publisher of the newspaper, telling him that in the future he wanted his artists to be critiqued only by knowledgeable people. He did not want their accomplishments judged by one who had no understanding of artistic tasks. From that day forth the official paper printed no more reviews, and the other local newspaper followed suit.

29. Karl Frenzel, "Wie ich zu den Meiningern kam," *Bühne und Welt* 1, no. 15 (June 1899): 687–690.

30. Frenzel's reviews were later collected in book form. The first review cited here is from Karl Frenzel, *Berliner Dramaturgie* (Hannover: Carl Rümpler, 1877) 2: 100–103.

31. Ibid., pp. 103–108.

32. Friedmann, "Gastspiel," pp. 329–31.

33. "Das nenne ich Regie! Mir ist, als kämen wir aus Posemuckel an ein erstes Hoftheater!"

34. Alois Wohlmuth, *Ein Schauspielerleben* (Munich: Parcus & Co., 1918), pp. 101–13. Perhaps Wohlmuth, ill–befitting his name (meaning "good–humor"), was bitter because Georg permitted him to do a one–man performance on his stage only once (January 21, 1873).

35. Ludwig Barnay, *Erinnerungen* (Berlin: Egon Fleischel & Co., 1903), 1: 246–56. Also Ludwig Barnay, "Mein Debut in Meiningen," *Bühne und Welt* 8, pt. 2, no. 14 (April 1906): 584–86.

36. Frenzel, "Wie ich," pp. 689–90.

37. The terms "visit" and "tour" will be used extensively, in place of the German terms *Gastspiel* and *Gastspielreise*. "Visit" *(Gastspiel)* is used here to mean a series of performances in one city. The term "tour" *(Gastspielreise)* refers to an entire year's schedule, hence comprising several "visits."

38. "Aus dem Werdegang," unpaginated.

39. Grabowsky had no actual duties at the theater from this time on, but he was free to assist if he so desired. He received a pension in 1879 and died in 1883 at the age of 79. Paul Lindau "Vergangene Zeiten," *Neue Freie Presse* (Vienna), No. 14,244 (21 April 1904), p. 1.

40. Barnay, *Erinnerungen,* 1: 256–57.

41. Frenzel, "Wie ich," p. 690.

42. That is, time for the ducal court theater to become a traveling theater. Ferdinand Gregori, "Georg von Meiningen," *Kunstwart und Kulturwart* 27, no. 20 (Munich: July 1914): 131.

43. M. Grube, *Geschichte,* pp. 70–73.

44. Franz Wallner, "Meine Erinnerungen an Meiningen," *Volksspielkunst* 7, no. 7 (July 1926): 109.

45. The term "Meininger" was apparently not used to refer to the Meiningen theater until Paul Lindau's review of May 9. The word was immediately adopted by the public, although Frenzel was careful not to use it during their first visit to Berlin, feeling that the use of a nickname detracted somewhat from the respect he felt was due the theater.

46. Monty Jacobs, ed., *Deutsche Schauspielkunst: Zeugnisse zur Bühnengeschichte klassischer Rollen,* 2nd ed. (Berlin: Henschel, 1954), pp. 103–104. Georg's modifications are discussed in a section dealing with changes made to Molière's play through the years.

47. M. Grube, *Geschichte,* p. 80.

48. Based upon figures recorded in Hans Hopfen, *Streitfragen und Erinnerungen* (Stuttgart: J. G. Cotta, 1876), p. 237.

49. Letter quoted in Barnay, *Erinnerungen,* 1: 268.

50. Max Grube erroneously gives the Meininger credit for being the first to perform Grillparzer's fragment *(Geschichte,* p. 84); it was actually first performed in 1840 (Heinz Politzer, "Franz Grillparzer," in *Handbook of Austrian Literature,* ed. Frederick Ungar [New York: Frederick Ungar, 1973], p. 101).

51. Reported in K. Grube, p. 8.

52. Von Hülsen's intrigue is outlined by Friedrich Rüffer in *Die Meininger und ihre Bedeutung, eine dramatische Skizze* (Seperat-Abdruck aus dem *Leipziger Sonntagsblatt)* (Leipzig: Leopold & Bär, 1882), pp. 20–21.

53. Ibid., p. 21.

54. Details of the Budapest trip were recorded by an actor who accompanied the troupe: Aloys Prasch, "Erinnerungen eines ehemaligen Meiningers," *Bühne und Welt* 1, no. 15 (June 1899): 695.

55. Charles Waldstein, "The Court Theatre of Meiningen," *Harper's New Monthly Magazine* 82 (April 1891): 750. Waldstein had a lengthy interview with Georg about his theater and the way in which he managed it.
    One of the special trains used by the Meininger comprised 18 freight cars and sufficient sleeping cars for nearly 100 people *(General–Anzeiger* [Düsseldorf], 1880, No. 167, cited in Alfred Kruchen, *Das Regieprinzip bei den Meiningern zur Zeit ihrer Gastspielepoche,* Diss. Danzig 1933 [Danzig: A. W. Kafemann, 1933], p. 79).

56. Georg Laub, Director of the Munich Theater Museum, feels that this was one of Georg's most important contributions to the theater (Personal interview with Georg Laub, Munich, 8 July 1976).

57. M. Grube, *Geschichte,* p. 91.

58. "Ibsen und die Meininger," *Die deutsche Bühne* 1, no. 19 (December 1909): 319.

59. Joseph Kainz recorded the glamour of that evening, and his reminiscences were later recalled in Helene Richter, *Kainz,* 2nd ed. (Vienna & Leipzig: F. G. Speidel, 1931), p. 58. It was also recorded that Meiningen's hostelries were inadequate for the crowd, and so Georg provided lodging for many in his palace.

60. This method of acting, which bears similarity to the method later developed by Stanislavsky, is discussed in Wolfgang Drews, *Die Grossen des deutschen Schauspiels* (Berlin: Deutscher Verlag, 1941), p. 174.

61. Richter, *Kainz,* p. 59.

62. The evening's events were recorded by an actor who was present in the audience. Eugen Zabel, *Theatergänge* (Berlin: A. Hofmann & Comp., 1908), pp. 9–10.

63. Details are found in *Die Meiningen'sche Theater–Intendanz gegenüber dem deutschen Bühnenverein: Nach amtlichen Quellen* (Meiningen: n.p., 1879), unpaginated.

64. Joseph Kürschner, *Jahrbuch für das deutsche Theater* 2 (Leipzig: L. E. Foltz, 1880): 119–20.

65. The report of the fire was published in Joseph Kürschner, *Jahrbuch für das deutsche Theater* 1 (Leipzig: Hermann Foltz, 1879): 172–73.

66. *Preciosa* was a melodrama in the former sense of the word, i.e., a dramatic composition with music interspersed.

67. *The Taming of the Shrew* was advertised on the Meininger's theater placards as both *Die bezähmte Widerspenstige* and *Der Widerspenstigen Zähmung.* However, both titles refer to Deinhardtstein's German version.

68. Barnay, *Erinnerungen,* 1: 273–74.

69. See the review "The Meiningen Court Company," *The Times* (London), 7 July 1881. The author of the article was favorably inclined toward *Preciosa,* although mainly because of Weber's music. The leading lady, incidentally, was unable to sing, and so another sang for her from behind the scenery. It is perhaps surprising that the other roles did not require assistance in singing, considering that Georg had closed the opera fifteen years previously.

70. Compare, for example, the favorable statement, "that in spite of the tropical heat that prevailed at the time, there was no drop in attendance up to the end of the visit, while the Théâtre Français, visiting at the same time, had to close its doors after only three weeks because of poor attendance" (Rüffer, *Skizze,* p. 24) with the comment in the *Illustrated Sporting and Dramatic News* of July 4 that "plenty of places were vacant . . . ." The production discussed in the London newspaper was *Twelfth Night,* which should certainly have attracted a large audience in London if the public had felt it was worth seeing.

71. The Meininger performed only one play of each during their tours. *Iphigenia* was done twice in London during 1881, twice each in Nürnberg and Breslau and once in Berlin during 1882, once in Barmen during 1883, twice in Leipzig and twice again in Breslau during 1889, and once apiece in St. Petersburg and Odessa during 1890. *Miss Sara Sampson* was performed three times in Berlin and twice each in Breslau and Dresden during 1884.

72. K. Grube, *Meininger,* p. 5.

73. One English writer was, indeed, of the opinion that, "I am glad that 'Faust' was not given. Having seen Emil Devrient and Hendrichs as Faust, Döring and Kühn as Mephistopheles, I feel that the Meininger troupe did not comprise an adequate Faust or a competent fiend." H. Schütz Wilson, "Our Play–Box: Die Meininger," *The Theatre,* n.s. 4 (1881): 104–05.

   In a 1932 interview with Alfred Kruchen, Max Grube stated that Hebbel was not done by the Meininger on tour because they had no actors strong enough to carry the parts (Kruchen, *Regieprinzip,* p. 50).

74. Along with *Two Foscari, Marino Faliero* has been considered by some to be the weakest of Lord Byron's plays. See, for example, Ernst Leopold Stahl, *Das englische Theater im 19. Jahrhundert: Seine Bühnenkunst und Literatur,* Die Kultur des modernen England in

Einzeldarstellungen, ed. Ernst Sieper, (Munich & Berlin: R. Oldenbourg, 1914), 5: 47.

75. Max Grube informs his readers that the planned trip to America never took place because of Chronegk's poor health *(Geschichte,* p. 43), while the historian Hans Calm lists the foreign countries where the Meininger performed as Austria, Switzerland, Holland, England, Russia, and America in his *Kulturbilder aus der deutschen Theatergeschichte* (Leipzig: Koehler und Amelang, 1925), p. 349.

The discussion that follows is based on a letter from Paul Richard in the *Frankfurter Zeitung,* 204 (1886), and Ludwig Chronegk's letters to Georg dated April 20, May 7, July 10, and July 28, 1886, in the Cologne theater museum. See also Carl Niessen, "Weshalb die Meininger nicht in Amerika gastierten," *Theater der Welt: Zeitschrift für die gesamte Theaterkultur* 1, no. 12 (December 1937): 596–602. There are, however, several incorrect dates listed in Niessen's article.

76. *Julius Caesar, The Winter's Tale, Twelfth Night, The Merchant of Venice, The Taming of the Shrew, Wilhelm Tell, The Robbers, Maria Stuart,* the *Wallenstein* trilogy, *Fiesco, Lydia, Die Bluthochzeit, Die Ahnfrau, Der Herrgottschnitzer von Ammergau,* and *Marino Faliero.*

77. Lindau and the Duke had become such good friends that Georg bought the Berlin critic a new American typewriter in 1885, and one can be certain that Georg would not have done Lindau the favor to allow him to continue vitriolically attacking the Meininger with the conveniences of the latest office equipment. Lindau demonstrated extreme pleasure over the gift, and thanked the Duke by typing a letter to him telling how proud he was of his new typewriter. He was also, incidentally, proud of the fact that he could type almost as fast as he could write, and that his secretary was twice as fast as he (Paul Lindau, letter to Georg II, 30 October 1885, Nachlass Georg II, Deutsche Staatsbibliothek, Berlin).

78. M. Grube, *Geschichte,* pp. 119–20.

79. Paul Lindau, *Nur Erinnerungen* (Stuttgart & Berlin: J. G. Cotta Nachfolger, 1917), 2: 375.

80. M. Grube, *Geschichte,* p. 115.

81. M. Grube, *Geschichte,* pp. 48–49.

82. For a thorough discussion of the Meininger's 1888 visit to the Netherlands, see H. H. J. de Leeuwe, *Meiningen en Nederland: Proeve van vergelijkende Toneelgeschiedenis,* Studia Litteraria Rheno–Traiectina, 6 (Groningen: J. B. Wolters, 1959).

83. "Verschiedenes," *Die deutsche Bühne* 1, No. 19 (December 1909): 334. This article is part of the special "Meininger issue" spoken of on page 41.

84. M. Grube, *Geschichte,* p. 121.

85. Hans Calm, *Kulturbilder aus der deutschen Theatergeschichte* (Leipzig: Koehler und Amelang, 1925), pp. 349–50, and Berthold Litzmann, *Das deutsche Drama in den litterarischen Bewegungen der Gegenwart: Vorlesungen, gehalten an der Universität Bonn* (Hamburg & Leipzig: Leopold Voss, 1894), p. 43.

86. "Es ist nicht mehr nötig. Was die deutschen Theater lernen sollten, das haben sie gelernt" (M. Grube, *Geschichte,* p. 121).

87. Max Kurnik, *Ein Menschenalter* (Berlin: Janke, 1883), p. 334.

88. Paul Richard, *Chronik sämmtlicher Gastspiele des Herzoglich Sachsen–Meiningen'schen Hoftheaters während der Jahre 1874–1890: Statistische Übersicht* (Leipzig: Friedrich Conrad, 1891), p. 164.

89. Kürschner, *Jahrbuch,* 2: 325.

90. Lindau, *Erinnerungen,* 2: 341–42.

91. One year earlier Helene was already hoping that the Meininger's tours could be discontinued:

> "I would prefer giving up the tours, for some years, at least; but it is so difficult to change to a smaller company, and so things will probably stay as they are" (Letter to Max Grube, 30 June 1889, in *Fünfzig Jahre Glück und Leid: Ein Leben in Briefen aus den Jahren 1873–1923,* ed. Johannes Werner [Leipzig: Koehler und Amelang, 1926], p. 54).

Her wish fulfilled, Helene told Arthur Fitger in a letter dated 31 August 1890 the reasons why the Meininger would be touring no more:

> "The Meninger are no longer 'the Meininger!' The main reason for disbanding was Chronegk's health. In addition, the rehearsing of new plays and the eternal necessity of training the actors have become more and more burdensome to the Duke and me. We had only work, others had the pleasure; and in the past three years this work has cost the Duke a tidy sum, because except for the first season with [Schiller's] *Jungfrau,* the theater hasn't paid for itself in spite of long tours. It was quite natural for us to give Chronegk a well-deserved rest and to allow ourselves some pleasure from the theater— and so it has come to this" (Ibid., p. 55).

92. Hugo Dinger, "Meiningen," *Die Schaubühne* 6 (1910): 18.

93. "Theater reforms that are to have a wide and lasting influence must come from a large, rich, pace–setting theater metropolis." ("Reformen im Theaterwesen, die eine breite und nachhaltige Wirkung ausüben sollen, müssen von einer grossen, reichen und tonangebenden Theatermetropole ausgehen." Heinrich Laube, *Briefe über das deutsche Theater,* vol. 29 of *Gesammelte Werke in 50 Bände,* ed. Heinrich Houben [Leipzig: Max Hesse, 1909], pp. 16–17.)

94. Bab, *Das Theater,* p. 30.

95. Christian Eckelmann, *Vom Nachtwächter zur Bühne: Tatsachenbericht* (Berlin: Voco–Verlag, 1942), pp. 96–115. The section noted forms a chapter of Eckelmann's biography and discusses, without much detail, how he joined the "Meininger" and traveled with them throughout the United States in 1891 and 1892.

96. Richard, *Chronik,* pp. 154–59.

    It is interesting to see Carl Grube's name on Eckelmann's list. Grube (no relation to Max Grube) was a member of the German–speaking St. Louis Stadttheater in 1891, having left Georg's employ some years earlier. He left Meiningen feeling that Georg repressed individual ability in his quest for harmony (K. Grube, *Meininger,* pp. 72–73), and yet in America he was billed as one of the Duke's disciples.

97. "[The company's] advent in America was cordially welcomed, not only by the German but also the American audience . . . ." William Winter, "The Saxe–Meiningen Production in America," in *Shakespeare on the Stage,* 2nd ser. (New York: Moffat, Yard & Co., 1915), pp. 612–16.

98. Excerpts from Winter's review: "In respect to the felicity of exhibition which results from competent stage management, the Meiningen Company justified its high repute. In other respects it proved a disappointment. The acting did not, in any particular, transcend the level of respectable mediocrity. No member of the company evidenced either exceptional talent or special charm." "They taught nothing which was not already known, and their acting, at its best, was not in any way superior to that which has ordinarily been seen . . . on the American stage."

99. Letter in *Fünfzig Jahre,* p. 76.

100. The history of Grabbe's play is thoroughly discussed in Eugen Kilian, "Grabbes Don Juan und Faust auf der Bühne," *Dramaturgische Blätter,* 1st series (München & Leipzig: Georg Müller, 1905), pp. 248–60. Of Wolzogen's version, Kilian said, "In some parts of the play, hardly a single stanza of the original was spared the alleged improvements of the editor."

101. "[Georg and Helene] entered their box on the evening of March 13, not suspecting a thing" (Lindau, *Nur Erinnerungen,* 2: 354). However, the other two extant accounts of the evening make it clear that details of the performance were published beforehand. Max Grube, *Am Hofe der Kunst* (Leipzig: Grethlein und Co., 1918), pp. 317–18, and J[sidor] Landau, "Ein Festabend der Meininger," *Bühne und Welt* 1, no. 15 (June 1899): 684–86.

102. Paul Lindau, *Nur Erinnerungen* 2: 357–60. Lindau's plan was part of a general movement to produce *Faust II. Faust I* had disappeared from the stage by 1899, while the second part was produced 121 times in Germany between 1899 and 1905, according to Georg Witkowski, *The German Drama of the Nineteenth Century,* L. E. Horning, trans. (New York: Henry Holt, 1909), p. 206.

103. Rolf Prasch, Meiningen director from 1936 to 1940, mentions in passing that the scenery for Shaw's play was still in good condition in 1955 and showed that the Hoftheater considered Shaw important enough to acquire scenery and props for his play. Rolf Prasch, "Festtage in Meiningen," *Die Bühnengenossenschaft* 7, no. 6 (September 1955): 147.

104. In the document awarding Georg the honorary degree, he is described as:

> His Majesty Georg II, Duke of Sachsen–Meiningen,
> Who has always thought of the welfare of his *Vaterland,*
> Prince richly bedecked with the love of his subjects,
> Noble benefactor of this university,
> A noble branch of the Ernestinian house,
> Closely joined with Germany's leading spirits,
> At all times protector of all arts and sciences,
> Admirable interpreter of the noblest works,
> Particularly those of the poets and musicians,
> Joyous reformer of Germany's dramatic arts,
> Who has, with great success, truly made the dramas
> And characters of our Schiller dear to the hearts
> Of all Germans . . . .

(Otto v. Kurnatowski, *Georg II., Herzog von Sachsen–Meiningen und Hildburghausen* [Hildburghausen: F. W. Gadow und Sohn, 1914], p. 86.)

105. The events at the theater were recorded by Gotthard Zarnke, "Die Feier des 80. Geburtstages Herzog Georgs II. im Meininger Hoftheater," *Bühne und Welt* 8, part 2, no. 14 (April 1906): 589–90. Georg's eightieth birthday also loosed a torrent of tributary newspaper articles throughout Germany, many of which are listed in this work's bibliography.

106. N. H. W., "Kunstreis der Meiningers in ons land," *Het Leven* 1 (1906): 314.

107. News of the fire was reported to the theater world by A. Leinhos, "Der Brand des herzoglichen Hoftheaters in Meiningen," *Bühne und Welt* 10 part 2, no. 13 (April 1908): 557–59, and J. Dischner, "Allgemeine Rückschau, 5. März 1908," *Neuer Theateralmanach* 20 (1909): 120.

108. Letters of Georg II to Paul Lindau, dated 7 March and 15 March 1908, in Lindau, *Erinnerungen* 2: 362.

109. Letter to Max Grube dated 6 October 1908 in M. Grube, *Am Hofe*, pp. 313–14.

110. Lindau, *Erinnerungen*, 2: 361.

111. Dinger, "Meiningen," pp. 16–17.

112. There were several articles published either anticipating the theater's re–opening or describing the December 17, 1909, performance and discussing the importance of Meiningen for the current theater world. See, for example: Max Grube, "Meininger Kunst," *Die Woche* 11 (1909): 2113–15; Artur Wolff, "Meiningen," *Die deutsche Bühne* 1 (1909): 336–37; and H. W., "Meiningen," *Das Theater* 1 (1910): 198–201. H. W.'s article gives a rather detailed description of the new building. The reviewer also interestingly states that he found the performances of the old Meininger, who had returned for one more evening on the Duke's stage, to be less than satisfactory. He noted, though, that the younger actors hired by Grube lent hope that Meiningen might continue as an important influence on the theater world.

113. Letter to Max Grube, dated February 1910, in *Fünfzig Jahre*, p. 65.

114. Letter to Cosima Wagner, dated 12 May 1912, in *Fünfzig Jahre*, p. 71.

115. M. Grube, *Am Hofe*, p. 336.

116. Paul Lindau, "Herzog Georg von Meiningen: Ein Lebensbild," *Die deutsche Bühne* 6 (1914): 403–407.

117. The celebration is described in "Die Gedenkfeier in Meiningen," *Der neue Weg* 55 (1926): 145. For a brief history of the Meininger Theater since 1926, consult Rolf Prasch, "Festtage in Meiningen." The article, written for the opening of the Meininger Theater Museum in 1955, also traces the history of the museum, first opened during Georg's centennial. One (unconfirmed) item of passing interest in Prasch's article is the assertion that the Meininger Theater was the first German theater to reopen in 1945.

Chapter 3

1. "Welch eine Fülle der Kunstfreude verdankt das deutsche Volk diesem erlauchteten, geliebten Fürsten und seiner Gemahlin!" (letter from Peter Rosegger to Georg II, 31 March 1906, Nachlass Georg II, Deutsche Staatsbibliothek, Berlin.)

2. J. W. von Goethe, "Betrachtungen im Sinne der Wanderer," *Wilhelm Meisters Wanderjahre.*

3. Oscar G. Brockett, *History of the Theater,* 2nd ed. (Boston: Allyn and Bacon, 1974), provides a concise summary of the developments in the German theater during the eighteenth and nineteenth centuries. For more detailed information about directors whose work anticipated Duke Georg's, see: Ernst Leopold Stahl, *Shakespeare und das deutsche Theater* (Stuttgart: W. Kohlhammer, 1947); Walter Lohmeyer, *Die Dramaturgie der Massen* (Berlin & Leipzig: Schuster & Loeffler, 1913); L. Lichterfeld, *Entwicklungs–Geschichte der deutschen Schauspielkunst* (Erfurt: Fr. Bartholomäus, 1882); August Klingemann, *Kunst und Natur,* 3 vols. (Brunswick: 1819–1828); Klingemann, "Über die Notwendigkeit eines allgemeinen Kunststudiums für den Schauspieler," *Zeitung für die elegante Welt,* 1816, Nos. 97 and 98; Heinrich Kopp, *Die Bühnenleitung August Klingemanns in Braunschweig,* Theatergeschichtliche Forschungen, vol. 27, ed. Berthold Litzmann (Hamburg & Leipzig: Leopold Voss, 1901); Julius Petersen, *Das deutsche Nationaltheater* (Leipzig & Berlin: B. G. Teubner, 1919); Friedrich Rosenthal, *Unsterblichkeit des Theaters* (Munich: Fritz Klopp, 1924); Rudolf Roennecke, *Franz Dingelstedts Wirksamkeit am Weimarer Hoftheater,* Diss. Greifswald 1912 (Greifswald: Hans Adler, 1912); Georg Altmann, *Heinrich Laubes Prinzip der Theaterleitung,* Diss. Jena 1908 (Dortmund: Fr. Wilh. Ruhfus, 1908); and Rudolph K. Goldschmidt, *Eduard Devrients Bühnenreform am Karlsruher Hoftheater,* Theatergeschichtliche Forschungen, vol. 32, ed. Berthold Litzmann (Leipzig: Leopold Voss, 1921).

4. Kean maintained a staff of historical researchers who were responsible for discovering trifles as picayune as what Shakespeare's favorite tune was—"Lightie Love Ladies," according to their findings; Kean wished to use that melody as intermission music (Stahl, *Shakespeare,* p. 439). Program notes at the Princess Theatre enumerated the pains to which Kean had gone and the experts he had consulted in order to present a scene that appeared to be taken from real life. As an example, the program for *A Winter's Tale* gravely noted that "the existence of bears in the East is exemplified in the 2nd chapter of the Second Book of Kings." Hence, Kean used an actual bear in his production, and Dutton Cook recalled that the animal "figures conspicuously, chasing the Antigonius of the time . . . with peculiar zest." *Punch* stated authoritatively that Kean's bear was "an archaeological copy from the original bear of Noah's Ark" (Arthur Colby Sprague, *Shakespeare and the Actors* [Cambridge: Harvard University Press, 1948], p. 68).

5. Josef Dischner, "Vom Meininger Theater," *Dramaturgische Beilage zur Deutschen Bühnengenossenschaft* 37, no. 40 (3 April 1908): 158.

6. Adolph L'Arronge, *Deutsches Theater und deutsche Schauspielkunst* (Berlin: Concordia, 1896), pp. 58–64.

7. L'Arronge termed the productions "Gesammt–Aufführungen."

8. "Der Eindruck, den die Darstellungen der Meininger auf mich gemacht haben, ist ein bleibender geworden und der Wunsch, das, was sie mich gelehrt, weiter auszubauen, an solchen Werk meine eigene Kraft zu erproben, hat mir den Mut gegeben, im Verein mit verschiedenen bedeutenden Bühnen–Künstler die Begründung des 'Deutschen Theaters zu Berlin' zu wagen" (L'Arronge, *Deutsches Theater,* p. 65).

9. Brahm's comments, which appeared in the *Vossische Zeitung* and *Die Nation,* are collected in Otto Brahm, *Kritische Schriften über Drama und Theater* (Berlin: S. Fischer Verlag,

1913), 1: 40–87.

10. "Die Anregungen der Meininger haben hier nachgewirkt, und massvoll hat man auch die Erfahrungen jener Gesellschaft zunutze gemacht" (Ibid., p. 40).

11. Brahm's terms are "Drängen und Stossen und Meiningisches Schreien," which he terms "Meiningertum."

12. L'Arronge, *Deutsches Theater,* p. 74.

13. Petersen, *Nationaltheater,* p. 88.

14. Hugh Frederic Garten, *Modern German Drama* (London: Methuen, 1959), pp. 23–30; Alfred Kerr, *Das Mimenreich,* vol. 1, no. 5 of *Gesammelte Schriften* (Berlin: S. Fischer, 1917), pp. 18–19.

15. Maxim Newmark, *Otto Brahm, The Man and the Critic* (New York and London: G. E. Stechert and Co., 1938), pp. 144–45; Arthur Kutscher, *Die Ausdruckskunst der Bühne* (Leipzig: Fritz Eckhart Verlag, 1910), p. 40.

16. "Die Wahrheit, die auf einem beschränkten Gebiete des Theaterlebens Herzog Georg so tapfer erstritt,—die Freie Bühne fordert sie für die gesammte dramatische Kunst" (Otto Brahm, "Kunstlerische Sendungen. Bei Gelegenheit der Meininger," *Die Freie Bühne* 1, no. 30 [1890]: 805).

17. Wolfgang Drews, *Theater* (Vienna, Munich, and Basel: Kurt Desch, 1961), pp. 125–26.

18. Dischner, p. 158.

19. Siegfried Jacobsohn, *Das Theater der Reichshauptstadt* (Munich: Albert Langen, 1904), pp. 46–47. Robert Prölss, *Das Herzoglich Meiningen'sche Hoftheater und die Bühnenreform* (Erfurt: Fr. Bartholomäus, n.d.), p. 71.

20. Julius Bab, *Das Theater der Gegenwart* (Leipzig: J. J. Weber, 1928), p. 37.

21. Friedrich Rüffer, *Geschichte des Leipziger Stadttheaters unter der Direction Dr. Förster* (Leipzig: Bernhard Freyer, 1880), p. 39.

22. Bab, *Gegenwart,* pp. 30–31.

23. Bab, *Gegenwart,* p. 31; Stahl, *Shakespeare,* p. 468.

24. Stahl, *Shakespeare,* p. 464.

25. Georg's set was directly copied from Irving's. *Romeo and Juliet* had been done in Meiningen since 1867, but Georg redesigned the sets in 1897. A comparison of his design (plate 27) with Irving's (plate 26) leaves no doubt of Georg's plagiarism. If Georg is given the benefit of the doubt, it is interesting to see that as late as 1897 he was still drawing on any source he found appropriate for betterment of his stage. The question must also be raised, though, of how much of Georg's work was derivative, and if he often took credit for work done originally by others. Future research must determine the answer.

26. Max Grube, "Von Meininger Art und Kunst," *Bühne und Welt* 8, part 2, no. 14 (April 1906): 582.

27. Ibid., p. 583.

28. Stahl, *Shakespeare,* pp. 473–75.

29. William Archer, *Study and Stage* (London: Grant Richards, 1899), pp. 98–99.

30. Such an opinion has been voiced in many scholarly works, such as: Margot Berthold, *Weltgeschichte des Theaters* (Stuttgart: Alfred Kröner, 1968), p. 419; Paul Fritsch, *Influence du Théâtre français sur le théâtre allemand de 1870 jusqu'aux approches de 1900,* (Paris: Jouve & Cie., 1912), p. 133; Ann Marie Best Koller, "Georg II, Duke of Saxe–Meiningen, and the German Stage," Ph.D. diss. Stanford 1965; and Barrett H. Clark and George Freedly, *A History of Modern Drama* (New York: Appleton–Century, 1947), p. 244. A more balanced view is found, however, in Denis Bablet, *Esthétique Générale du Décor de théâtre de 1870 à 1914* (Paris: Editions du centre national de la recherche scientifique, 1965), pp. 48–49.

31. The original letter was published by Sarcey in *Le Temps,* 23 July 1888. Antoine also published it in *Mes Souvenirs sur le Théâtre–Libre* (Paris: 1921), pp. 108–113. A translation may be found in A. M. Nagler, *A Source Book in Theatrical History* (New York: Dover, 1959), pp. 580–82. Jules Claratie, administrator of the Comédie Française, also saw the Meininger in 1888. He admired little except the troupe's discipline. His report was published as "Les Meininger et leur mise en scène," *Le Temps,* 13 July 1888.

32. The contention that the Meininger "made a profound impression on the young Stanislavski" with their first visit (Clark and Freedly, *History,* p. 401) is erroneous.

33. Constantin Stanislavsky, *My Life in Art,* J. J. Robins, trans. (Boston: Little, Brown, 1938), p. 197.

34. Ibid., p. 199.

35. David Magarshack, *Stanislavsky* (New York: Chanticleer Press, 1951), p. 74.

36. Stanislavsky, *My Life,* p. 201.

37. Christine Edwards, *The Stanislavsky Heritage* (New York: N.Y.U. Press, 1965), p. 50.

38. Stanislavsky, *My Life,* pp. 236–37.

39. Edwards, *Heritage,* p. 71.

40. Magarshack, *Stanislavsky,* p. 248.

41. Friedrich Düsel, "Dramatische Rundschau. Vom Gastspiel des Mrskauer Künstlerischen Theaters," *Westermanns Monatshefte,* No. 8 (May 1906), p. 295. Also, Felix Emmel, *Das Ekstatische Theater* (Prien: n.p., 1924), pp. 256–60.

42. Stanislavsky, *My Life,* p. 447.

43. Ibid., p. 448.

44. Max Grube, *Am Hofe der Kunst* (Leipzig: Grethlein & Co., 1918), pp. 264–65.

45. Stanislavsky, *My Life,* p. 201.

46. Many of these messages are now located in Georg's literary remains at the Deutsche Staatsbibliothek, East Berlin.

47. "So mag man ermessen, was für eine total geknechtete, aller Illusion beraubte, in ihrem dunklen Drange nach grossen Eindrücken lechzende Knabenseele die Erlebnisse Macbeth,

Julius Caesar, die Wallenstein–Trilogie und Kleists Hermannsschlacht von dieser Bühne bedeuten mussten" (Gerhart Hauptmann, *Das Abenteuer meiner Jugend* [Berlin: S. Fischer, 1937] 2: 280).

48. Based on Paul Richard, *Chronik sämmtlicher Gastspiele* (Leipzig: Friedrich Conrad, 1891).

49. "Kein Wort der Verehrung reicht an den Wert dieses Ereignesses für meine entleerte, ausgehungerte Seele heran. Kein Wort ermisst den Umfang des geistigen Gutes, mit dem ich in diesen wenigen Abendstunden für mein ganzes Leben ausgestattet wurde" (Gerhart Hauptmann, "Jugenderinnerungen," *Berliner Börsen-Courier,* No. 533 [13 November 1932]. Reported in Felix Alfred Voight and Walter A. Reichert, *Hauptmann und Shakespeare,* Deutschkundliche Arbeiten, gen. series, vol. 12 [Breslau: Maruschke & Berenat, 1938], pp. 8–9. Hauptmann's account was shortened in *Das Abenteuer meiner Jugend.* The full text of the 1932 version appears in the Appendix.)

50. Hauptmann, *Abenteuer* 2: 349–50.

51. Georg Witkowski, *The German Drama of the Nineteenth Century,* L. E. Horning, trans. (New York: Henry Holt, 1909), pp. 102–103.

52. W. H. Eller, *Ibsen in Germany* (Boston: Richard C. Badger, 1918), p. 133, gives 1875 as the date of this performance, using Emil Reich, *Ibsens Dramen* (Dresden: 1906), p. 48, as his justification. However, the Cologne collection of playbills shows that January 30, 1876, is the actual date. On the bill for that night is listed "Die Kronprätendenten—zum ersten Male" ("Pretenders–for the first time"). The playbills for 1875 include no productions of Ibsen's plays. In Eller's Table B (p. 139), he lists a performance of *Pretenders* at the Schwerin Hoftheater on November 15, 1875, after the Meininger according to him, but two and one-half months before them, if the date is correct. The Schwerin performance is mentioned nowhere else, however.

53. Letter to Ludwig Josephson, "Ibsen und die Meininger," *Die deutsche Bühne* 19 (December 1909): 319. For further critical comment, see Philipp Stern, *Henrik Ibsen—zur Bühnengeschichte seiner Dichtung* (Berlin: Otto Elsner, 1901), p. 3.

54. *Ghosts* was first produced in Chicago, in the summer of 1882. Near the end of 1883 it was done four times in Sweden and Denmark.

55. David George, *Henrik Ibsen in Deutschland,* Palestra, vol. 251 (Göttingen: Vandenhoek & Ruprecht, 1968): 19, incorrectly states that the Meininger gave the closed performance in Augsburg.

56. Henrik Ibsen, letter to Georg, 13 November 1886, Georgs Nachlass, Cologne Theater Museum. The text of their correspondence is translated in the Appendix.

57. Ludwig Chronegk, letter to Profs. Brückner, 15 November 1886, Georgs Nachlass, Cologne Theater Museum.

58. Ibid.

59. Ludwig Chronegk, letter to Profs. Brückner, 13 December 1866, Georgs Nachlass, Cologne theater museum.

60. Ludwig Chronegk, telegram to Profs. Brückner, 18 December 1866, Georg's Nachlass, Cologne Theater Museum. The set had not arrived at 3:30 p.m., and rehearsal was scheduled to begin at 5:00. The play went on as scheduled, though, so it must have arrived soon

thereafter.

61. Richard Voss, *Aus einem phantistischen Leben: Erinnerungen* (Stuttgart: J. Engelhorns Nachfolger, 1922), p. 175.

62. M. Grube, *Am Hofe,* pp. 75–76.

63. "Pfui, ein Stück für Nähmamsells!" (Friedrich Trinks, *Erinnerungen an Herzog Georg II.* [Saalfeld a. S.: Adolf Nieses Nachf., 1925], p. 28).

64. Voss, *Leben,* pp. 176–77.

65. Described by Gotthilf Weissstein, *Meininger Erinnerungen* (Berlin: Edmund Meyer, 1906), pp. 8–21.

66. "Ibsen und die Meininger," *Die deutsche Bühne* 1, no. 19 (December 1909): 319.

67. Franz Wallner, quoted in Eller, *Ibsen,* p. 60.

68. Eller, *Ibsen,* pp. 60–65.

69. Witkowski, *German Drama,* p. 104.

70. Voss, *Leben,* p. 168.

71. Ibid., pp. 177–78.

72. Richard Voss, "Erinnerungen an Herzog Georg von Meiningen," *Velhagen und Klasings Monatshefte* 29 (1914–15): 232–37.

73. A term of endearment meaning "little Voss;" Helene, letter to Helene Jachmann, 1 December 1894. *Fünfzig Jahre Glück und Leid* (Leipzig: Koehler und Amelang, 1926), p. 76.

74. Voss, *Leben,* pp. 298–99.

75. Heinrich Bulthaupt, *Dramaturgie des Schauspiels,* 3rd ed. (Oldenburg–Leipzig: Schulzesche Hof-Buchhandlung, 1908), 3: 246–47.

76. Karl Frenzel, *Berliner Dramaturgie* (Hannover: Carl Rümpler, 1877), 2: 135–39.

77. Max Grube, "Georg II. und Otto Ludwig," *Otto–Ludwig-Kalendar 1929* (Weimar: Hermann Böhlaus Nachfolger, 1928), pp. 47–50.

78. The first German performance of Björnson was not in spring of 1873 in Berlin, as Eller claims (p. 23). My research indicates that the first performance was six years earlier.

79. Helene, letter to Max Grube, 13 August 1920, in *Fünfzig Jahre,* p. 68.

80. Max Martersteig, *Das deutsche Theater im neunzehnten Jahrhundert,* 2nd ed. (Leipzig: Breitkopf und Härtel, 1924), p. 650.

81. Bulthaupt, *Dramaturgie* 4: 212–13, 418–19; Berthold Litzmann, *Das deutsche Drama in den literarischen Bewegungen der Gegenwart* (Hamburg and Leipzig: Leopold Voss, 1894), pp. 68–70.

82. Friedrich Rüffer, *Die Meininger und ihre Bedeutung* (Leipzig: Leopold & Bär, 1882), p. 15.

Chapter 4

1. "Mein Ingrimm ist und wird gerichtet sein, so lange ich lebe, gegen alles Frivole in der Kunst" (letter from Georg, before he had become Duke, to Carl von Stein, 1862 [no more specific date given], in Carl, Freiherr von Stein, *Die Kunst in Meiningen unter Herzog Georg II.* [Meiningen: Karl Keyssner, 1909], p. 8).

2. The full text of this letter may be found in the Appendix.

3. Paul Lindau, "Herzog Georg von Meiningen als Regisseur," *Die deutsche Bühne* 1, no. 19 (Dec. 1909): 313–318. The instructions, as compiled by Lindau, appear in aphoristic form.

4. Ernst Leopold Stahl, *Shakespeare und das deutsche Theater* (Stuttgart: W. Kohlhammer, 1947), p. 449; Josef Dischner, "Vom Meininger Theater," *Dramaturgische Beilage zur Deutschen Bühnengenossenschaft* 37, no. 40 (3 April 1908): 158.

5. *Dienst–Regeln für die Mitglieder des Herzogl. Sachsen–Meiningenschen Hoftheaters* (1880; reprint ed., Meiningen: H. Marbach, 1905), par. 36.

6. Dischner, "Theater," p. 158.

7. Karl Weiser, "10 Jahre Meiningen," *Schriften der Gesellschaft für Theatergeschichte/Archiv für Theatergeschichte,* ed. Hans Devrient (Berlin: Egon Fleischel & Co., 1904), 1: 124.

8. The local garrison was the 32nd Regiment, 2nd Thuringian Infantry, but this group of soldiers who felt it more their duty to defend the muses than the local territory was popularly known as the "Meininger Theater Regiment." Walter Lohmeyer, *Die Dramaturgie der Massen* (Berlin and Leipzig: Schuster und Loeffler, 1913), p. 250.

9. Karl Grube, *Die Meininger,* Das Theater, vol. 9 (Berlin and Leipzig: Schuster & Loeffler, 1904), pp. 30–32; Hans Knudsen, "Das Werk des Theaterherzogs," *Die Volksbühne,* 1 April 1926, 2nd sheet.

10. Max Grube, *Jugenderinnerungen eines Glückskindes* (Leipzig: Grethlein & Co, 1917), p. 198. Paul Lindau ("Herzog Georg als Regisseur," p. 318) did not mention even this one exception.

11. Ibid., pp. 199–200.

12. *Dienst–Regeln für die Mitglieder des Herzogl. Sachsen–Meiningenischen Hof–Theaters* (Meiningen: H. Marbach, 1868), pars. 17 and 22 + Addendum. Par. 22 (par. 26 in the 1880 edition) reads: "No one is relieved of playing walk–on parts. As a rule, the leading members should not have to."

13. M. Grube, *Jugenderinnerungen,* p. 347. By the end of the century the practice of referring to actors and actresses only by their full names had become general throughout Germany, following the example of the Meininger (Eugen Kilian, *Dramaturgische Blätter,* 1st series [Munich and Leipzig: Georg Müller, 1905], p. 351).

14. M. Grube, *Jugenderinnerungen,* p. 203.

15. Letter dated 27 August 1877. *Der Junge Kainz: Briefe an seine Eltern,* Arthur Eloesser, ed. (Berlin: S. Fischer, 1912), pp. 196–97.

16. Josef Nesper, "Zum 2. April 1926," *Thüringen* 2, no. 1 (April 1926): 23.

17. Hans Doerry personally inspected Grube's Meiningen contracts and found this information therein. Hans Doerry, *Das Rollenfach im deutschen Theaterbetrieb des 19. Jahrhunderts,* Diss. Erlangen 1926, Schriften der Gesellschaft für Theatergeschichte (Berlin: Selbstverlag der Gesellschaft für Theatergeschichte, 1926) 35: 124.

18. M. Grube, *Jugenderinnerungen,* pp. 197–98. Reiterated by Hartmut Gerstenhauer, "Das Meininger Hoftheater—zu seinem 125jährigen Jubiläum," *Mitteldeutsches Jahrbuch,* eds. Mitteldeutscher Kulturrat e.V., Bonn (Meisenheim am Glan: Anton Hain Verlag, 1956), pp. 81–82. Much of Gerstenhauer's article is, however, of no value, it being a plagiarism of Grube's *Geschichte der Meininger.*

19. M. Grube, *Jugenderinnerungen,* p. 212.

20. *Dienst–Regeln,* 1880, par. 33.

21. Ibid., par. 30.

22. Such lengthy rehearsals were still the practice in 1895, when Paul Lindau became director. Paul Lindau, *Nur Erinnerungen,* 2nd ed. (Stuttgart & Berlin: J. G. Cotta Nachfolger, 1916), 2: 343–44.

23. Letters dated 23 January and 1 May 1878 in *Der junge Kainz,* pp. 199 and 204–205.

24. Otto von Kurnatowski, *Georg II. von Sachsen–Meiningen und Hildburghausen* (Hildburghausen: F. W. Gadow und Sohn, 1914), pp. 83–84.

25. *Fünfzig Jahre Glück und Leid,* Johannes Werner, ed. (Leipzig: Koehler und Amelang, 1926), p. 21. Lindner's description of dinner breaks, just as Lindau's above (note 22), contradicts Grube's claim that no breaks were ever taken: "Even the longest rehearsal was never interrupted by a dinner break." Max Grube, *Geschichte der Meininger* (Stuttgart: Deutsche Verlags–Anstalt, 1926), p. 46.

26. Auguste Prasch–Grevenberg, "Unser Herzog," *Thüringen* 2, no. 1 (April 1926): 25. Kurnatowsky tells the same story, ascribing a somewhat sterner tone to the Duke's words. According to him, Georg said, "We'll try the entire act once more! I will be staying until the end of the rehearsal, standing bolt upright in the last row of seats; pull yourselves together as I do." (Kurnatowski, *Georg,* pp. 69–70).

27. "[Duke Georg] never directed, any more than Otto Brahm did; like Brahm, he was epoch–making in the history of stage direction. Ludwig Chronegk conveyed the Duke's directions to the actors . . ." (Wolfgang Drews, *Theater* [Vienna, Munich, Basel: Kurt Desch, 1961], p.124). "Georg did not direct" (Georg Laub, personal interview with author, 8 July 1976). Laub, director of the Munich Theater Museum, is the son of a Meininger actor, and was himself named after the Duke. He grew up in Meiningen, and remembers many stories about Georg and the Meininger.

28. M. Grube, *Geschichte,* p. 46.

29. Franz Wallner, Sen., "Meine Erinnerungen an Meiningen," *Volksspielkunst* 7, no. 7 (July 1926): 108.

30. Charles Waldstein, "The Court Theatre of Meiningen," *Harper's New Monthly Magazine* 82 (April 1891): 751–53. Waldstein was in attendance at an 1890 rehearsal of Schiller's *Die*

Braut von Messina. Acting as producer for the production was Paul Richard.

31. Georg Laub, interview.

32. Constantin Stanislavsky, *My Life in Art,* J. J. Robbins, trans. (Boston: Little, Brown & Co., 1938), pp. 196–201. Stanislavsky saw the Meininger in Moscow in 1885, but his description is based on information from, as he puts it, "persons who dealt with him [Chronegk] and who were present at his rehearsals."

33. *Dienst–Regeln,* 1880, par. 31.

34. Stanislavsky, *My Life,* pp. 199–200.

35. Ibid.

36. Kainz makes special mention of this in his memoirs. Helene Richter, *Kainz,* 2nd ed. (Vienna & Leipzig: F. G. Speidel'sche Verlagsbuchhandlung, 1931), p. 45.

37. Amanda Lindner, "Erinnerungen," *Thüringen* 2, no. 1 (April 1926): 20–21.

38. Robert Prölss, *Das Herzoglich Meiningen'sche Hoftheater und die Bühnenreform* (Erfurt: Fr. Bartholomäus, n.d. [1878]), pp. 24–25.

39. Lindner, "Erinnerungen," p. 20.

40. Arthur Kraussneck, "Wie ich zu den Meiningern kam," *Thüringen* 2, no. 1 (April 1926): 17–18. Kraussneck, who joined the troupe in 1880, tells an interesting story of his fear being calmed by Helene's kindness at his tryout. Even when she was disappointed in the way he read an unfamiliar role, she tried to make him feel good about his effort.

41. *Fünfzig Jahre,* p. 20.

42. Often Georg would include in his sketches facial details of the actor for whom the drawing was intended; sometimes the drawings would be in caricature (M. Grube, *Jugenderinnerungen,* p. 202).

43. M. Grube, *Geschichte,* p. 62.

44. Drews, *Theater,* pp. 124–25.

45. Luitpold Nusser, "Max Brückner," *Das Welttheater,* 1924/25, No. 3 (November): 33–35. The two Brückners remained the set painters for Georg throughout the Meininger's most famous period. Max continued painting for Georg until 1912, when he had to retire due to failing eyesight. At that time Georg honored his work with the words: "There will never be another Max Brückner." Georg had earlier given him the honorary titles of "Professor" and "Privy Councilor."

    Grube's assertion that Gotthold died young *(Geschichte,* p. 63) is erroneous, for he did not die until 1892. Gotthold, whom Georg also named "Professor," was seriously wounded in a hunting accident in November 1884, at which time he was forced to give up painting. Louis Walter, "Gotthold Brückner, ein Coburger Künstler," *Aus der Heimat. Wochenbeilage zu den Heimatglocken,* 1 Feb. 1931 and 8 Feb. 1931, n. pag. See also: Fritz Mahnke, "Theaterfamilie Brückner," in *150 Jahre Coburger Landestheater,* Festschrift, Coburg: Landestheater, 1977.

46. Letter from Georg to Max Brückner, 24 January 1875, quoted in (first name not given) Peters–Marquardt, "Zum 100jährigen Geburtstage Max Brückners," *Coburger Heimatblätter,* No. 14 (June 1936): 81.

47. Dischner, "Theater," p. 157.

48. Reported to Max von Boehn by Max Grube. Max von Boehn, *Das Bühnenkostüm in Altertum, Mittelalter, und Neuzeit* (Berlin: Bruno Cassirer, 1921), p. 438. *Macbeth* was, incidentally, performed only ten times by the Meininger.

49. Max Grube, "Die Magenfrage auf der Bühne," *Neue Freie Presse* (Vienna), no. 14,269 (16 May 1904), unpaginated. He also mentions that the scene was not helped by the partial deafness of Otto Lehfeld, who was in the role of Othello. Either everyone was silent or all began to speak at once.

50. Eugen Isolani, "Herzog Georg von Meiningen," *Deutsches Bühnen–Jahrbuch* 26 (1915): 62.

51. Reported in Oscar Blumenthal, *Theatralische Eindrücke* (Berlin: A. Hofmann & Comp., 1885), p. 334. The Meininger presented *Maria Stuart* in Berlin nine times between August 31 and October 12, 1884.

52. K. Grube, *Meininger,* p. 46.

53. Rudolph K. Goldschmidt, *Eduard Devrients Bühnenreform am Karlsruher Hoftheater,* Theatergeschichtliche Forschungen, vol. 32 (Leipzig: Leopold Voss, 1921), p. 83.

54. Robert Prölss, *Das Herzoglich–Meiningen'sche Hoftheater, seine Entwicklung, seine Bestrebungen und die Bedeutung seiner Gastspiele* (Leipzig: F. Conrad, 1887), p. 23.

55. In his letters, Kainz mentions being called out by the audience several times: after one scene in *Die Räuber* (2 May 1878), twice a day during *Die Räuber* (7 May 1878), fifteen times during *Prinz Friedrich von Homburg* (12 May 1878), and four to six times after each act of *Twelfth Night* (19 November 1878). Kainz was young when he wrote these letters, and perhaps he exaggerated his popularity somewhat in them.

56. *Dienst–Regeln,* 1880, par. 60.

57. Max Grube, *Am Hofe der Kunst* (Leipzig: Grethlein & Co., 1918), p. 91.

58. Ibid., p. 92.

59. Told by Herbert Eulenberg, "Der Theaterherzog: 1826–1914," in *Der Guckkasten: Deutsche Schauspielbilder* (Stuttgart: J. Engelhorns Nachf., 1922), pp. 242–47. Eulenberg reports the story seriously as theater history.

60. The results of Wolff's survey are reported in "Rhabarber," *Der Neue Weg* 55, no. 8 (16 August 1926): 274. Therein, Grube contradicts his earlier descriptions of Georg's attention to backstage noises by saying: "[the Meininger] placed absolutely no value on noises behind the scenes." See also Max Grube, "Kleine Erinnerungen an einen grossen Künstlerfürsten," in *Im Theaterland* (Berlin: A. Hofmann & Comp., 1908), p. 201, and Grube, *Am Hofe,* pp. 91–92.

    Hugo Thimig of Vienna was able to tell Wolff whence *Rhabarber* came. The use of the word was instigated by an actor named Ferdinand Kracher at the Burgtheater, who as a joke "gurgled" the word backstage during a rehearsal. His fellow actors liked the sound so much that they adopted it.

61. Lohmeyer, *Dramaturgie,* p. 249.

62. In German, *äussere Regie* or *Rahmen–Regie.* Its opposite is inward direction— *innere Regie* or *Text–Regie.* Outward direction refers to everything that forms the framework for

the play itself, everything that creates a mood in the audience. The term originated in Adolf Winds, *Geschichte der Regie* (Stuttgart, Berlin & Leipzig: Deutsche Verlagsanstalt, 1925), pp. i ff., and has been used by others, such as Alfred Kruchen, *Das Regieprinzip bei den Meiningern zur Zeit ihrer Gastspielepoche,* Diss. Danzig 1933 (Danzig: A. W. Kafemann, 1933), pp. 32–74.

63. Paul Lindau, "Wintermärchen," *Dramaturgische Blätter, Neue Folge: 1875–1878* (Breslau: S. Schottlaender, 1879), 2: 137–47.

64. "This, my dear sir, is most assuredly not the intent of my efforts, although I do not wish to deny that it matters to me in which bowl a golden fruit is offered. I also do not want to claim that I never make a mistake about how far one may go in terms of scenery; views about this point are, of course, quite subjective! However, I can assure you that the painterly, the scenery, is never the main focus when dealing with a play. On the contrary, such a concentration on the outward elements would find in me a most worthy opponent" (letter from Georg to Paul Lindau, 23 October 1879, in Lindau, *Nur Erinnerungen,* 2: 332).

65. "Gehet heim, dienet dem Staate, werdet nützliche Bürger" (Karl Zeiss, "Die Bühnenreform der Meininger," *Neuphilologische Blätter* 2, no. 3 [20 December 1894]: 50).

66. These "Meininger editions" have become extremely rare. In thirty volumes, with two publishers, the collection was entitled *Repertoire des herzoglich Meiningen'schen Hoftheaters, officielle Ausgabe nach dem Scenarium des Herzogl. Sachsen–Meiningen'schen Hoftheaters bearbeitet,* R. von Grumbkow, ed. (Dresden: Hof-Verlagsbuchhandlung, 1879 ff.; Leipzig: Friedrich Conrad, n.d.). Volume titles may be found in the Appendix.

A discussion of the Meininger version of *The Merchant of Venice,* which serves as an example of Georg's work in textual revision and staging, is found in Wolfgang Iser, "Der Kaufmann von Venedig auf der Illusionsbühne der Meininger," *Shakespeare Jahrbuch* 99 (1963): 72–94.

67. The title page of this version read: *Die Räuber, ein Trauerspiel* von Friedrich Schiller. Neue für die Mannheimer Bühne verbesserte Auflage. Mannheim, in der schwanischen Buchhandlung, 1782.

68. Heinrich Bulthaupt, "Die Räuber," in *Dramaturgie des Schauspiels,* vol. 1, 10th ed. (Oldenburg–Leipzig: Schulzesche Hof–Buchhandlung und Hof–Buchdruckerei, 1905): 254–55.

69. Vol. 8 of the Meininger *Repertoire* was not available for consultation. The reconstruction is based on scenes mentioned in Bulthaupt, "Die Räuber," and in a review by Paul Lindau, "Die Räuber," in *Dramaturgische Blätter, neue Folge: 1875–1878,* (Breslau: S. Schottlaender, 1879), 2: 14–16. In the reconstruction listed, prefix m refers to passages taken from the *Mannheimer Bühnenbearbeitungen;* prefix d, from the *Druckausgabe.*

Editions used:
Druckausgabe: *Schillers sämtliche Werke in zehn Bänden* (Stuttgart and Tübingen: J. G. Cotta'scher Verlag, 1844), 2: 1–140. *Bühnenbearbeitung:* Friedrich Schiller, *Die Räuber,* Walter Hess, ed., Rowohlts Klassiker der Literatur und der Wissenschaft: Deutsche Literatur 15 (n.p.: Rowohlt, 1965): 145–186.

70. Bulthaupt, "Räuber," 1: 283–84; M. Grube, *Geschichte,* pp. 85–89.

71. Based on Lindau, *Blätter* 2: 44–45; and M. Grube, *Geschichte,* pp. 90–91.

72. "The Duke's meritorious service is the reawakening of the classical authors . . ." (Georg Altmann, *Heinrich Laubes Prinzip der Theaterleitung,* Diss. Jena 1908, Schriften der literaturhistorischen Gesellschaft Bonn, vol. 5 [Dortmund: Fr. Wilh. Ruhfus, 1908]: 77). "The propagation of Shakespeare throughout the entire European world was completed with the deeds of the Meininger" (Stahl, *Shakespeare,* p. 444).

　　Of the 41 plays presented in 2887 performances on tour, 9 were by Schiller (1250 performances), 3 by Kleist (222 performances), 2 by Grillparzer (153 performances), 1 by Goethe (14 performances), and 1 by Lessing (7 performances). Shakespeare was represented by 6 plays (820 performances); Molière, by 2 (112 performances); and Lord Byron, by 1 (19 performances).

73. Stahl, *Shakespeare,* pp. 458–59.

74. "Ich ärgerte mich, dass in Deutschland Shakespeare so schlecht gespielt wurde" (M. Grube, "Kleine Erinnerungen," p. 180).

75. "Unser Hauptzug bestand darin, dass unsere Vorstellungen die richtige Stimmung im Zuschauer erzeugten" (Aloys Prasch, "Erinnerungen eines ehemaligen Meiningers," *Bühne und Welt* 1, no. 15 [June 1899]: 697). The author quotes Georg directly.

76. Walter Bormann, "Reformen und Reformbestrebungen der deutschen Bühne im letzten Jahrhundert," *Deutsches Theaterjahrbuch* (Berlin: Cassirer und Danziger, 1892), pp. 16–17.

77. Isolani, "Herzog Georg," pp. 62–63.

78. Max Kurnik, *Ein Menschenalter: Theater Erinnerungen 1845–1880,* 2nd ed. (Berlin: Otto Janke, 1883), pp. 326–28.

79. Hans Herrig, *Die Meininger, ihre Gastspiele und deren Bedeutung für das deutsche Theater* (Dresden: R. von Grumbkow Hofverlagbuchhandlung, 1880 and 1881 [both dates in imprint]), pp. 24–30, 32.

80. Thomas Hahm has discussed the critical reaction to the Meininger in Berlin during their tours of 1874, –75, –76, –78, –82, –84, and –87; and in Vienna during 1875, –79, and –83. Thomas Hahm, *Die Gastspiele des Meininger Hoftheaters im Urteil der Zeitgenossen,* Diss. Cologne, 1970. De Leeuwe has done the same, but more thoroughly, for the 1880 visit to Amsterdam and the 1888 Rotterdam visit. H. H. J. de Leeuwe, *Meiningen en Nederland. Proeve van vergelijkende Toneelgeschiedenis,* Studia Litteraria Rheno–Traiectina, vol. 6 (Groningen: J. B. Wolters, 1959). Muriel St. Claire Byrne has discussed London reviews of the Meininger visit during 1881, but her article seems based on the premise that if the Meininger had done anything well, it would reflect negatively on the English stage. Muriel St. Claire Byrne, "What We Said about the Meiningers in 1881" in *Essays and Studies 1965* (London: John Murray, 1965), pp. 45–72.

81. Karl Frenzel, *Berliner Dramaturgie* (Hannover: Carl Rümpler, 1877), 2: 109–114.

82. The earliest review of a Meininger performance was Wilhelm Oechelhäuser's 1868 discussion of their Shakespeare performances. His comments, as well as those Karl Frenzel made during his 1870 visit to Meiningen, were discussed in chapter 2 and will not be mentioned further here.

83. Frenzel, *Dramaturgie* 2: 112.

84. Ibid.

85. Paul Lindau, "Aus der Haupstadt. Gesammtgastpiel der Meininger Hofschauspieler," *Die Gegenwart* 5, No. 19 (9 May 1874): 301–02.

86. Frenzel, *Dramaturgie* 2: 118–19.

87. Paul Lindau, "Aus der Hauptstadt. Dramatische Aufführungen. 'Pabst Sixtus V,' " *Die Gegenwart,* 5, No. 21 (23 May 1874): 331–33.

88. Frenzel, *Dramaturgie* 2: 121–25.

89. Paul Lindau, "Aus der Hauptstadt. Dramatische Aufführungen." *Die Gegenwart* 5, no. 22 (30 May 1874): 349–51.

90. Ibid. p. 351.

91. Frenzel, *Dramaturgie* 2: 125–26.

92. M.v. Szesiski, "Aus der Hauptstadt. Dramatische Aufführungen. Das Gastspiel der Meininger," *Die Gegenwart* 5, no. 25 (20 June 1874): 396–98.

93. Frenzel, *Dramaturgie* 2: 128–30.

94. Szesiski, "Hauptstadt," p. 398.

95. Hans Hopfen, "Die Meininger in Berlin," *Streitfragen und Erinnerungen* (Stuttgart: J. G. Gotha, 1876), pp. 239–51.

96. Ibid.

97. Reviews examined include: Paul Lindau, "Aus der Hauptstadt," *Die Gegenwart* 7, no. 17 (24 April 1875): 265–68; no. 19 (8 May 1875): 299–302; no. 20 (15 May 1875): 316–18. F. H. Kugler, "Aus der Hauptstadt," *Die Gegenwart* 7, no. 24 (24 June 1875): 381. "Das Gastspiel der Meininger," *Pester Lloyd* (Budapest) 22, no. 254 (4 Nov. 1875): 2–3; no. 257 (7 Nov. 1875): 2–3; no. 259 (10 Nov. 1875): 2–3; no. 264 (Beilage) (16 Nov. 1875): 1; no. 268 (20 Nov. 1875): 3 and Beilage, p. 1. Ludwig Speidel, "Die Meininger in Wien," in *Schauspieler,* Ludwig Speidels Schriften, 4 (Berlin: Meyer & Jessen, 1911): 47–62. Rudolf Génee, "Das Gastspiel der Meininger in Berlin," *Deutsche Rundschau* 1, no. 9 (June 1875): 457–63.

98. Lindau, *Blätter,* 2: 34–37.

99. Theodor Fontane, *Plaudereien über Theater* (Berlin: G. Grote'sche Verlagsbuchhandlung, 1926), pp. 35, 91–92, 257–58.

100. Ibid., p. 35.

101. Reviews examined include: Karl Frenzel, "Berliner Chronik," *Deutsche Rundschau* 3 (1876): 151–55; Frenzel, *Berliner Dramaturgie* (Hannover: Carl Rümpler, 1877), pp. 130–35, 135–39, 139–44, 144–51, 151–56; Lindau, *Blätter* 2: 14–25, 41–47, 129, 137–47; Frenzel, "Das Gastspiel der Gesellschaft des Meiningen'schen Hoftheaters," *Deutsche Rundschau* 16 (1878): 145–52; H. Jacoby, *Die Meininger in Leipzig. Seperat–Abdruck aus dem "Grenzboten" 1878, Nr. 44 & 47* (Leipzig: Friedrich Ludwig Herbig, 1878), pp. 4–21; "Theater und Kunst. Deutsches Theater in der Wollgasse," *Pester Lloyd* (Budapest), no. 342 (Beilage) (13 Dec. 1879): 1; "Drama," *The Athenaeum* (London), no. 2797 (4 June 1881): 762, no. 2798 (11 June 1881): 796, no. 2799 (18 June 2881): 826, no. 2800 (25 June 1881): 858, no. 2801 (2 July 1881): 25, no. 2802 (9 July 1881): 58, no. 2804 (23 July 1881):

123; "The Meiningen Company and the London Stage," *Blackwood's Edinburgh Magazine* 130, no. 790 (July–Dec. 1881): 248–63; H. Schütz Wilson, "Our Play–Box. Die Meininger," *Theatre,* 4, n.s. (July–Dec. 1881): 102–05; "The Meiningen Court Company," *The Times* (London) 7 July 1881; Otto Brahm, "Meininger: Wallenstein," *Vossische Zeitung* (Berlin), 25 April 1882; "Meininger: Julius Cäsar," *Vossische Zeitung,* 25 May 1882; "Die Jungfrau von Orleans der Meininger," *Die Nation,* 5 Feb. 1887.

102. N. H. W., "Kunstreis der Meiningers in ons Land," *Het Leven,* (Amsterdam) 1, no. 10 (27 April 1906): 314.

103. "Die Künstler sind nichts, sondern nur die Kunst hat Wert, das heisst, nur der Künstler verdient Unterstützung, der die Kunst als solche fördert zum Frommen der Menschheit. Der andere Künstler aber, der mit Leichtsinn an die Kunst tritt und dieselbe dazu gebraucht, die Menschen zu betören, dem gebührt, dass man ihn bekriege und unschädlich mache" (letter, Georg to Karl von Stein, in Stein, *Kunst,* p. 8).

Appendix A

1. Adapted by Wilbrant.

2. Translated by Vost.

3. Translated by Schlegel.

4. There are two programs listed for February 14, 1867.

5. Initial production

6. Performance for the benefit of the town's poor.

7. Performance in honor of Goethe's birthday.

8. Adapted by Wilbrandt.

9. Adapted by Wilbrandt.

10. Adapted by Wilbrandt.

11. Translated by Schlegel and Bodenstedt.

12. Translated by Bodenstedt.

13. Translated by Gries.

14. Program change due to the illness of Ellen Franz.

15. adapted by Bodenstedt; translated by Schlegel.

16. Translated by Schlegel.

17. Shortened version.

18. Translated by Schlegel.

19. Adapted by Wilbrant.

20. Opera by Gounod. Balcony scene, parting scene, and Juliet's dream.

21. Translated by Dingelstedt.

22. Translated by Lindner.

23. Translated by Rossmann.

24. There are two programs listed for November 23, 1868.

25. Adapted by Bodenstedt.

26. Translated by Schlegel.

27. Translated by Schlegel.

28. Adapted by Herrmann.

29. Duke Bernhard's birthday.

30. With the opera staff of the Court Theater of Saxe-Coburg Gotha.

31. Translated by Tieck and Schlegel.

32. Adapted by Deinhardtstein.

33. Adapted by Schlegel.

34. There are two programs listed for November 24, 1874.

35. In honor of Duke Bernhard's birthday celebration.

36. In honor of the golden anniversary of Bernhard and Marie.

37. Georg's birthday.

38. Bernhard's birthday.

39. Premiere performance; adapted by Adolf Strodtmann.

40. Georg's birthday.

41. Georg's birthday.

42. In honor of the birthday celebration of his majesty, Duke Bernhard.

43. For the benefit of the Widows' and Orphans' Relief Fund.

44. In celebration of C. v. Holtei's eightieth birthday.

45. For the benefit of the German Theatrical Guild.

46. For the birthday celebration of his Majesty, Duke George II.

Bibliography

A. Works with Author Given:

Allers, Christian Wilhelm. *Die Meininger, (Zeichnungen) mit einem Vorwort von Aloys Prasch.* Hamburg: Dahlström, 1890.

———. "Die Meininger." *Die Gartenlaube* 38 (1890): 716–19.

Altmann, Georg. *Heinrich Laubes Prinzip der Theaterleitung: Ein Beitrag zur Ästhetik der dramatischen Kunst im XIX. Jahrhundert.* Schriften der Literatur-Gesellschaft Bonn, Vol 5. Dortmund: Fr. Ruhfus, 1908.

Archer, William. *Study and Stage: A Year–Book of Criticism.* London: Grant Richards, 1899.

Arnold, Robert F. *Bibliographie der deutschen Bühnen seit 1830.* Vienna: C. W. Stern, 1908.

———. *Das Deutsche Drama.* Munich: C. H. Beck'sche Verlags-Buchhandlung, 1925.

———. *Das moderne Drama.* Strassbourg: Karl J. Trübner, 1908.

Bab, Julius. *Das Theater der Gegenwart: Geschichte der dramatischen Bühne seit 1870.* Leipzig: J. J. Weber, 1928.

Bamberg, Eduard von. *Otto Lehfeld, ein Erinnerungsblatt für seine Freunde.* Halle a. d. Saale: Beyer und Ronnger, 1886.

Barnay, Ludwig. "Bei den Meiningern hinter den Coulissen." *Heimatgarten* 6 (February 1882).

———. *Erinnerungen.* Berlin: Egon Fleischel und Co., 1903.

———. "Mein Debut in Meiningen." *Bühne und Welt* 8 (1906): 584–86.

———. "Die Meininger in London." *Die Deutsche Bühne* 1 (1909): 325–26.

———. "Mit den Meiningern in London. Erinnerungen." *Bühne und Welt* 6 (1903): 12–17.

Bartmann, H. "Die Entwicklung der deutschen Theaterfreiheit." *Masken* 4: 19.

Bechstein, R. "Jubiläum des Meiningen'er Hoftheaters." *Wissenschaftliche Beilage zur Leipziger Zeitung,* 1882, p. 49.

Behlert, Karl. *Das Herzogliche Hoftheater in Meiningen. Denkschrift zur Eröffnung am 17. Dez. 1909.* Meiningen: Junghanss & Koritzer, 1909.

Bergmann, Ernst. *Der Geist des XIX. Jahrhunderts.* Breslau: Ferdinand Hirt, 1927.

Berlin. Theaterhistorische Samlung Walter Unruh. "148 Kostüm–Entwürfe (Originale) des Herzogs Georg II von Sachsen–Meiningen 1874 bis 1878. Die Kostüme sind unter meiner personlichen Leitung ausgeführt" [by Ludwig Raupp].

Bernstein, A. "Persönliche Erinnerungen." *Vossische Zeitung* (Berlin), 26 June 1914.

Berthold, Margot. *Weltgeschichte des Theaters.* Stuttgart: Alfred Kröner, 1968.

Bessel, L. v. "Unveröffentlichte Briefe des Theaterherzogs." *Kölnische Zeitung* (Cologne), 25/26 May 1934.

Bloem, Walter. *Komödiantinnen.* Berlin & Vienna: Ullstein & Co., 1914. (a novel featuring the Meininger)

Blumenthal, Oscar. *Theatralische Eindrücke.* Berlin: A. Hofmann & Comp., 1885.

Boehn, Max von. *Das Bühnenkostüm in Altertum, Mittelalter und Neuzeit.* Berlin: Bruno Cassirer, 1921.

Bormann, Walter. "Das deutsche Theater und die Meininger." *Die Gartenlaube* 27 (1879): 234–238.

————. "Reformen und Reformbestrebungen der deutschen Bühne im letzten Jahrzehnt." *Deutsches Theaterjahrbuch,* ed. Karl Biesendahl. Berlin: Cassirer und Danziger, 1892.

Bourlier, George. *Almanach des Herz. S.–Meiningen'schen Hoftheaters. Saison 1877–1878.* Meiningen: H. Marbach, 1878.

————. *Almanach des Herzogl. Sachsen–Meiningen'schen Hoftheaters. Saison 1880–81.* Meiningen: H. Marbach, 1881.

Brahm, Otto. "Grillparzer: Die Ahnfrau (Meininger)." *Vossische Zeitung* (Berlin), 15 October 1882.

————. "Heinrich v. Kleist: Die Hermannsschlacht (Meininger)." *Vossische Zeitung* (Berlin), 14 October 1882.

————. *Kritische Schriften über Drama und Theater,* vol. 1. Berlin: S. Fischer Verlag, 1913.

————. "Künstlerische Sendungen. Bei Gelegenheit der Meininger." *Die Freie Bühne* 1 (1890): 804–6.

————. "Die Jungfrau von Orleans der Meininger." *Nation,* 5 February 1887.

————. "Lessing: Miss Sara Sampson (Meininger)." *Vossische Zeitung* (Berlin), 3 October 1884.

————. "Maria Stuart (Meininger)." *Vossische Zeitung* (Berlin), 2 September 1884.

————. "Meininger: Julius Cäsar." *Vossische Zeitung* (Berlin), 25 May 1882.

————. "Schiller: Fiesko (Meininger)." *Vossische Zeitung* (Berlin), 30 September 1882.

————. "Schiller: Tell (Meininger)." *Vossische Zeitung* (Berlin), 15 September 1882.

————. "Schiller: Wallenstein (Meininger)." *Vossische Zeitung* (Berlin), 25 April 1882.

————. "Shakespeare: Ein Wintermärchen (Meininger)." *Vossische Zeitung* (Berlin), 22 September 1882.

————. "Wolff: Preziosa (Meininger)." *Vossische Zeitung* (Berlin), 9 September 1882.

Brand, Wilhelm F. "The Meiningen Actors and Their Visit to London." *The Theatre: A Monthly Review of the Drama, Music, and the Fine Arts* 3, n.s. (1881): 328.

Braun, Julie. *Almanach des herzoglichen Sachsen–Meiningen'schen Hoftheaters. Saison 1883.* Meiningen: Dr. H. Marbach, 1883.

Brockett, Oscar G. *History of the Theatre.* 2nd ed. Boston, London, and Sydney: Allyn and Bacon, Inc., 1974.

————. *The Theatre: An Introduction.* 3rd ed. New York: Holt, Rinehart & Winston, Inc., 1974.

Bulthaupt, Heinrich. *Dramaturgie des Schauspiels.* Oldenburg–Leipzig: Schulzesche Hof–Buchhandlung und Hof–Buchdruckerei, vol. 1, 10th ed., 1905; vol. 2, 9th ed., 1907; vol. 3, 8th ed., 1908; vol. 4, 4th ed., 1905.

Byrne, Muriel St. Claire. "Charles Kean and the Meininger Myth." *Theatre Research/Recherches Thèâtrales* 4 (1964): 137–53.

————. "What We Said about the Meiningers in 1881." In *Essays and Studies 1965. Being volume eighteen of the new series of essays and studies collected for the English Association by Sybil Rosenfeld.* London: John Murray, 1965, pp. 45–72.

Calm, Hans. *Kulturbilder aus der deutschen Theatergeschichte.* Leipzig: Koehler und Amelang, 1925.

C. E. S. "Ludwig Barnay of the Meiningen Court Company." *The Theatre: A Monthly Review of the Drama, Music, and the Fine Arts* 3, n.s. (1881): 344–46.

Chronegk, Ludwig. Letter to Professors Brückner. 15 November 1886. Georgs Nachlass. Institut für Theaterwissenschaft der Universität Köln (Cologne Theater Museum).

_____. Letter to Professors Brückner. 13 December 1886. Georgs Nachlass. Institut für Theaterwissenschaft der Universität Köln (Cologne Theater Museum).

_____. Telegram to Professors Brückner. 18 December 1886. Georgs Nachlass. Institut für Theaterwissenschaft der Universität Köln (Cologne Theater Museum).

Clark, Barrett H. and George Freedly. *A History of Modern Drama.* New York and London: D. Appleton–Century, Inc., 1947.

Cole, Toby, and Helen Krich Chinoy. *Directing the Play. A Source Book of Stagecraft.* Indianapolis: Bobbs–Merrill, 1953.

Davies, Hugh Sykes. *Realism in the Drama.* Cambridge: University Press, 1934.

DeHart, Steven A. "The History and Legacy of Georg II. von Sachsen–Meiningen and His Theater." Ph.D. dissertation, Johns Hopkins University, 1979.

Devrient, Eduard. *Geschichte der deutschen Schauspielkunst. Neubearbeitet und bis in die Gegenwart fortgeführt als "Illustrierte deutsche Theatergeschichte" von W. Stuhlfeld.* Zurich: Eigenbrödler Verlag, 1929.

Dietrich, Felix. "Bibliographie der deutschen Zeitschriftenliteratur." *Daheim* 50, No. 40.

Dinger, Hugo. "Meiningen." *Die Schaubühne* 6, (1910): 16–19.

_____. "Zum 2. April 1906." *Deutscher Bühnen–Genossenschaft. Amtliche Zeitung der Genossenschaft Deutscher Bühnen–Angehörigen* 35 (1906): 117–119, 129–131.

Dischner, Josef. (Untitled article) *Neuer Theateralmanach* 20 (1909): 120.

_____. "Vom Meininger Theater." Dramaturgische Beilage zur *Deutschen Bühnen–Genossenschaft* 37 (1908): 157–158.

Doerry, Hans. *Das Rollenfach im deutschen Theaterbetrieb des 19. Jahrhunderts.* Schriften der Gesellschaft für Theatergeschichte, vol. 35. Berlin: Selbstverlag der Gesellschaft für Theatergeschichte, 1926.

Drach, M. "Erinnerungen an die Meininger." *Berliner Lokal–Anzeiger,* 11 March 1905.

Drews, Wolfgang. *Die Grossen des deutschen Schauspiels.* Berlin: Deutscher Verlag, 1941.

_____. *Theater.* Vienna, Munich, Basel: Kurt Desch, 1961.

Düsel, Friedrich. "Dramatisch Rundschau. Vom Gastspiel des Moskauer Künstlerischen Theaters. Zum achtzigsten Geburtstage des Herzogs von Meiningen." *Westermanns Monatshefte,* May 1906, pp. 291–296.

Eckelmann, Christian. *Vom Nachtwächter zur Bühne. Tatsachenbericht.* Berlin: Voco–Verlag, 1942.

Edwards, Christine. *The Stanislavsky Heritage. Its Contribution to the Russian and American Theatre.* New York: New York University Press, 1965.

Ehrlich, Moriz. *Das Gastspiel der Meininger oder die Grenzen der Bühnenausstattung. Ein freundschaftliches Gespräch.* Berlin: Mitscher und Röstell, 1874.

E. K. [Emil Knechke] "Das Meininger Hoftheater und seine Mitglieder." *Illustrierte Zeitung* (Leipzig), 20 April 1878, pp. 311, 314.

Eller, William Henri. *Ibsen in Germany 1870–1900.* Boston: Richard G. Badger, 1918.

Eloesser, Arthur, ed. *Der junge Kainz: Briefe an seine Eltern.* Berlin: S. Fischer, 1912.

Emmel, Felix. *Das Ekstatische Theater.* Prien, n.p., 1924.

Engel, Fr. "Der Tag von Meiningen." *Berliner Tageblatt,* No. 632 (1909).

Eulenberg, Herbert. *Mein Leben für die Bühne.* Berlin: Bruno Cassirer, 1919.

———. "Der Theaterherzog, 1826–1914." *Der Guckkasten. Deutsche Schauspielbilder.* Stuttgart: J. Englehorns Nachf., 1922.

Feigenspan, Bruno. *Thüringer Warte,* 12 March 1906, pp. 536–543.

Fontane, Theodor. *Plaudereien über Theater.* Berlin: G. Grote'sche Verlagsbuchhandlung, 1939.

Frenzel, Karl. "Berliner Chronik." *Deutsche Rundschau* 3 (1876): 151–155.

———. *Berliner Dramaturgie.* Hannover: Carl Rümpler, 1877.

———. "Das Gastspiel der Gesellschaft des Meiningen'schen Hoftheaters." *Deutsche Rundschau* 16 (1878): 145–152.

———. "Der Herzog von Meiningen." *National Zeitung* (Berlin), Feuilleton, 1870.

———. "Wie ich zu den Meiningern kam." *Bühne und Welt* 1 (1899): 687–690.

Frenzel, Karl W. T. *Die Wandegemälde Wilhelm von Kaulbachs im Treppenhaus des neuen Museums in Berlin.* Berlin: Schauer, 1870.

Friedmann, Siegward. "Das erste Gastspiel in Meiningen." *Die Deutsche Bühne* 1 (1909): 329–331.

———. "Die Gastspiele der Meininger in Leipzig." *Leipziger Illustrierte Zeitung.*

Friedrich, L. "Das echte auf der Bühne." *National Zeitung* (Berlin), No. 30 (July 1905).

Fritsch, Paul. *Influence du théâtre français sur le théâtre allemand de 1870 jusqu'aux approches de 1900.* Diss. Paris, 1912. Paris: Jouve & Cie., Editeurs, 1912.

Fuchs, Georg. *Die Revolution des Theaters. Ergebnisse aus dem Münchner Künstler-Theater.* Munich & Leipzig: Georg Müller, 1909.

Fulda, Carl. *Die dramatische Kunst auf der deutschen Bühne: Festrede zu Goethes 127. Geburtstag im Freien Deutschen Hochstifte für Wissenschaften, Künste und allgemeine Bildung.* Frankfurt am Main: Verlag des freien Deutschen Hochstiftes, 1877.

Garten, Hugh Frederic. *Modern German Drama.* London: Methuen, 1959.

Gassner, John. *Masters of the Drama.* New York: Random House, 1940.

Geisshörner. "Georg II., Herzog von Meiningen." *Illustriertes Musik und Theater Journal,* 1875.

———. "Mit den Meiningern kreuz und quer durch Europa, aus den Errinerungen des Theater-Garderobiers Geisshörners." *Meininger Heimatklänge,* December 1934.

Genée, Rudolph. "Das deutsche Theater und die Reform Frage." *Deutsche Zeit- und Streit-Fragen* 7 (1878).

———. *Die Entwicklung des szenischen Theaters und die Bühnenreform in München.* Stuttgart: J. G. Cotta, 1889.

———. "Das Gastspiel der Meininger in Berlin." *Deutsche Rundschau* 1 (1875): 457–463.

Georg II., Herzog von Sachsen-Meiningen. "Aus Briefen des Herzogs Georg." *Die Deutsche Bühne* 1 (1909): 323.

———. Letter to Direktion des Theaters in Meiningen. 25 November 1912. Theatersammlung. Österreichische Nationalbibliothek (Austrian National Library Theater Collection).

———. Diplom anlässlich der Verleihung des Ritterkreuzes II. Klasse an Josef Kainz. Theatersammlung. Österreichische Nationalbibliothek (Austrian National Library Theater Collection).

———. Letter to Gebrüder Brückner. 15 November 1886. Institut für Theaterwissenschaft der Universität Köln (Cologne Theater Museum).

George, David E. R. *Henrik Ibsen in Deutschland. Rezeption und Revision.* Palaestra, vol. 251. Göttingen: Vandenhoeck & Ruprecht, 1968.

Gerstenhauer, Hartmut. "Das Meininger Hoftheater—zu seinem 125 jährigen Jubiläum." *Mitteldeutsches Jahrbuch,* 1956, pp. 75–87.

GFHe. "Die Meininger." *Kölnische Zeitung* (Cologne), No. 658, 1942; No. 4, 1943.

Gilder, Rosamund and Georg Freedley. *Theatre Collections in Libraries and Museums. An International Handbook.* London: B. F. Stevens and Brown, Ltd., 1936.

Glaser, Adolf. "Das Meininger Hoftheater." *Westermanns Jahrbuch der Illustrirten Deutschen Monatshefte* 36 (1874): 593–597.

Goldschmit, Rudolph K. *Eduard Devrients Bühnenreform am Karlsruher Hoftheater.* Theatergeschichtliche Forschungen edited by Berthold Litzmann, vol. 32. Leipzig: Leopold Voss, 1921.

Grans, Heinrich. *Fünfzehn Jahre in Weimar. Erlebtes und Erlittenes.* Leipzig: Otto Spamer, 1889.

Gregor, Josef. *Weltgeschichte des Theaters.* Zurich: Phaldon, 1933.

Gregori, Ferdinand. "Georg von Meiningen." *Kunstwart und Kulturwart* 27 (1914): 129–131.

Greiner, Wilhelm. *Georg II von Meiningen und die Freifrau, ein Erinnerungsblatt zum 25. Todestag des Herzogs und zum 100. Geburtstag der Freifrau.* Grüne Herzbücherei, edited by Julius Kober. Gotha: Englehard–Keyher, 1939.

Grube, Karl. "Herzog Georg von Meiningen und das deutsche Schauspiel." *Bühne und Welt* 16, (1914): 455–458.

―――. "Ein Künstler auf dem Herzogthron." Weltrundschau, Beilage zum *Universum,* 1914, p. 283.

―――. *Die Meininger.* Das Theater, vol. 9. Berlin and Leipzig: Schuster & Loeffler, 1904.

Grube, Max. *Am Hofe der Kunst.* Leipzig: Grethlein und Co., 1918.

―――. "Aus dem Tierleben des Theaters." *Velhagen und Klasings Monatshefte* 23 (1909): 347–350.

―――. "Georg II. als Landschafter." *Thüringen; Eine Monatsschrift für alte und neue Kultur* 2(1926): 5–7.

―――. "Georg II und Otto Ludwig." *Otto–Ludwig–Kalendar 1929: Jahrbuch des Otto–Ludwig–Vereins* 1 (1928): 47–50.

―――. *Geschichte der Meininger.* Stuttgart, Berlin and Leipzig: Deutsche Verlags–Anstalt, 1926.

―――. "Heil, Herzog Georg." *Bühne und Welt* 8 (1906): 573–574.

―――. *Jugenderinnerungen eines Glückskindes.* Leipzig: Grethlein und Co., 1917.

―――. "Kleine Erinnerungen an einen grossen Künstlerfürsten." *Im Theaterland.* Berlin: A. Hoffman & Comp., 1908.

―――. "Die Magenfrage auf der Bühne." *Neue Freie Presse* (Vienna), 16 May 1904.

―――. "Meininer Kunst." *Die Woche* 11 (1909): 2113–2115.

―――. "Meiningertum und Meiningerei." *Die Deutsche Bühne* 1 (1909): 319–323.

―――. *Oh Theater!* Leipzig & Zurich: Grethlein & Co., 1921. (novel)

―――. *Spemanns goldenes Buch des Theaters. Eine Hauskunde für Jedermann. Herausgegeben unter Mitwirkung von R. Genee, M. Grube, Robert Hessen, P. Lindau, V. Ottman, E. v. Possart, G. Weissstein, E. Zabel u.a.* Berlin & Stuttgart: W. Spemann, 1902.

―――. "Von Meininger Art und Kunst." *Bühne und Welt* 8 (1906): 573–583.

―――. "Von Meininger Art und Kunst." *Der Neune Weg* 55, (1926): 126–127.

von Grumbkow, R., ed. *Repertoire des herzoglich Meiningen'schen Hoftheaters, officielle Ausgabe nach dem Scenarium des Herzogl. Sachsen–Meiningen'schen Hoftheaters bearbeitet.* Dresden: Hof–Verlagsbuchhandlung, 1879ff.

Günther, Max Hermann. *Die soziologischen Grundlagen des naturalistischen Dramas der jüngsten deutschen Vergangenheit.* Dissertation, Leipzig, 1912. Weida i. Th.: Thomas & Hubert, 1912.

Guthke, Karl. *Gerhart Hauptmann. Weltbild im Werk.* Göttingen: Vandenhoeck & Ruprecht, 1961.

————. *Geschichte und Poetik der deutschen Tragikomödie.* Göttingen: Vandenhoeck & Ruprecht, 1961.

Gutknecht. "Neueröffnung des Meininger Theatermuseums." *Meininger Kulturspiegel,* 1955.

Haase, Friedrich. *Ungeschminkte Briefe.* Dresden & Leipzig: Heinrich Minden, 1883.

————. *Was ich erlebte, 1846–1896.* Berlin, Leipzig, Vienna & Stuttgart: Richard Bong, 1897.

Hagemann, Carl. *Moderne Bühnenkunst.* Vol. 1: "Regie, die Kunst der szenischen Darstellung." Berlin and Leipzig: Schuster & Loeffler,1918.Vol. 2: "Der Mime, Schauspiel–und Opernkunst." Berlin and Leipzig: Schuster & Loeffler, 1921.

————. *Regie, Studien zur dramatischen Kunst.* Berlin and Leipzig: Schuster & Loeffler, 1902.

Hahm, Thomas. "Die Gastspiele des Meininger Hoftheaters im Urteil der Zeitgenossen. Unter besonderer Berücksichtigung der Gastspiele in Berlin und Wien." Ph.D. dissertation, University of Cologne, 1970.

Harden, Max. "Herzog Georg." *Die Zukunft* 14 (1906): 433–440.

————. "Die Meininger." *Die Zukunft* 88 (1914): 11–23.

Hartnoll, Phyllis, ed. *The Oxford Companion to the Theatre.* London: Oxford University Press, 1967.

Hauptmann, Gerhart. *Das Abenteuer meiner Jugend.* Berlin: S. Fischer, 1937.

————. "Aus den Jugenderinnerungen." *Berliner Börsen–Courier,* November 13, 1932.

Hawkins, C. Halford. "The Meiningen Court Theater." *Macmillan's Magazine,* April 1877.

Heine, Carl. "Vom neuen Stil auf dem Theater." *Neue Deutsche Rundschau* 8 (1897): 845–856.

Heldburg, Helene, Freifrau von. *Fünfzig Jahre Glück und Leid. Ein Leben in Briefen aus den Jahren 1873–1923.* Edited by Johannes Werner. Leipzig: Koehler und Amelang, 1926.

Hemsen, Th. (untitled article). *Tägliche Rundschau* (Berlin), 25 June 1914.

————. "Herzog Georg von Meiningen und seine Gesellschaft." *Alte Presse* (Vienna), 26 September 1875.

————. "Herzog Georg II. von Meiningen." *Der Neue Weg* 55 (1926): 125–126.

————. "Hoftheater Meiningen." *Berliner Börsen–Courier,* 6–7 April 1908.

————. "Das Meiningen Hoftheater." *Vorstadt–Zeitung* (Vienna), 3 October 1875.

Henderson, William James. *Richard Wagner: His Life and His Dramas.* New York: G. P. Putnam's Sons, n.d.

Herrig, Hans. *Die Meininger, ihre Gastspiele und deren Bedeutung für das deutsche Theater.* Dresden: R. von Grumbow, Hofverlagbuchhandlung, 1880 and 1881.

————. "Die Meininger, ihre Gastspiele und deren Bedeutung für das deutsche Theater. Eine Selbstanzeige." *Jahrbuch für das deutsche Theater* 2 (1880): 217–219.

————. "Die Meininger, ihre Gastspiele und deren Bedeutung für das deutsche Theater." *Die Deutsche Bühne* 1 (1909): 332–333.

Hirt, Anne Louise. "The Place of George II, Duke of Meiningen in the Unfoldment of Theatre Art." Ph.D. dissertation, University of Southern California, 1940.

Hopfen, Hans. "Die Meininger in Berlin." *Neue Freie Presse* (Vienna), May 30, 1874.

————. *Streitfragen und Erinnerungen.* Stuttgart: J. G. Cotta, 1876.

Hormann, Helmuth Winfrid. "From Weimar to Meiningen. A Century of Theatrical Direction in Germany." Ph.D. dissertation, Cornell University, 1943.

Houben, Heinrich Hubert. *Emil Devrient. Sein Leben, sein Wirken, sein Nachlass. Ein Gedenkbuch.* Frankfurt a. M.: Literarische Anstalt Rütten & Loening, 1903.

H. v. C. "Herzog Georg von Sachsen–Meiningen." *Die Gartenlaube* 27 (1879): 243–244.

H. W. "Meiningen." *Das Theater* 1 (1910): 198–201.

Ibsen, Henrik. Letter to Georg II. 13 November 1886. Institut für Theaterwissenschaft der Universität Köln (Cologne theater museum).

Ihering, Herbert. *Reinhardt, Jessner, Piscator oder Klassikertod?* Berlin: Ernst Rowohlt, 1929.

Iser, Wolfgang. "Der Kaufmann von Venedig auf der Illusionsbühne der Meininger." *Shakespeare Jahrbuch* 99 (1963): 72–94.

Isolani, Eugen. "Herzog Georg von Meiningen." *Deutsches Bühnen-Jahrbuch* 26 (1915): 60–66.

Isterheil, Heinz. "Die Bühnendekorationen bei den Meiningern." Ph.D. dissertation, University of Cologne, 1928.

Jacobs, Monty, ed. *Deutsche Schauspielkunst, Zeugnisse zur Bühnengeschichte klassischer Rollen.* Berlin: Henschel, 1954.

Jacobsohn, Siegfried. "Berlin und die Meininger." *Die Schaubühne,* April 1906, pp. 23–30.

———. *Das Theater der Reichshauptstadt.* Munich: Albert Langen, 1904.

Jacoby, H. "Die Meininger in Leipzig." *Der Grenzbote,* Nos. 44 & 47 (1878): 4–21.

Jansen, Marianne. "Meiningertum und Meiningerei—eine Untersuchung über die Aus– und Nachwirkungen der Meininger Theaterreform." Ph.D. dissertation, University of Berlin, 1948.

Jantsch, Heinrich. *Bühnenbearbeitung von Schillers Wilhelm Tell.* Hendels Bibliothek der Gesamtlitteratur, Nos. 1120–22. Halle a.d.S.: Otto Hendel, 1898.

Jellinek, Arthur L. *Bibliographie der Theatergeschichte.* Schriften der Gesellschaft für Theatergeschichte, vols. 1–2. Archiv für Theatergeschichte, edited by Hans Devrient. Berlin: Egon Fleischel & Co., 1904–1905.

Jeschke, Gerhard. "Die Bühnenbearbeitungen der Meininger während der Gastspielzeit." Ph.D. dissertation, University of Munich, 1922.

Junack, R. "Heinrich Laubes Entwicklung zum Reformator des deutschen Theaters." Ph.D. dissertation, University of Erlangen, 1922.

Junghans, Ferdinand. *Zeit in Drama.* Theater und Drama, vol. 1. Edited by Max Hermann, Julius Petersen, and Hans Knudsen. Berlin: Otto Elsner, 1931.

Karlyle, Charles. "Die Meininger in London." *Signale für die musikalische Welt* 60 (1902): 1193–1196.

Karpeles, Gustav. "Die Meininger." *Das Neue Blatt: eine illustrierte Familien–Journal* 29, No. 13.

Kerr, Alfred. *Das Mimenreich.* Vol. I, 5 of *Gesammelte Schriften.* Berlin: S. Fischer, 1920.

———. *Das neue Drama.* Erste Reihe der Davidsbündler–Schriften. Berlin: G. Fischer Verlag, 1905.

Kienzl, Hermann. "Vom deutschen Provinz–Theater." *Deutsche Revue* 31 (1906): 246–249.

Kilian, Eugen. *Aus der Theaterwelt. Erlebnisse und Erfahrungen.* Karlsruhe: C. F. Müller, 1924.

———. *Dramaturgische Blätter. 1. Reihe: Aufsätze und Studien aus dem Gebiete der praktischen Dramaturgie, der Regiekunst und der Theatergeschichte.* Munich & Leipzig: Georg Müller, 1905.

———. *Dramaturgische Blätter. 2. Reihe: Aus der Praxis der modernen Dramaturgie.* Munich & Leipzig: Georg Müller, 1914.

———. *Dramaturgische Blätter. 3. Reihe: Aus der Werkstatt des Spielleiters.* Munich: Georg Müller, 1931.

———. *Der einteilige Theater–Wallenstein. Ein Beitrag zur Bühnengeschichte von Schillers Wallenstein.* Forschungen zur neueren Literaturgeschichte, edited by Franz Muncker, vol. 28. Berlin: Alexander Duncker, 1901.

———. "Georg von Meiningen und seine Bühnenreform." *Dramaturgische Blätter. Zeitschrift des Hofs– und Landestheaters Meiningen,* 1920–1922.

———. *Münchener Neueste Nachrichten* (Munich), 26 June 1914.

———. *Schillers Wallenstein auf der Bühne. Beiträge zum Probleme der Aufführung und Inszenierung des Gedichtes.* Munich & Leipzig: Georg Müller, 1908.

Kindermann, Heinz. "Die literarische Entfaltung des 19. Jahrhunderts." *Monatsschrift* 14 (1926): 35–52.

———. *Theatergeschichte Europas.* Salzburg: Otto Müller Verlag, 1957.

Kirch, R. "Die Meininger." *Freiburger Zeitung,* 6 March 1909.

Kirsch, R. [Nowack, K. F.?] "Der Meininger." *Die Wage,* 9, No. 14.

Klaar, Alfred. "Herzog Georg von Meiningen." *Jahrbuch der deutschen Shakespeare–Gesellschaft* 51 (1915): 193–204.

———. "Der Vater der Meininger." *Vossische Zeitung* (Berlin), June 1914.

Knight, Joseph. *Theatrical Notes.* London: Lawrence & Bullen, 1893.

Knudsen, Hans. *Deutsche Theatergeschichte.* Stuttgart: Alfred Kröner, 1959.

———. "Das Werk des Theaterherzogs." *Die Volksbühne: Zeitung für soziale Theaterpolitik und Kunstpflege.* 1 April 1926.

———. "Massenszene" (p. 336) & "Meininger" (pp. 337–38). *Reallexikon der deutschen Literaturgeschichte.* Edited by Paul Merker and Wolfgang Stammler. 2nd ed., vol. 2. Berlin: 1964 ff.

Köberle, Georg. *Brennende Theater–Frage. Eine Denkschrift für alle kunstfreundlichen Patrioten.* Vienna: Adolph W. Künast, 1887.

———. *Dramaturgische Gänge. Der Verfall der deutschen Schaubühne und die Bewältigung der Theater–Calamität.* Leipzig: Paul Wolff, 1880.

Koch, Ernst. "Herzog Georg II. von Saxe–Meiningen." *Deutsches Fürstenbuch. Lebensbilder der zeitgenössischen deutschen Regenten.* Leipzig: Rengerische Buchhandlung, Gebhardt und Wilisch, 1889–1890, pp. 180–186.

Koller, Ann Marie Best. "Georg II, Duke of Saxe–Meiningen, and the German Stage." Ph.D. dissertation, Stanford University, 1965.

———. trans. *Max Grube's "The Story of the Meininger."* Edited by Wendell Coles. Coral Gables, Florida: University of Miami Press, 1963.

Kopp, Heinrich. *Die Bühnenleitung August Klingemanns in Braunschweig. Ein Beitrag zur deutschen Theatergeschichte des 19. Jahrhunderts.* Vol. 17 of Theatergeschichtliche Forschungen, edited by Berthold Litzmann. Vol 17. Hamburg & Leipzig: Leopold Voss, 1901.

Körting, Gustav. *Das Theater der Neuzeit.* Vol. 3 of *Geschichte des Theaters in seinen Beziehungen zu der dramatischen Dichtkunst.* Paderborn: Ferdinand Schöningh, 1905.

Kosch, Wilhelm. "Die Meininger." *Deutsches Theater–Lexikon.* Klagenfurt–Vienna: Ferd. v. Kleinmayr, 1951 ff.

———. *Das deutsche Theater und Drama im 19. Jahrhundert mit einem Ausblick auf die Folgezeit.* Leipzig: Verlag der Dykschen Buchhandlung, 1913.

Kraussneck, Arthur. "Wie ich zu den Meiningern kam." *Thüringen; eine Monatsschrift für alte und neue Kultur* 2 (1926): 17–18.

Kruchen, Alfred. *Das Regieprinzip bei den Meiningern zur Zeit ihrer Gastspielepoche.* Danzig: A. W. Kafemann, 1933.

Kugler, F. H. "Aus der Hauptstadt. Dramatische Aufführungen. Das Meiningensche und das Dresdner Residenz–Theater." *Die Gegenwart. Wochenschrift für Literatur, Kunst und öffentliches Leben* 7 (1875): 381.

———. "Aus der Hauptstadt. Dramatische Aufführungen. 'Rabagas'—'Der Kaufmann von Venedig'." *Die Gegenwart. Wochenschrift für Literatur, Kunst und öffentliches Leben* 7 (1875): 397–98.

Kurnatowski, Otto v. *Georg II., Herzog von Sachsen–Meiningen und Hildburghausen, ein Lebens– und Kulturbild.* Hildburghausen: F. W. Gadow und Sohn, 1914.

Kurnik, Max. *Ein Menschenalter. Theater Erinnerungen 1845–1880.* 2nd ed. Berlin: Otto Janke, 1883.

Kürschner, Joseph. "Bemerkenswertes aus dem Theaterjahr 1877/78." *Jahrbuch für das deutsche Theater. Eine umfassende Rundschau über die Zustände und Ereignisse auf Theatralischen und verwandten Gebieten während des letzten Theaterjahres. Nebst einem ausführlichen Register.* Vol. 1. Leipzig: Hermann Foltz, 1879. Vol. 2. Leipzig: L. E. Foltz, 1880.

————. *Kürschners biographisches Theater–Handbuch.* Edited by Herbert Frenzel and Hans Joachim Moser. Berlin: Walter de Gruyter & Co., 1956.

Kutscher, Artur. *Die Ausdruckskunst der Bühne. Grundriss und Bausteine zum neuen Theater.* Leipzig: Eckardt Verlag, 1910.

————. *Grundriss der Theaterwissenschaft.* 2nd ed. Munich: Kurt Desch, 1949.

Landau, Jsidor. "Ein Festabend der Meininger." *Bühne und Welt* 1 (1899): 684–686.

————. "Meiningen." *Die Deutsche Bühne* 1 (1909): 326–328.

Landsberg, Hans. "Die Meininger in der zeitgenössischen Kritik." *Der neue Weg* 39 (1910): 47–50.

L'Arronge, Adolph. *Deutsches Theater und deutsche Schauspielkunst.* Berlin: Concordia Deutsche Verlags–Anstalt, 1896.

Laub, Georg. Personal Interview. 8 July 1976.

Laube, Heinrich. *Gesammelte Werke in 50 Bände.* Edited by Heinrich Hubert Houben. Leipzig: Max Hesse, 1909.

————. *Theaterkritiken und dramaturgische Aufsätze.* Edited by Alexander von Weilen. Schriften der Gesellschaft für Theatergeschichte, vols. 7–8. Berlin: Selbstverlag der Gesellschaft für Theatergeschichte, 1906.

de Leeuwe, H. H. J. *Meiningen en Nederland. Proeve van vergelijkende Toneelgeschiedenis.* Studia Litteraria Rheno–Traiectina, vol. 6. Edited by H. Sparnay and W. A. P. Smit. Groningen: J. B. Wolters, 1959.

Leinhos, A. "Der Brand des herzoglichen Hoftheaters in Meiningen." *Bühne und Welt* 10 (1908): 557–559.

Liebscher, Otto. "Franz Dingelstedt, seine dramaturgische Entwicklung und Tätigkeit bis 1857 und seine Bühnenleitung in München." Ph.D. dissertation, University of Munich, 1909.

Lichterfeld, L. *Entwicklungs–Geschichte der deutschen Schauspielkunst.* Erfurt: Fr. Bartholomäus, 1882.

Lilie, Georg. *An der fränkischen Pforte. Vergangenes und Gegenwärtiges aus der Umgebung von Meiningen.* Meiningen: Brückner und Renner, 1929.

Lindau, Paul. "Aus der Hauptstadt. Dramatische Aufführungen. Das Gastspiel des herzoglich Meiningschen Hofschauspiels." *Die Gegenwart. Wochenschrift für Literatur, Kunst und öffentliches Leben* 7 (1875): 265–268.

————. "Aus der Hauptstadt. Dramatische Aufführungen. Das Gastspiel des meiningschen Hoftheaters. II." *Die Gegenwart* 7 (1875): 299–302.

————. "Aus der Hauptstadt. Dramatische Aufführungen. Das Gastspiel des herzoglich meiningenschen Hoftheaters. III. 'Fiesco' von Schiller." *Die Gegenwart* 7 (1875): 316–318.

————. "Aus der Hauptstadt. Dramatische Aufführungen. 'Pabst Sixtus V' " *Die Gegenwart* 5 (1874): 331–333.

————. "Aus der Hauptstadt. Dramatische Aufführungen. Vorstellung für die 'Berliner Presse'—Gäste—Die Meininger." *Die Gegenwart* 5 (1874): 348–351.

————. "Aus der Hauptstadt. Gesammtgastspiel der Meininger Hofschauspieler." *Die Gegenwart* 5 (1874): 301–302.

————. *Dramaturgische Blätter. Neue Folge. 1875–1878.* Breslau: S. Schottlaender, 1879.

————. "Helene, Freifrau von Heldburg." *Die Deutsche Bühne* 1 (1909): 323–325.

————. "Herzog Georg von Meiningen als Regisseur." *Die Deutsche Bühne* 1 (1909): 313–319.

————. "Herzog Georg von Meiningen als Regisseur." *Die Deutsche Bühne* 18 (1926): 79–82.

————. "Herzog Georg von Meiningen, ein Lebensbild." *Die Deutsche Bühne* 6 (1914): 403–407.

————. Letter to Georg II. 30 October 1885. Nachlass Georg II. Deutsche Staatsbibliothek, Berlin (German State Library).

————. "Ludwig Chronegk." *Die Deutsche Bühne* 1 (1909): 331–332.

————. *Nur Erinnerungen.* Stuttgart & Berlin: J. G. Cotta Nachfolger, 1916.

————. "Vergangene Zeiten." *Neue Freie Presse* (Vienna), I. April 3, 1904, pp. 34–37. II. April 8, 1904, pp. 1–5. III. April 21, 1904, pp. 1–5.

————. "Vergangene Zeiten." *Neue Freie Presse* (Vienna), No. 14751 (16 September 1905); No. 14762 (27 September 1905); No. 14769 (4 October 1905); No. 14786 (21 October 1905).

————. "Vergangene Zeiten. Dem Herzog Georg von Sachsen–Meiningen zum 80. Geburtstag." *Neue Freie Presse* (Vienna), No. 14943 (30 March 1906), No. 14947 (3 April 1906), No. 14949 (5 April 1906).

Lindenberg, Paul. "Berliner Stimmungsbilder." n.p., n.d.

————. "Herzog Georg II von Sachsen–Meiningen und Hildburghausen. Zu seinem achtzigsten Geburtstage." *Illustrierte Zeitung* (Leipzig), March 29, 1906.

Lindner, Albert. "Die Meininger und ihr Kunstprinzip." *Westermanns Jahrbuch der Illustrirten Deutschen Monatshefte* 44 (1878): 436–442.

Lindner, Amanda. "Erinnerungen." *Thüringen. Eine Monatsschrift für alte und neue Kultur* 2(1926): 20–22.

Litto, Fredric. *American Dissertations on the Drama and the Theatre. A Bibliography.* Kent, Ohio: Kent State University Press, 1969.

Litzmann, Berthold. *Das deutsche Drama in den litterarischen Bewegung der Gegenwart. Vorlesungen, gehalten an der Universität Bonn.* Hamburg and Leipzig: Leopold Voss, 1894.

Lohmeyer, Walther. *Die Dramaturgie der Massen.* Berlin and Leipzig: Schuster und Loeffler, 1913.

Lusztig, J. C. "Aus der Berliner Musikwelt 1902/03." *Bühne und Welt* 5 (1903): 387.

Magarschack, David. *Stanislavsky. A Life.* New York: Chanticleer Press, 1951.

Mahnke, Fritz. "Theaterfamilie Brückner." In *150 Jahre Coburger Landestheater.* Festschrift. Coburg: Landestheater, 1977.

von Maixdorff, Carl. "Zwei 'Räuber'–Proben: Kleinigkeiten aus Meiningens grosser Zeit." *Thüringen. Eine Monatsschrift für alte und neue Kultur* 2 (1926): 19–20.

Martersteig, Max. *Das deutsche Theater im neunzehnten Jahrhundert. Eine Kulturgeschichtliche Darstellung.* Leipzig: Breitkopf und Härtel, 1904.

Max, Hero [E. H. Peter]. "Herzog Georg II. von Meiningen." *Bühne und Welt* 16 (1914): 432–433.

————. "Das Meiningensche Hoftheater." *Wiener Abendblatt* (Vienna), Nos. 70ff., 1878.

————. "Die Meininger." *Deutsche Zeitung* (Vienna), September 25, 1875.

————. "Die Meininger." *Hamburger Zeitung,* October 1, 1875.

————. "Die Meininger." *Illustriertes Wiener Extrablatt* (Vienna), October 31, 1875.

————. "Die Meininger." *Neues Pester Journal* (Budapest), November 4, 1875.

————. "Die Meininger." *Berliner Tageblatt,* December 17, 1909.

————. "The Meininger Theatre." *The London Times,* October 14, 1876.

————. "Ein Nachwort über die Meininger." *Die Presse* (Vienna), November 4, 1875.

McNamee, Lawrence F. "The Meininger Players and Shakespeare." *Drama Survey* 3 (1963): 164–175.

Merbach, Paul Alfred. *Bibliographie für Theatergeschichte 1905–1910.* Schriften der Gesellschaft für Theatergeschichte, vol. 21. Berlin: Schriften der Gesellschaft für Theatergeschichte, 1913.

Merchant, W. Moelwyn. "On Looking at *The Merchant of Venice.*" In *Essays on Nineteenth Century British Theatre,* edited by Kenneth Richards and Peter Thompson. London: Methuen & Co. Ltd., 1971.

Michael, Friedrich. *Deutsches Theater.* 1923; *Geschichte des deutschen Theaters.* Reprint. Stuttgart: Reclam, 1969.

Mueller, Ernst. *Übersicht über die Bestände des Landesarchivs Meiningen.* Weimar: Böhlau, 1960.

Mühlfeld, Christian. "Georg II. und die Musik." *Thüringen* 2 (1926): 8–13.

Müller, Johannes. "Das Meininger Theatermuseum und sein Archiv." *Kleine Schriften der Gesellschaft für Theatergeschichte* 18 (1962): 57–62.

Nagler, A. M. *A Source Book in Theatrical History.* New York: Dover Publications, Inc., 1959.

Nesper, Josef. "Zum 2. April 1926." *Thüringen. Eine Monatsschrift für alte und neue Kultur* 2(1926): 22–24.

Newmark, Maxim. *Otto Brahm, the Man and the Critic.* New York & London: G. E. Stechart & Co., 1938.

N. H. W. "Kunstreis der Meiningers in ons Land." *Het Leven. Algemeen Geïllustreerd Weekblad* 1 (1906): 314.

Niessen, Carl. *Das Bühnenbild. Ein kulturgeschichtlicher Atlas.* Bonn, Leipzig: F. Klopp, 1925.

————. "Ein Jahrhundert Meininger Theater." *Kölnische Zeitung* (Cologne), June 1, 1931.

————. *Kleine Schriften zur Theaterwissenschaft und Theatergeschichte.* Festschrift. Günter Seehaus, ed. Emsdetten/Westfalen: Lechte, 1971.

————. "Weshalb die Meininger nicht in Amerika gastierten." *Theater der Welt. Zeitschrift für die gesamte Theaterkultur* 1 (1937): 596–602.

Nippold, Erich. *Das deutsche Theater von seinen Anfängen bis zur Gegenwart.* Gotha & Stuttgart: F. A. Perthes, 1924.

————. "Herzog Georg II von Sachsen–Meiningen." *Pflüger. Thüringer Heimatblätter* 3 (1926): 152–158.

————. "Die Meininger." *Dramaturgische Blätter des Landestheaters* (Meiningen), 1921/22.

————. *Thüringer Volkstum und Thüringer Geistesleben. Vortrag vom 16. und 17. April 1922 gehalten im Meininger Landestheater.* Stuttgart: F. A. Perthes A. G., 1922.

Norman, Henry. *An Account of the Greek Play.* Boston: James R. Osgood & Co., 1882.

Nusser, Luitpold. "Max Brückner." *Das Welttheater. Monatsschrift der Münchner Volksbühne,* No. 3 (November 1924).

————. "Schinkel und Brückner in ihrer Bedeutung für die Bühnenmalerei im 19. Jahrhundert." Ph.D. dissertation, University of Würzburg, 1923.

Oechelhäuser, Wilhelm. "Die Shakespeare Aufführungen in Meiningen." *Jahrbuch der deutschen Shakespeare–Gesellschaft* 3 (1868): 383.

Oesterheld, Herta. "Dokumente zur Musikgeschichte Meiningens. 6 Briefe von Richard und Cosima Wagner an Georg II." In *Neue Beiträge zur Regerforschung und Musikgeschichte Meiningens: Südthüringer Forschungen* 5, No. 6. Meiningen: Staatliche Museen Meiningen, 1970.

Oppenheim, H. B. "Offene Briefe und Antworten." *Die Gegenwart: Wochenschrift für Literatur, Kunst und öffentliches Leben* 5 (1874): 366–367.

Otto, Alex. "Zwei Erinnerungen." *Thüringen: Eine Monatsschrift für alte und neue Kultur* 2(1926): 24–25.

Peters–Marquardt. "Zum 100jährigen Geburtstage Max Brückners." *Coburger Heimatblätter* 14 (1936): 73–89.

Petersen, Julius. *Das deutsche Nationaltheater. Fünf Vorträge, gehalten im Februar und März 1917 im Freien deutschen Hochstift zu Frankfurt a.M. Zeitschrift für den deutschen Unterricht, 14. Ergänzungsheft.* Leipzig, Berlin: B. G. Teubner, 1919.

Phelps, W. May and John Forbes–Robertson. *The Life and Life–Work of Samuel Phelps.* London: Sampson Low, Marston, Searle & Rivington, 1886.

Piscator, Erwin. *Das Politische Theater.* Reinbek b. Hamburg: Rowohlt, 1963.

P. L. [Paul Lindau] *Zur silbernen Hochzeit Sr. Hoheit des Herzogs Georg II. von Sachsen–Meiningen und der Frau Helene Freifrau von Heldburg. Ode.* n.p. 18 March 1898.

P. L–d. "Echo der Zeitungen." *Das Literarische Echo* 8 (1906), column 1081.

Poppen, Hermann. "Fünfzig Jahre Maininger Musikgeschichte." *Neue Beiträge zur Geschichte deutschen Altertums.* Edited by dem hennebergischen altertumsforschenden Verein, Meiningen. Lieferung 34 (1929), 33–50.

Possart, Ernst von. *Erstrebtes und Erlebtes. Erinnerungen aus meiner Bühnentätigkeit.* Berlin: Ernst Siegfried Mittler und Sohn, Königliche Hofbuchhandlung, 1916.

Prasch, Aloys. "Erinnerungen eines ehemaligen Meiningers." *Bühne und Welt* 1 (1899): 691–702.

————. "Herzog Georg II. als dankbarer Theaterleiter." *Bühne und Welt* 8 (1906): 587–588.

————. "Der Prinz von Homburg auf der Meiningenschen Bühne." *Die Grenzbote* 37, 1st semester, part 2 (1878).

Prasch, Rolf. "Festtage in Meiningen." *Die Bühnengenossenschaft* 7 (1955): 147–148.

Prasch-Grevenberg, Augusta. "Unser Herzog." *Thüringen. Eine Monatsschrift für alte und neue Kultur* 2 (1926): 25–26.

Prölss, Robert. *Geschichte des neueren Dramas.* Vol. 3, part 2. Leipzig: Verlag von Bernhard Schlicke, 1883.

————. *Das Herzoglich–Meiningen'sche Hoftheater, seine Entwicklung, seine Bestrebungen und die Bedeutung seiner Gastspiele. Ein Führer durch das Repertoire der Meininger.* Leipzig: Friedrich Conrad, 1887.

————. *Das Herzoglich Meiningen'sche Hoftheater und die Bühnenreform.* Erfurt: Fr. Bartholomäus, 1878.

————. "Das Meiningensche Hoftheater und die Entwicklung und kulturhistorische Bedeutung seiner Gastspiele." *Bühne und Welt* 1 (1899): 673–678.

Prutz, Robert Eduard. *Vorlesungen über die Geschichte des Theaters.* Berlin: Duncker & Humblot, 1847.

Pullmann, Wilhelm. *Die Bearbeitungen, Fortsetzungen und Nachahmungen von Schillers 'Räubern' (1782–1802).* Schriften der Gesellschaft für Theatergeschichte, vol. 15. Berlin: Selbstverlag der Gesellschaft für Theatergeschichte, 1910.

Rath, Willy. "Die Meininger." *Eckhardt, ein deutsches Literaturblatt* 5: 447–454.

Reger, Max. *Briefwechsel mit Herzog Georg II. von Sachsen–Meiningen.* Hedwig & E. H. Müller von Asow, eds. Weimar: Verlag Hermann Böhlans Nachfolger, 1949.

Révy, Richard. "Züricher Shakespeare–Aufführungen im Jahre 1916." *Jahrbuch der deutschen Shakespeare–Gesellschaft* 53 (1917): 146.

Richard, Paul. *Chronik sämmtlicher Gastspiele des Herzoglich Sachsen–Meiningen'schen Hoftheaters während der Jahre 1874–1890. Statistische Übersicht.* Leipzig: Friedrich Conrad, 1891.

————. *Die Gastspiele des herzoglich Meiningen'schen Hoftheaters während der Jahre 1874–1883. Chronologisch–Statistische Übersicht.* Dresden: R. v. Grumbkow, 1884.

Richter, Helene. *Josef Lawinsky. Fünfzig Jahre Wiener Kunst und Kultur. Zum 150. Jubiläum des Burgtheaters.* Vienna, Leipzig, New York: Deutscher Verlag für Jugend und Volk, 1926.

———. *Kainz.* Vienna & Leipzig: F. G. Speidel'sche Verlagsbuchhandlung, 1931.

Roenneke, Rudolf. "Franz Dingelstedts Wirksamkeit am Weimarer Hoftheater. Ein Beitrag zur Theatergeschichte des 19. Jahrhunderts." Ph.D. dissertation, University of Greifswald, 1912.

Rojek, Hans Jürgen. *Bibliographie der deutschsprachigen Hochschulschriften zur Theaterwissenschaften von 1953 bis 1960.* Schriften der Gesellschaft für Theatergeschichte, vol. 61. Berlin: Selbstverlag der Gesellschaft für Theatergeschichte, 1962.

Rosegger, Peter. Letter to Georg II. 31 March 1906. Nachlass Georg II. Deutsche Staatsbibliothek, Berlin.

Rosenthal, Friedrich. *Unsterblichkeit des Theaters. Versuch einer Kulturgeschichte der deutschen Bühne.* Bonn: Fritz Klopp, 1927.

———. *Zwei Reden von der Not des deutschen Theaters: 203. Flugschrift des Dürerbands.* Munich: Georg D. W. Callwey, 1926.

Rössing, J. H. "De Meiningers te Rotterdam." *De Amsterdammer,* May 6, 1888.

Rube, W. "Herzog Georg II als Regisseur." *Meininger Kulturspiegel,* 1957: 379–388.

Rüffer, Friedrich. *Geschichte des Leipziger Stadttheaters unter der Direction Dr. Förster. Ein Beitrag zur Specialgeschichte des deutschen Theaters.* Leipzig: Bernhard Freyer, 1880.

———. *Die Meininger und ihre Bedeutung. Eine dramaturgische Skizze: Seperat-Abdruck aus dem Leipziger Sonntagsblatt.* Leipzig: Leopold & Bär, 1882.

Rumpf, Fritz. "Die geschichtliche Treue des Theaterkostüms." *Masken,* 1905, No. 11.

Rupprecht, Heinrich. "Erinnerungen an Herzog Georg II. von Sachsen–Meiningen." *Thüringen. Eine Monatsschrift für alte und neue Kultur* 2 (1926): 26–27.

Russo, Wilhelm. "Die Meininger. Ein Wort zum 100. Geburtstag des Herzogs Georg II. von Meiningen am 2. April 1926." *Die Scene: Blätter für Bühnenkunst herausgegeben von der Vereinigung künstlerische Bühnenvorstände* 16 (1926): 97–99.

Schäfer-Widmann, J. V. "J. V. Widmann und der Herzog von Meiningen." *Basler Nachrichten* (Sonntagsblatt No. 23), 1939.

Schanze, Helmut. *Drama im bürgerlichen Realismus (1850–1890). Theorie und Praxis.* Studien zur Philosophie und Literatur des neunzehnten Jahrhunderts, vol. 21. Frankfurt: Vittorio Klosterman, 1973.

Scharrer, E. "Herzog Georg II. als Bühnenreformator." *Neue Preussische Kreutzzeitung* (Berlin), No. 146, 1926.

Schasler, Max. *Die Wandgemälde im Treppenhaus des neuen Museums zu Berlin.* Berlin: Allgemeine Deutsche Verlags–Anstalt, 1854.

Schlenther, Paul. *Botho von Hülsen und seine Leute. Eine Jubiläumskritik über das Berliner Hofschauspiel.* Berlin: Internationale Buchhandlung, 1883.

———. *Theater im 19. Jahrhundert. Ausgewählte theatergeschichtliche Aufsätze.* Hans Knudsen, ed. Schriften der Gesellschaft für Theatergeschichte, vol. 40. Berlin: Selbstverlag der Gesellschaft für Theatergeschichte, 1930.

Schöne, Günter. *Tausend Jahre deutsches Theater. 914–1914.* München: Prestel, 1962.

Schuberth, Ottmar. *Das Bühnenbild–Geschichte, Gestalt, Technik.* München: Georg D. W. Callwey, 1955.

Schwanbeck, Gisela. *Bibliographie der deutschsprachigen Hochschulschriften zur Theaterwissenschaften von 1885 bis 1952.* Schriften der Gesellschaft für Theatergeschichte, vol. 58. Berlin: Selbstverlag der Gesellschaft für Theatergeschichte, 1956.

Schwarz, Adolf, Paul Lindau, and "ein deutscher Schauspieler." "Offene Briefe und Antworten in Sachen der Meininger." *Die Gegenwart. Wochenschrift für Literatur, Kunst und öffentliches Leben* 6, No. 27 (4 July 1874): 14–15.

Seldmayr, Hans. *Verlust der Mitte. Die bildende Kunst des 19. und 20. Jahrhunderts als Symbol der Zeit.* Salzburg: Otto Müller Verlag, 1948.

Shaw, Leroy Robert. *The Playwright and Historical Change. Dramatic Strategies in Brecht, Hauptmann, Kaiser and Wedekind.* Madison: University of Wisconsin Press, 1970.

Simonson, Lee. *The Stage is Set.* New York: Harcourt, Brace and Company, 1932.

Speidel, Ludwig. "Die Meininger (1879)." In Buschbeck, Erhard, *Der Thespiskarren.* Vienna: Wilhelm Andermann, 1943.

―――. *Schauspieler.* Ludwig Speidels Schriften, vol. 4. Berlin: Meyer & Jessen, 1911.

Sp. L. [Speidel, Ludwig]. *Neue Freie Presse* (Vienna) November 15, 1879.

Sprague, Arthur Colby. *Shakespeare and the Actors. The Stage Business in His Plays (1660–1905).* Cambridge: Harvard University Press, 1948.

Stadtplan of Meiningen. *Theaterstadt Meiningen und Umgebung.* Meiningen: Städtisches Verkehrsamt, 1937.

Stahl, Ernst Leopold. *Das englische Theater im 19. Jahrhundert. Seine Bühnenkunst und Literatur.* Die Kultur des modernen England in Einzeldarstellungen, edited by Ernst Sieper, vol. 5. Munich & Berlin: R. Oldenbourg, 1914.

―――. "Der englische Vorläufer der Meininger." *Beiträge zur Literatur- und Theatergeschichte. Festgabe für Ludwig Geiger zum 70. Geburtstage 5. Juni 1918.* Edited by Heinrich Stümcke. Berlin–Steglitz: S. Behr's Verlag, 1918.

―――. "Der englische Vorläufer der Meininger (Charles Kean als Bühnenreformator)." *Kölnische Zeitung* (Sonntagsbeilage) (Cologne), Nos. 14 and 21 (1913).

―――. *Shakespeare und das deutsche Theater. Wanderung und Wandelung seines Werkes in dreieinhalb Jahrhunderten.* Stuttgart: W. Kohlhammer, 1947.

Stanislavsky, Constantin. *My Life in Art.* Translated by J. J. Robbins. Boston: Little, Brown and Company, 1938.

Stein, Carl, Freiherr von. *Die Kunst in Meiningen unter Herzog Georg II.* Meiningen: Karl Keyssner, 1909.

Stein, Philipp. *Henrik Ibsen. Zur Bühnengeschichte seiner Dichtungen.* Berlin: Otto Elsner, 1901.

Stoever, Wilhelm. *Wilhelm von Kaulbachs Bilderkreis der Weltgeschichte im Treppenhaus des Berliner Neuen Museums.* Steglitz–Berlin: Verlag der Kaulbachstiche, n.d.

Storz, Gerhard. *Das Theater in der Gegenwart.* Wissen und Wirken. Einzelschriften zu den Grundfragen des Erkennens und Schaffens. Edited by Adolph Kistner und Emil Ungerer, vol. 43. Karlsruhe: G. Braun, 1927.

Stuart, Donald Clive. *The Development of Dramatic Art.* New York & London: D. Appleton & Co., 1928.

Stümcke, Heinrich. "Herzog Georg II. von Sachsen–Meiningen und das Theater." *Die Persönlichkeit. Monatsschrift für Lebensund geistesgeschichtliche Forschung* 1 (1914): 558–566.

―――. "Das neue Hoftheater in Meiningen." *Bühne und Welt* 12 (1910): 285–292.

Sylge, Max. "Das deutsche Theater in London." *Die Schaubühne,* 2, No. 28 (1906): 41–43.

Symons, Arthur. "The Meiningen Orchestra." *The Academy and Literature,* No. 1595 (29 November 1902): 581–582.

―――. "The Meiningen Orchestra." *Plays, Acting, and Music: A Book of Theory.* London: Duckworth, 1903; New York: E. P. Dutton & Co., 1909.

Szesiski, M. v. "Aus der Hauptstadt. Dramaturgische Aufführungen. Das Gastspiel der Meininger." *Die Gegenwart. Wochenschrift für Literatur, Kunst und öffentliches Leben* 5 (1874): 396–398.

Thalmann, Marianne. "Nachwort." *Die Märchen aus dem Phantasus.* Darmstadt: Wissenschaftliche Buchgesellschaft, 1977.

Trinks, Friedrich. *Erinnerungen an Herzog Georg II. und Zeitbilder aus und für Saalfeld–Saale.* Saalfeld a.S.: Adolf Nieses Nachf., 1925.

Tyrolt, Rudolf. *Aus der Theater–Welt. Ernste und heitere Bilder.* Leipzig: Richard Eckstein, 1879.

Uhlig, Karl. "Proben–Erinnerungen." *Thüringen. Eine Monatsschrift für alte und neue Kultur* 2 (1926): 27–29.

Unruh, Walter, ed. *Ein Brief des Herzogs Georg II. von Sachsen–Meiningen an Joseph Nesper.* Privately printed, 1936.

Varneke, Boris Vasilevich. *History of the Russian Theatre. Seventeenth through Nineteenth Century.* Translated by Boris Brasol. New York: Macmillan, 1951.

Voight, Felix Alfred und Walter A. Reichert. *Hauptmann und Shakespeare; ein Beitrag zur Geschichte des Fortlebens Shakespeares in Deutschland.* Deutschkundische Arbeiten. Veröffentlichungen aus dem Deutschen Institut der Universität Breslau. Allgemeine Reihe, vol. 12. Breslau: Maruschke & Berendt, 1938.

Voss, Richard. *Aus einem phantastischen Leben. Erinnerungen.* Stuttgart: J. Engelhorns Nachfolger, 1922.

——. "Erinnerungen an den Herzog Georg von Meiningen." *Velhagen und Klasings Monatshefte* 29 (1914): 232–237.

Vovour, O. "Hoftheater." *Illustrierte Zeitung,* No. 3469 (23 December 1909).

Wagner, Richard. *Gesammelte Schriften und Dichtungen,* vol. 7, 3rd edition. Leipzig: E. W. Fritsch, 1898.

Waldstein, Charles, "The Court Theatre of Meiningen." *Harper's New Monthly Magazine* 82 (1891): 743–758.

Wallner, Franz. "Bei den 'Meiningern.' Zum 100. Geburtstage des Herzog Georg II. von Sachsen–Meiningen." *Thüringen. Eine Monatsschrift für alte und neue Kultur* 2 (1926): 29–30.

——. "Meine Erinnerungen an Meiningen." *Volksspielkunst* 7 (1926): 107–109.

——. (or Hugo Dinger). "Die Weihe des Meininger Hoftheaters." *Deutsche Tageszeitung* (Berlin), December 31, 1903.

Walter, Louis. "Gotthold Brückner, ein Coburger Künstler." *Aus der Heimat. Wochenbeilage zu den Heimatglocken* (Coburg), No. 5 (1 February 1931), No. 6 (8 February 1931).

"Die Wartburgstimmen," eds. *Herzog Georg II. und die Meininger Kunst. Festschrift zum 80. Geburtstage Herzog Georgs am 2. April 1906.* Hildburghausen & Leipzig: Thüringische Verlags–Anstalt, 1906.

Weddigen, Otto. *Geschichte der Theater Deutschlands.* Berlin: Ernst Frensdorff, 1904 (vol. 1), 1906 (vol 2).

Weilen, Alexander von. "Laube und Shakespeare." *Jahrbuch der Shakespeare Gesellschaft* 33 (1909).

Weiser, Karl. "Herzog Georg als Regisseur." *Illustrierte Zeitung,* No. 3469 (23 December 1909).

——. "10 Jahre Meiningen." In *Archiv für Theatergeschichte.* Schriften der Gesellschaft für Theatergeschichte, vols. 1 & 2. Edited by Hans Devrient. Berlin: Egon Fleischel & Co., 1904–1905.

Weiss, J. "Das Meininger Theatermuseum." *Meininger Kulturspiegel,* 1956, pp. 432–434.

Weissstein, Gotthilf. *Meininger Erinnerungen.* Berlin: Edmund Meyer, 1906.

Well, P. "Brahms Beziehungen zu Meiningen." *Meininger Kulturspiegel,* 1958, pp. 115–120.

Wilbrandt, Adolf. *Erinnerungen.* Stuttgart & Berlin: J. G. Cotta'sche Buchhandlung Nachfolger, 1905.

——. trans. *Sophokles' und Euripedes' ausgewählte Dramen, mit Rücksicht auf die Bühne übertragen.* Nördlingen: C. H. Beck, 1866.

Wildberg, Bodo. *Das Dresdener Hoftheater in der Gegenwart.* Dresden and Leipzig: E. Piersons Verlag, 1902.

von Wildenbruch, Ernst. *Schwester–Seele.* Stuttgart and Berlin: J. G. Cotta'sche Buchhandlung Nachfolger, 1909. (Novel).

————. "Von Weimar nach Meiningen." *Berliner Tageblatt,* 1909, Nos. 199 and 202.

Wilson, H. Schütz. "Our Play–Box. Die Meininger." *Theatre. A Monthly Review of the Drama, Music, and the Fine Arts,* vol. 4, n.s. (1 August 1881).

Winds, Adolf. *Geschichte der Regie.* Stuttgart, Berlin & Leipzig: Deutsche Verlagsanstalt, 1925.

————. "Shakespeares 'Bezähmte Widerspenstige' und ihre deutschen Bearbeitungen." *Bühne und Welt* 5 (1903): 755–764.

Winter, William. *Shakespeare on the Stage.* New York: Moffat, Yard, & Co., 1915.

Winterstein, Eduard von. *Jungendjahre. Mein Leben und mein Zeit,* vol. 1. Berlin: Oswald Arnold, 1947.

Witkowski, Georg. *Das deutsche Drama des 19. Jahrhunderts in seiner Entwicklung dargestellt.* Aus Natur und Geisteswelt, vol. 51. Leipzig: B. G. Tuebner, 1913.

————. *The German Drama of the Nineteenth Century.* Translated by L. E. Horning. New York: Henry Holt, 1909.

Wohlmuth, Alois. *Ein Schauspielerleben.* Munich: Parcus & Co., 1918.

Wolff, Artur. "Meiningen." *Die deutsche Bühne 1 (1909): 336–337.*

————. "Der Theaterherzog." *Die deutsche Bühne 18 (1926): 77–79.*

Wolff, Eugen. "Georg II, Herzog von Sachsen–Meiningen." *Deutsches Biographisches Jahrbuch,* vol. 1. Berlin & Leipzig: Deutsche Verlags–Anstalt Stuttgart.

Wolff, Fritz. "Bildniss deutscher Schauspieler." *Die Schaubühne* 5 (1909): 241–244.

Zabel, Eugen. *Theatergänge.* Berlin: A Hofmann & Comp., 1908.

————. *Zur modernen Dramaturgie.* Oldenburg: Schulze, 1903.

Zarnke, Gotthard. "Die Feier des 80. Geburtstages Herzogs Georgs II. im Meininger Hoftheater." *Bühne und Welt* 8 (1906): 589–590.

von Zedlitz, Konstantin. "Das deutsche Theater in London." *Die Woche* 8, Nr. 6 (1906).

Zeiss, Karl. "Die Bühnenreform der Meininger." *Neuphilologische Blätter. Organ des Cartell–Verbandes Neuphilologischer Vereine deutscher Hochschulen,* vol. 2: October 20, 1894; December 20, 1894; February 20, 1895.

————. "Lebenslauf." *Das Welttheater* 1 (1924/25): 5–7.

————. "Zur Reform der Bühnendekorationen." *Bühne und Welt,* 1904?

Zucker, Paul. *Die Theaterdekorationen des Barocks. Eine Kunstgeschichte des Bühnenbilds.* Berlin: Rudolf Kaemmerer, 1925.

B. Works with No Author Given:

The Academy, 29 April 1876.

The Athenaeum Journal of Literature, Science, and Fine Arts, 1881.

June 4, No. 2797, 762.

June 11, No. 2798, 796.

June 18, No. 2799, 826.

June 25, No. 2800, 858.

July 2, No. 2801, 25.

July 9, No. 2802, 58.

July 23, No. 2804, 123.

Augsburger Allgemeine Zeitung, May 25, 1874.

Beilage zur Pester Lloyd (Budapest), December 13, 1879.
Das Bühnenbild im 19. Jahrhundert. Ausstellungskatalog. Munich: Theatermuseum München, 1959.
Deutsche Kultur 2, No. 13.
Deutsche Zeitung (Vienna), September 28, 1875 *(Beilage);* October 8, 1875; October 17, 1875.
Deutsches Zeitgenossenlexikon. Biographisches Handbuch deutscher Männer und Frauen der Gegenwart. Leipzig: Schulze, 1905.
Dienst–Regeln für die Mitglieder des Herzogl. Sachsen–Meiningenischen Hof–Theaters. Meiningen: H. Marbach, 1868.
Dienst–Regeln für die Mitglieder des Herzogl. Sachsen–Meiningischen Hoftheaters. Meiningen: H. Marbach, 1905.
Das Echo, 1914, pp. 2376–2377.
Festschrift zur Feier des 100. Geburtstages Herzog Georg II von Sachsen–Meiningen vom 2. bis 4. April 1926. Meiningen: n.p. [Landestheater Meiningen], 1926.
Das "Gastspiel der Meininger" *Pester Lloyd* (Budapest) 22 (1875),
No. 254 (4 November): 2–3;
No. 257 (7 November): 2–3;
No. 259 (10 November): 2–3;
No. 264 (Beilage) (16 November): 1;
No. 268 (20 November): 3;
No. 268 (Beilage) (20 November): 1.
"Die Gedenkfeier in Meiningen." *Der Neue Weg* 55 (1926): 145.
"Georg, Herzog von Meiningen." *Deutsche Schaubühne. Vierteljahresschrift für Theater, Kunst und Musik* 2, No. 1 (1878).
"Georg II., Herzog von Sachsen–Meiningen. Zum 100. Geburtstag am 2. April 1926." *Thüringen. Eine Monatsschrift für alte und neue Kultur* 2 (1926): 1–5.
"Georg II und das Theater." *Thüringen* 2 (1926): 14–16.
Gesellschaft 7: 1430–1447.
Haus–Ordnung für das Herzogliche Hoftheater in Meiningen. Meiningen: Keyssner, 1909.
"Herzog Georg II. von Meiningen." *Der neue Weg* 55, No. 7 (1926).
"Herzog Georg II. von Sachsen–Meiningen." *Neue Freie Presse* (Vienna), June 25, 1914, p. 3.
"Ibsen und die Meininger." *Die deutsche Bühne* 1 (1909): 319.
Jahresbericht für neuere deutsche Litteraturgeschichte 2 (1891): 113.
"Juni 1914." *Deutsches Bühnen–Jahrbuch* 26 (1915): 139.
"Die kommende Festwoche in Meiningen." *Der neue Weg. Halbmonatsschrift für das deutsche Theater* 55 (1926): 111.
Life. London: 1881.
"The Meiningen Company and the London Stage." *Blackwood's Edinburgh Magazine* 130 (1881): 248–263.
"The Meiningen Court Company." *The Times* (London), July 7, 1881.
Die Meiningen'sche Theater–Intendanz gegenüber dem deutschen Bühnenverein. Nach amtlichen Quellen. Meiningen: n.p. 1879.
"The Meininger Theatre." *The Times* (London), July 7, 1881.
Militärzeitung, 1914, pp. 431–432.
Münchner Allgemeine Zeitung, 1914, pp. 428–429.
Münchener Neueste Nachrichten (Munich), July 28, 1883.
National Zeitung (Berlin), June 8, 1874.

Neue Musikzeitung 35: 393.
Die Presse (Vienna), September 28, 1875; October 17, 1875.
"Rhabarber." *Der neue Weg* 55 (1926): 274.
"Sachsen Meiningen und Hildburghausen." *Gothaischer Genealogischer Hofkalendar 83.* Gotha: Justus Perthes, 1915.
Sechs Handzeichnungen Georgs II. Leipzig: K. F. Kochlers Antiquariat, n.d.
Sonntags–Blatt (Vienna), September 26, 1875.
Tag 1914: 151.
"Verschiedenes." *Die deutsche Bühne* 1 (1909): 333–334.
Volks–Zeitung (Berlin), May 27, 1874.
Wer Ist's? Unsere Zeitgenossen, 7, A 36 (1914).
Zweite Beilage zur Allgemeinen Zeitung (Munich). No. 213 (2 August 1883); No. 195 (16 July 1887).

C. Newspaper Articles Commemorating Georg's 80th Birthday (April 2, 1906):

Barnay, Ludwig. "Der Herzog von Meiningen." *Die Woche* 8 (1906): 539–541.
Besozzi, Max. "Ein König im Reiche der Kunst." *Grazer Tagblatt,* April 2, 1906.
Bleysteiner, Georg. "Herzog Georgs v. Meiningen 80. Geburtstag." *Leipziger Abendzeitung,* April 3, 1906.
Ch. F. "Herzog Georg von Meiningen." *Münchener Zeitung* (Munich), March 30, 1906.
Falk, Norbert. "Der Meininger." *Berliner Morgenpost,* April 1, 1906.
Frenzel, Karl. "Der Herzog v. Meiningen." *National Zeitung* (Berlin), April 1, 1906.
Heilmann, Hans. "Zum 80. Geburtstage des Herzogs von Meiningen." *Königsberger Allgemeine Zeitung,* April 1, 1906.
Hemsen, Th. "Der Herzog Georg v. Meiningen." *Tägliche Rundschau* (Berlin), No. 77 (1906).
Kilian, Eugen. "Der Herzog v. Meiningen." *Frankfurter Zeitung,* April 1, 1906.
——— . "Ein Künstler auf dem Thron." *Münchener Neueste Nachrichten* (Munich), April 1, 1906.
Klaar, Alfred. "Herzog Georg v. Meiningen." *Vossische Zeitung* (Berlin), April 1, 1906.
Kreuschner, Jurt Rudolf. "Der Theaterherzog. Zum 80. Geburtstage Herzog Georgs II. v. Sachsen–Meiningen." *Elbinger Zeitung & Elbinger Anzeiger, Sonntags–Beilage,* April 1, 1906.
——— . "Zum 80. Geburtstage Herzog Georgs II. von Sachsen–Meiningen." *Hildburghausen Dorfzeitung,* April 1, 1906.
Nowak, Karl Fr. "Georg II. und die Meininger." *Weser–Zeitung* (Bremen), April 1, 1906.
Prasch, Aloys. "Herzog Georg II. von Sachsen–Meiningen. Ein Gedenkblatt zu seinem 80. Geburtstage." *Berliner Lokalanzeiger,* April 1, 1906.
R. Br. "Herzog Georg von Meiningen. Zum 80. Geburtstag." *Münchener Neueste Nachrichten* (Munich), March 30, 1906.
Stübler, Arthur. "Herzog Georg von Sachsen–Meiningen. Zu seinem 80. Geburtstage." *General– Anzeiger* (Mannheim), March 31, 1906.
v. W. "Herzog Georg II. und Ellen von Heldburg." *Neue Badische Landeszeitung* (Mannheim), April 1, 1906; *Jenaischer Zeitung,* April 7, 1906; *Hamburgischer Correspondent,* April 2, 1906; *Neue Hamburger Zeitung,* April 2, 1906; *Freiburger Zeitung,* April 3, 1906; *Dresdner Nachrichten,* April 1, 1906; *Bremer Courier,* April 11, 1906.
——— . "Hier und dort." *Berlinger Börsen–Courier,* April 1, 1906.
Widmann, J. V. "Meininger Erinnerungen." *Neue Freie Presse* (Vienna), April 15, 1906.

Wolff, Artur. "Der Theaterherzog." *Berliner Zeitung am Mittag,* March 30, 1906.

Zieler, Gustav. "Die Meininger und ihr Herzog, zum 80. Geburtstag Herzog Georgs v. Meiningen." *Tagespost* (Graz) March 31, 1906; *Dresdner Anzeiger,* April 1, 1906; *4. Beilage zu Nr.77 des Anhaltischen Staats–Anzeigers* (Dessau), April 1, 1906; *Casseler Tageblatt & Anzeiger,* April 2, 1906; *Jenaische Zeitung,* April 1, 1906; *Neckar–Zeitung* (Heilbronn), April 1, 1906; *Hildesheimer Allgemeine Zeitung,* March 28, 1906; *1. Beilage zum Grossenhainer Tageblatt,* April 1, 1906 and April 3, 1906; *Geraer Zeitung,* April 1, 1906; *General–Anzeiger* (Frankfurt am Main), April 3, 1906; *2. Beilage zum Täglichen Anzeiger für Berg und Mark,* April 1, 1906; *Bote aus dem Wonnegau,* No. 13 (1906); *Rigaer Tageblatt,* April 1, 1906; *Nachrichten für Stadt und Land Oldenburg,* April 2, 1906; *Landes–Zeitung* (Neu–Strelitz), April 1, 1906; *Leipziger Neueste Nachrichten,* March 30, 1906; *Kölner Tageblatt* (Cologne) March 31, 1906; *Kieler Zeitung,* March 30, 1906; *Hamburger Nachrichten,* 232 (1906); *Sonntagsblatt. Unterhaltungs–Beilage der Danziger Zeitung,* April 1, 1906; *Ostdeutsche Zeitung* (Bromberg), March 30, 1906; *2. Beilage zu Nr. 152 der Breslauer Morgenzeitung,* March 31, 1906; *Bremer Courier,* April 1, 1906; *Braunschweiger Landeszeitung,* April 1, 1906; *Deutsche Tages–Zeitung* (Berlin), March 29, 1906; *Berliner neueste Nachrichten,* April 2, 1906; *Barmer Zeitung,* March 31, 1906; *Altenburger Zeitung,* April 1, 1906; *Augsburger Abend–Zeitung,* March 31, 1906.

"Aus den Jugendjahren des Herzogs Georg." *2. Beiwagen zu Nr. 78 der Dorfzeitung* (Hildburghausen), April 3, 1906.

"Herzog Georg II. von Sachsen–Meiningen. Ein Gedenkblatt." *Tägliche Rundschau* (Berlin), March 31, 1906.

"Der Herzog von Meiningen." *Beilage zur Allgemeinen Zeitung* (Munich) April 1, 1906; *Allgemeine Zeitung,* April 3, 1906; April 5, 1906; April 9, 1906.

D. *Nachlässe* (Literary Remains):

The "Meininger Kodex," a bound volume of Georg's Costume sketches, at the Theaterhistorische Sammlung Walter Unruh, Berlin

Nachlass Georg II. Deutsche Staatsbibliothek (German State Library), Berlin.

Georgs Nachlass. Theatermuseum des Instituts für Theaterwissenschaft der Universität Köln (Cologne Theater Museum).

Index